S0-ASN-963

Ancient Peoples and Places

EARLY INDIA AND PAKISTAN

General Editor

DR GLYN DANIEL

Ancient Peoples and Places

EARLY INDIA AND PAKISTAN

TO ASHOKA

Sir Mortimer Wheeler, C.I.E.

57 PHOTOGRAPHS
25 LINE DRAWINGS
AND 7 MAPS

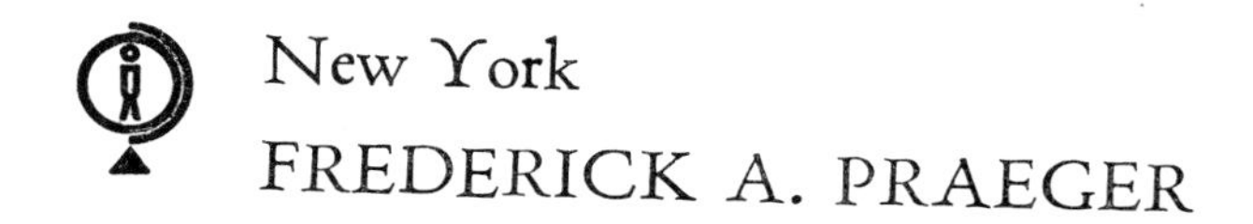

THIS IS VOLUME TWELVE IN THE SERIES
Ancient Peoples and Places

GENERAL EDITOR: DR GLYN DANIEL

ALREADY PUBLISHED

1 PERU
G. H. S. Bushnell

2 THE SCYTHIANS
T. Talbot Rice

3 SICILY BEFORE THE GREEKS
L. Bernabò Brea

4 DENMARK BEFORE THE VIKINGS
O. Klindt-Jensen

5 THE LOW COUNTRIES
S. J. De Laet

6 THE CELTS
T. G. E. Powell

7 THE ETRUSCANS
Raymond Bloch

8 EARLY CHRISTIAN IRELAND
Máire and Liam de Paor

9 WESSEX BEFORE THE CELTS
J. F. S. Stone

10 JAPAN BEFORE BUDDHISM
J. Edward Kidder Jr

11 MALTA
J. D. Evans

BOOKS THAT MATTER
Published in the United States of America
in 1959 by Frederick A. Praeger, Inc.,
Publishers, 15 West 47th Street,
New York 36, N.Y.

Library of Congress Catalog Card Number: 59-7045
Printed in Great Britain

CONTENTS

CONTENTS

ILLUSTRATIONS

FIGURES

To my Colleagues of the old Archaeological Survey of India

Preface

THIS BOOK is a tentative sketch of a large and growing subject. Much of its material is, in the present stage of research, fragmentary and disjointed; in fact, the archaeology of the subcontinent is passing through that phase of increasing complexity which inevitably precedes a more comprehensive synthesis. The examples here presented are chosen mainly as representative of the cultural trends in the arterial valleys and on the great plains and plateaux, where the major developments took place. Apart from incidental references, no attempt is made to describe the static communities which still, in the highlands and backwoods, occupy an appreciable part of India and often preserve their tribal usages and techniques surprisingly intact in a closing world. There is much about these remote peoples that the archaeologist would like to know but does not. His turn will come; meanwhile the anthropologist holds the field.

I have ended my survey with Ashoka for the good reason that it is thereby possible to anchor Indian prehistory to the first firmly documented epoch of Indian history. The common division of the study of human cultures into 'prehistoric' and 'historic' categories is an unhappy one; often enough, the interrelationships and vagaries which are intelligible enough on the historic scene are useful reminders in the interpretation of undocumented material and help to bring it to much-needed life. Ashoka's era seems to me, in that fashion, to illumine much that went before it.

No logical system has here been followed in the transcription of Indian names. Since 1947 a number of them have been corrected from the sort of Hobson-Jobson into which time and the British had corrupted them. In some instances this revision has perhaps been tinged with pedantry, in others a blundered or Anglicized spelling has merely been corrected. I have pursued a middle course which will please no one. Thus for Yamunā and Gangā I have retained the more widely familiar Jumna and Ganges. On the other hand, I have used the more seemly spelling of Mathurā for Muttra. In the case of the old Benares I have gone so far as to adopt Banaras but have shrunk from the archaistic Vārāṇasī. My aim has been to retain sufficient affinity between old and new to ensure recognition by the English reader, for whom this book is primarily intended.

References in an outline of this kind are necessarily reduced to a minimum, but the list at the end is sufficient to enable the persistent student to verify and extend the text.

My indebtedness to others is necessarily extensive. In particular, I have received every possible assistance from Shri A. Ghosh, Director General of Archaeology in India, and his colleagues, especially Shri B. B. Lal; from Dr. F. A. Khan, Director of Archaeology in Pakistan; from Dr. H. D. Sankalia, Director of the Deccan College Research Institute at Poona; from Professor B. Subbarao, Head of the Department of Archaeology at the M.S. University of Baroda; and from Shri G. R. Sharma, Head of the Department of Ancient History, Culture and Archaeology, at Allahābād University. Apart from personal contacts, I have drawn widely upon the periodical reports and studies issued by the Indian Department of Archaeology, which sets a pattern of punctual and systematic publication.

R. E. M. W.

Chapter I
The Scene

If to far India's coast we sail, we encounter today insistent barriers which have nothing to do with a study of the subcontinent's ancient past. Variant uniforms and graces meet us at the gates of West and East Pakistan and of the thousand miles of the new India that divide them. Adam's Bridge has long ceased to offer the most tenuous and symbolic link with Ceylon. The antique fortress of Goa still wears the alien flag of Portugal. At Kātmāndu the traveller, who may now indeed arrive by air, is confronted by the guardians of Nepal, if less obdurately than of old. The Afghan sentry leans warily upon the closed gate at the head of the Khyber Pass, though little heeded by the nomads who were already passing that way from season to season long before his advent. In no sense, ancient or modern, does the term 'India' nominally contain this vast and changing amalgam. At the outset our artificial usage of the word in the context of this book must therefore be defined.

India was the land of the great river Sindhu or Indus which, paradoxically, flows mostly within the modern state of Pakistan. The name or its substance was anciently extended, however vaguely, to the whole subcontinent, and even across the present Khyber barrier to the range of the Hindu Kush, north of Kābul. In that enlarged geographical connotation it will on occasion be used in these pages, without reference to the modern political map. It will relate to the whole subcontinent south of the Himālayas and the Hindu Kush, east of the Helmand Desert, and west of the Chin Hills. No doubt so cavalier a disregard of barbed wire will be resented, and resentment is readily intelligible. But even the clumsy carpet-bag term 'Indo-Pakistan subcontinent' fails to meet the case, and there is indeed no practical alternative to the retention and even the expansion of the traditional name. As one with good friends in Pakistan, India and Afghanistan, I can only beg forgiveness for crossing and recrossing so many proud frontiers without passport. I must plead that my sole concern is with prehistoric and protohistoric geography prior to the 2nd century B.C.

Within that vast territory of some two million square miles the familiar outlines may usefully be recalled. At first sight, the formidable mountain-ranges of the north give the subcontinent an aspect of exclusiveness which it does not in fact possess. For example, there are routes from China to the Brahmaputra in Assam; through Sikkim it is possible to reach the Tibetan plateau; farther west a number of feasible if arduous routes enter Kashmir from Turkestan. The most notable of these routes uses the famous Karakoram Pass, a desolate highway, if such it can be called, from High Asia into trans-Indus Kashmir. But neither this nor any other of these northern approaches has played any dominant rôle in the formation of Indian civilization. Their importance lay rather in the reverse direction, in that they were among the chosen channels for the diffusion of Buddhism and certain aspects of Buddhistic art from India into central Asia and China during the early centuries A.D.

On the north-western frontier of India and thence southward to the Arabian Sea the picture is a very different one. Here the approaches to the subcontinent, though not always easy, are still frequented, with a preference for two or three main routes. They may be grouped into two series: a northern and a southern. The northern group links north Iran and the Oxus region with Kābul and the central reaches of the Indus; the southern group links central and south Iran alternatively with Kandahār, north Baluchistan and the more southerly regions of the Indus, or with Makrān and the Indus delta. These two groups are significant in the cultural relations of Iran and Mesopotamia with India, supplemented less tangibly by the bypass of the Persian Gulf.

The northern group today converges on the Khyber Pass, which has been a major traffic-axis since the establishment of Peshāwar, the ancient Purushapura, as a metropolis about A.D. 100. An important earlier route, after penetrating the Hindu Kush south-east of the ancient Bactra and the modern Mazar-i-Sharif, followed the more northerly and devious line of the Kābul river with Chārsada, the ancient Pushkalāvatī (twenty miles north-east of Peshāwar), as its immediate goal. South of the Khyber alternative tracks used and still use the Kurram valley and the Peiwar Pass; and farther south again the Tochi, Gumal and other valleys carry ancient thoroughfares from the direction of the Ghaznī-Kandahār uplands. At this point, feeders from the southern group spread delta-like towards the Indus plain. The Zhob valley carries or carried a modest traffic north-north-eastwards from the direction of Quetta, itself the northernmost of the three focal points of the southern group; the others being Kalāt and Las Bela. South-eastwards from Quetta a route, now followed approximately by the railway, enters the plains *via* Sibi. Westwards from Quetta a camel-route leads towards Kirman and southern and western Iran. And at the southern end of our series, Las Bela, now 'an insignificant Baluch town, . . . must have stood full in the tide of human immigration into India for centuries in the past. It is a true gateway'.[1]

We have then a well-known geographical picture of a sub-continent mainly barred from the north but accessible in the north-west to the plodding traffic of Asia throughout most of the year from the Iranian plateau and the Oxus valley. Commerce, migration and invasion have recurrently come this way in historical times, and similar movement is implicit in our prehistoric evidence.

South of the northern barriers lie the Great Plains of India, with an average width from north to south of some 200 miles and an average height of 500 feet above the sea. On the map their shape is that of a leaning gable, with the ridge in the neighbourhood of Siālkot, north of Lahore. The shorter and more westerly slope of the gable is the Plain of the Indus, the more easterly the Plain of the Ganges, with Ambālā and Simla in the divide. The prehistory and much of the history of the two plains, in spite of their superficial continuity, is strikingly different, for reasons which must be discussed in due course. Here it will suffice to observe that the land of the middle and lower Indus, with the lost rivers of the Sarasvatī or Ghaggar system which at one time ran parallel or perhaps tributary to it, is barred by desert towards the south-east and was alternatively threatened or reinforced from the Baluch highland towards the west; it remained essentially submontane. The obstructive desert, the Thar, may not in the earlier part of our period have been of its present large dimensions, but at least its mountainous south-eastern flank, the Arāvalli Range, was a durable barrier to the spread of early cultures. Round the northerly end of the Range there was, in the Bronze Age (earlier half of the 1st millennium B.C.) some interconnection between Bikaner and the Jumna-Ganges plains, as is shown by the distribution of the Painted Grey Ware (p. 26); and, round the southerly end of the Range and the desert, the Indus Civilization crept from the mouths of the Indus into Kāthiāwāḍ and beyond. The Ganges, on the other hand, with the mighty Jumna to the west of it and a host of imposing tributaries along its great length, culminating in the maze-like mingling of its delta with that of the Brahmaputra, escapes into a more leisurely landscape, choked at one time with the vast jungles that form the background of the Indian epics. Invasion from the passes of the north-west frontier—its normal source—surged laterally across the middle Indus plain but then encountered the Jumna-Ganges

Fig. 3

plain at the head of its longer axis. There, in the environs of Pānīpat north of Delhi, the passage narrows between the Jumna and the Ghaggar, and further progress eastwards was liable to challenge. The barrier once passed, the Ganges valley lay open towards Bihār and Bengal, though distance and jungle were still substantial obstacles to penetration.

The northern Plains are bounded towards the south by the Vindhya Range which, with its outliers and extensions (notably, the Arāvallis on the west and the Kaimur Range on the east), divides northern India from Gujarāt, the Deccan and the South. Parallel with the Range lies the Narbadā or Narmadā river, which may be regarded as the equivalent riverine frontier, though it is also the axis of a Central India with cultural problems of its own. Thence southwards the core of peninsular India is the great plateau which rises to an average height of 2,000 feet or more, with occasional peaks in the neighbourhood of 9,000 feet. On the west the plateau tumbles steeply to a narrow coastal strip in what are known as the Western Ghāṭs, which receive the full impact of the summer monsoon. On the east a broader plain, between the Eastern Ghāṭs and the Bay of Bengal, is enlarged by the valleys of the major rivers which cut back deeply into the central highland. Towards the southern end, at Pālghāṭ and Coimbatore, rivers falling east and west actually combine to lower a pass through the upland, thus providing an easy cross-country route of considerable interest in the protohistoric period. Through this gap in the 1st century A.D. Roman trafficking, represented by hoards of Roman coins, penetrated from the west coast to the east, avoiding the troublesome navigation of Cape Comorin.[2] By the same accepted way a legend brought St. Thomas to Madras. The pass is marked today by the passage of a trans-peninsular railway.

Such are the outstanding features of the Indian map. They comprise the Indus basin, with southerly extension into Gujarāt;

the Ganges basin; the Bengal-Assam borderland of riverine plain, hill and jungle; central India with north-westerly extension into Gujarāt; and the southern plateau with its flanking coastlands. Other features will be noted as need arises, but at this point a plea may be inserted. The time has come for a careful study of the human geography of the subcontinent in far smaller sub-units than have hitherto been attempted with any approach to systematic completeness. Professor B. Subbarao has made a useful beginning in Gujarāt, but more is needed. Areas, say, a hundred miles—or even five hundred miles—square, selected arbitrarily at any point of the map and analysed in respect of settlement and traffic at all periods down to the present day, would be of incalculable value to our understanding of the land, its peoples, and their secular interaction. Such analysis is an urgent preamble to further progress in the studies with which this little book is concerned.

Chapter II

Time

LIFE ON THIS PLANET originated, we are told, over two thousand million years ago. Somewhere within the last of all those millions, creatures in whom we can recognize a simulacrum of ourselves, with emergent ideas and capacities, came in their turn upon the scene and hesitantly assumed command of the world about them: so hesitantly that, as it seems, they became economically creative—and to that extent independent—only a dozen millennia ago, and civilized in any comprehensive sense only some five or six millennia ago. Advancing science will move these 'dates' a little this way or that but is unlikely now to revolutionize them. The general framework of human endeavour is set.

But within that framework there is infinite scope for subtlety and differential change. The significance and the circumstance of man's major—not to say minor—triumphs are of the essence of the story, and these involve a close reading and re-reading of the evidence as it slowly accumulates. Today in India this accumulation is proceeding at a faster pace than in many other parts of the world, and precise interpretation of the new evidence in relation to the old is proportionately necessary. Without an exact timetable, the tremendous achievement which our evidence reflects cannot be brought into sharp and significant perspective; its phases cannot be interrelated, nor can its position and meaning in the wider context of human effort be established with assurance. *Relative* dates and sequences are useful, but only *actual* dates, in terms of years from the present, are of substantive value. Since therefore most of our subject-matter relates to prehistory, an introductory note on chronological method is inevitable.

The simplest means of determining an archaeological date is naturally by the direct or indirect application of historical criteria. In India, it may be claimed that the earliest literature, the hymnal of the *Ṛigveda*, has something of the quality of history, since it portrays incidentally the earlier struggles and rivalries of the Aryan-speaking invaders of the north-western territories of the subcontinent, and gives a vivid picture of their social condition at the time. What precisely that time was, is less explicit. An Indian writer, enlarging a remark of Megasthenes by means of supposititious king-lists, would ascribe the Aryan Invasion to 6777 B.C., a fantasy which may be consigned to limbo with Archbishop Ussher's date for the Creation. More rational inference assigns the episode to the centuries following 1500 B.C., when, if not earlier, Aryan gods and men were on the move in western Asia. Of this movement it is reasonable to regard the invasions reflected in the *Ṛigveda* as an eastward extension; and their possible bearing upon the date and character of the latter end of the great Indus Civilization will be considered later.

Further back than that, the literature of India fails to carry us. But Mesopotamia is happier in its early chronology; there a widely agreed central date, that of Sargon of Akkad, who, it has been calculated, was reigning about 2350 B.C., is of special use to us. In and about his time there were recognizable contacts between the cities of Mesopotamia and those of the Indus Civilization, to which the Mesopotamian dating can to that extent be transferred.

Behind the latter half of the 3rd millennium there is at present no absolute moment or epoch upon which Indian archaeology can depend. Comparisons have been suggested between certain of the ceramic industries of the Indian borderland and those of Iran and Iraq, but without any pretence of certainty in a chronological sense. Differences are as plentiful as resemblances, and the duration of a local or even a regional industry is in any case incomputable without more collateral evidence than is at present forthcoming. For example, a distinctive ware to which the name of 'Quetta' has been given may, on typological analysis, be regarded as early but on stratigraphical analysis—such little as is available—may equally well be relatively late. For the time being, typology is indeed a fickle guide to the time-sequence of the border cultures of the 4th and 3rd millennia.

Nor, in relation to the earliest stone industries of India, has geology yet produced that measure of precision which, in Europe, is gradually emerging from modern geochronological method: for example, by equating ancient climatic fluctuations, deduced from the examination of loess-deposits and the analysis of river-gravels, with fluctuations of the intensity of solar-radiation calculated on an astronomical basis; or by computing the rates of weathering, denudation and sedimentation in the light of such evidence as that provided by varved clays or radiocarbon analysis.[3] A cross-reference of some of the European to some of the Indian evidence might be attempted if we could with any confidence equate the Himālayan glaciations with those of the Alps. But such equations as have in fact been postulated, however likely, remain guess-work; and even within the subcontinent itself the relation of the pluvials of the tropics to the glaciations of the north is still full of speculation. We are still adrift in time.

Unfortunately, one potential test which can, and will, help to regulate conjecture has not yet, except for occasional pioneer attempts,[4] been extended to the subcontinent. That is the now well-known method, introduced in 1949, of calculating the residual radioactive content of ancient organic material and thereby deducing the time-interval since the 'death' of that material, a method applicable under suitable conditions and controls to periods up to forty thousand years from the present.[5] This new technique, though still in the experimental stage, is in process of revolutionizing our understanding of the tempo and interrelationship of human achievement elsewhere, and its further application to Indian material by the National

Physical Laboratory of India, which is understood to have the matter in hand, is an outstanding need.

In the latter half of the 1st millennium B.C., however, history and archaeology at last become fully effective partners in this matter of timing, without the intervention of physical science. A datum-line is provided by the partially historic life of the Buddha, who, for our purpose, represents that miraculous upsurge of reflective and creative thought which swept across the world from Greece to China about 500 B.C. Sharing in this upsurge, Achaemenid Persia, with its systematized imperialism and its rich artistry, reached out to the Indus region about 518 B.C.* At this time, too, in the Ganges valley native kingdoms were already laying the foundations of the great literate Indian empire that was to emerge two centuries later. To them, Persia transmitted, directly or indirectly, not merely a pattern of empire but also important new skills and utilities: above all the use of iron and of coinage. It can be no mere coincidence that in northern India (as indeed in distant Britain) 500 B.C. or a little earlier marks the nominal beginning of the Iron Age, always with the proviso that cultural backwaters are a familiar feature of the Indian landscape. Nor is it likely to be chance that then or shortly afterwards the first Indian coinage appears in the Ganges valley as a new aid and incentive to organized commerce. And home-enterprise was in no way lacking. Following the arrival of iron—perhaps, indeed, literally reflecting the aspect of the new and fashionable metal—the Ganges craftsmen invented a distinctive and remarkable ceramic which is a godsend to the archaeologist: the so-called 'Northern Black Polished' or 'N.B.P.' Ware, of steel-like

* Gandhara (the Peshāwar plain and its environs) was already in Persian hands when the Behistūn inscription was cut for Darius, *c.* 520–518 B.C. It had either been acquired by Darius at the beginning of his reign or, more probably, by his grandfather Cyrus. Darius now extended his realm to the Indus valley, but his eastern frontier is not defined.

quality, which will constantly recur in later chapters. This pottery spread outwards from the Ganges Basin to the North-West Frontier, Bengal and the Deccan; its nuclear date seems to be 5th–2nd centuries B.C. (see p. 30). It followed an equally distinctive 'Painted Grey' or 'P.G.' Ware, often of comparable quality but less securely dated within the earlier half of the 1st millennium; 8th–5th centuries B.C. is a provisional bracket (p. 26). Of these and other crafts and industries more will be said; here they are mentioned as examples of an accumulation of data to which an approximate timetable can be attached.

And then came Alexander the Great. To describe his advent in the Punjab in 326 B.C.—with the loot of Asia in his haversack and his entourage of historians and philosophers—as an 'archaeological datum' is scarcely to add to the stature of the liveliest of the Nine Worthies. But the fact remains that he opened the way to an inrush of refugee craftsmanship from prostrate Persia and was thus indirectly responsible for lasting elements in Indian sculpture and architecture. The Lions of Sārnāth, the badge of the modern Republic, are in this sense his legacy no less than Ashoka's. And these lions and their kin are a part of the grammar of Mauryan and Shuṅga archaeology, as are the gems and ornaments which can be related to the same cultural tradition.

It was however in the first centuries B.C. and A.D. that the classical West contributed most emphatically to the repertory of the Indian archaeologist. The consolidation of the Roman Empire by Augustus and his successors brought Roman coinage and Graeco-Roman wares in great quantities to the Indian peninsula, where spices, gems and a middleman-trade with China were the main objectives. Backed by a considerable and circumstantial literature—Greek, Roman, Indian, Chinese—these imports of known date and origin have been identified archaeologically and have lent their precision to associated Indian cultures. It is no exaggeration to say that in recent years they have provided a fresh starting-point for the study of central and southern Indian materials of which the context was otherwise unknown. In particular the widespread 'Rouletted Ware' (p. 31) is due to them, and its association with Italic (Arretine) pottery and coins of the Roman principate gives it a valuable initial date in the first half of the 1st century A.D.

Such are some of the means whereby a great and growing mass of material of the prehistoric and protohistoric ages is now being sorted out and arranged in something approaching an absolute time-sequence. Under the stimulus of the Indian and Pakistani State Departments of Archaeology, aided by a few of the universities (notably Calcutta, Poona, Allahābād and Baroda) the work proceeds apace. There is far to go.

FURTHER NOTE ON THREE WARES OF SPECIAL CHRONOLOGICAL IMPORTANCE

Fig. 1

1. *Painted Grey Ware (P.G. Ware)*. This distinctive Bronze Age ware is of fine well-levigated clay, wheel-turned, thin and grey in section, well-fired, and grey to greyish brown, sometimes dark, in surface colour. On the surface are painted linear and dotted patterns, concentric circles, spirals, *sigmas* and *swastikas*, generally in matt black but occasionally red.

The commonest forms are straight-sided bowls, and dishes with upright convex sides and sagger-bases.

The ware is characteristic of the Jumna-Ganges *doāb* but occurs as far west as Bikaner and as far south as Ujjain.

At Ahichchhatrā in U.P., where the ware was first recognized, it occurred mainly below the Northern Black Polished or N.B.P. Ware (see below), though there was some likelihood of an overlap between the two. At the more carefully excavated Hastināpura on the Ganges, however, there was a stratigraphical gap between the P.G. Ware and the overlying N.B.P. Ware, and there is a hint of a similar gap at Kaushāmbī on the Jumna, though the evidence there is less abundant. Other sites

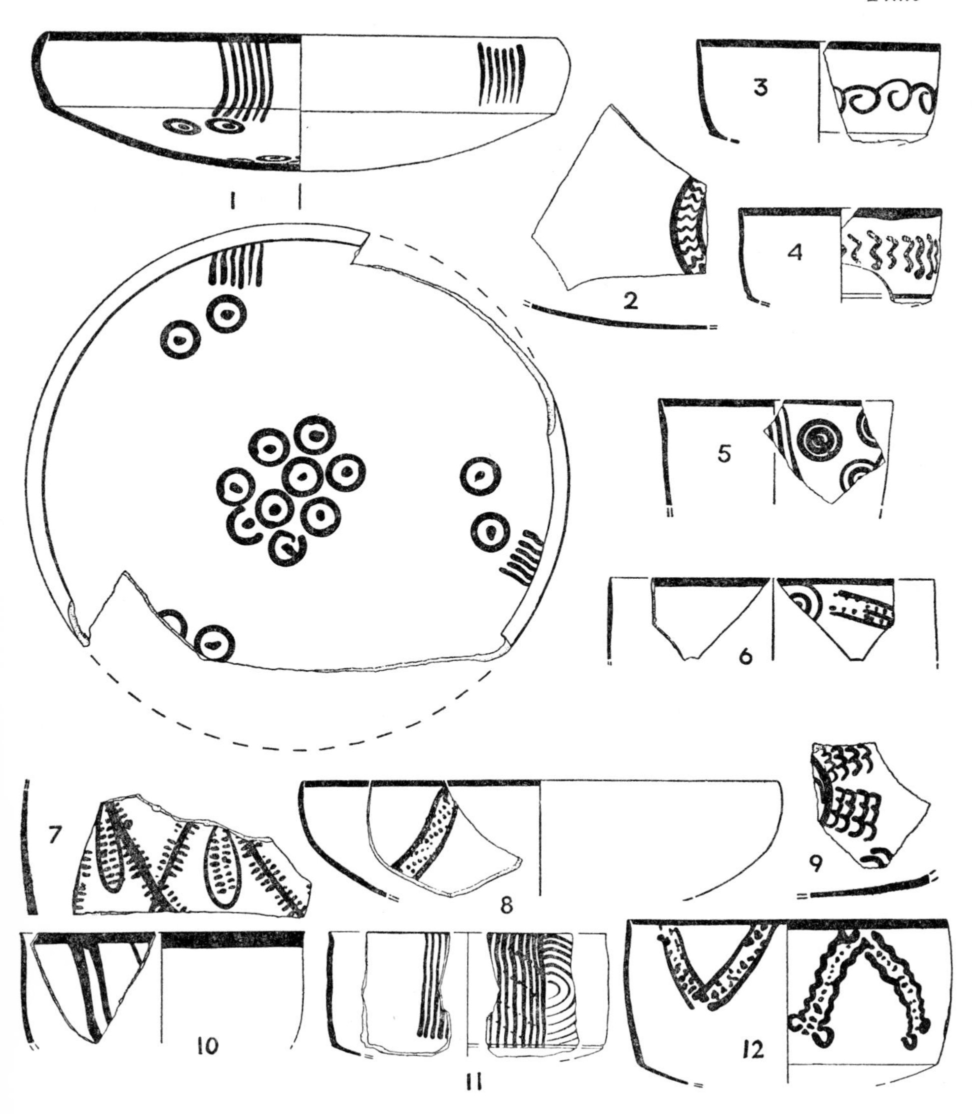

Fig. 1 Painted grey ware: 1–4, from Ahichchhatrā; 5–9, from Pānīpat; 10–12, from Hastināpura. $\frac{1}{4}$

confirm the general sequence of the two wares. Moreover, whilst the N.B.P. Ware is associated with iron implements, the P.G. Ware is found exclusively with copper or bronze: even the stone industries which often accompany the use of copper in India seem to be absent from P.G. Ware levels.

If the initial date of the N.B.P. Ware in the Ganges region be placed somewhere in the 5th century B.C. (see below), then the bulk of the P.G. Ware is certainly earlier than that date. At Hastināpura this ware extended downwards through 4–7 feet of occupational strata; what that represents in time can only be conjectured, but two or three centuries are a feasible guess. On this basis, and at this representative site, the beginning of the P.G. Ware might be ascribed to the 8th century B.C. The skilful excavator of Hastināpura would prefer to take it back to '*circa* 1100 B.C., with a probable margin on the earlier side'. This estimate is influenced by the fact that the P.G. Ware is the earliest reputable pottery known to us from a number of town-sites—Hastināpura amongst them—mentioned as already established before the *Mahābhārata* war, for which F. E. Pargiter suggested a date of *c.* 950 B.C. The equation may be right, but the available archaeological evidence scarcely carries so long a chronology. In any case, the date of the historical elements of the *Mahābhārata* is highly speculative.

At the upper limit of the dating, a clear archaeological gap has been established between the end of the Indus Civilization (*c.* 1500 B.C.?) and the beginning of the P.G. Ware at Rupar and other sites in N.W. India. Nevertheless, if as archaeologists we must be for ever tracing the steam-engine back to the tea-kettle, we may postulate a link, however tenuous, with Baluchistan, where the bowls from the secondary burials at Shāhi Tump seem to have a certain ancestral affinity with the Ganges material; and the Shāhi Tump burials post-dated the Indus Civilization at that spot. Certainly the sudden appearance of the high-class P.G. fabric in the Ganges basin suggests, or even proves, that its technique had already been perfected elsewhere. If Aryans must be dragged into this picture, it is possible to suppose that the P.G. Ware may represent the second phase of their invasion of India, when, from the Punjab, they entered and Aryanized the Middle Country of the Ganges-Jumna *doāb*, after picking up ideas and doubtless craftsmen in the Indus valley and the Baluch borderland. But see p. 126.

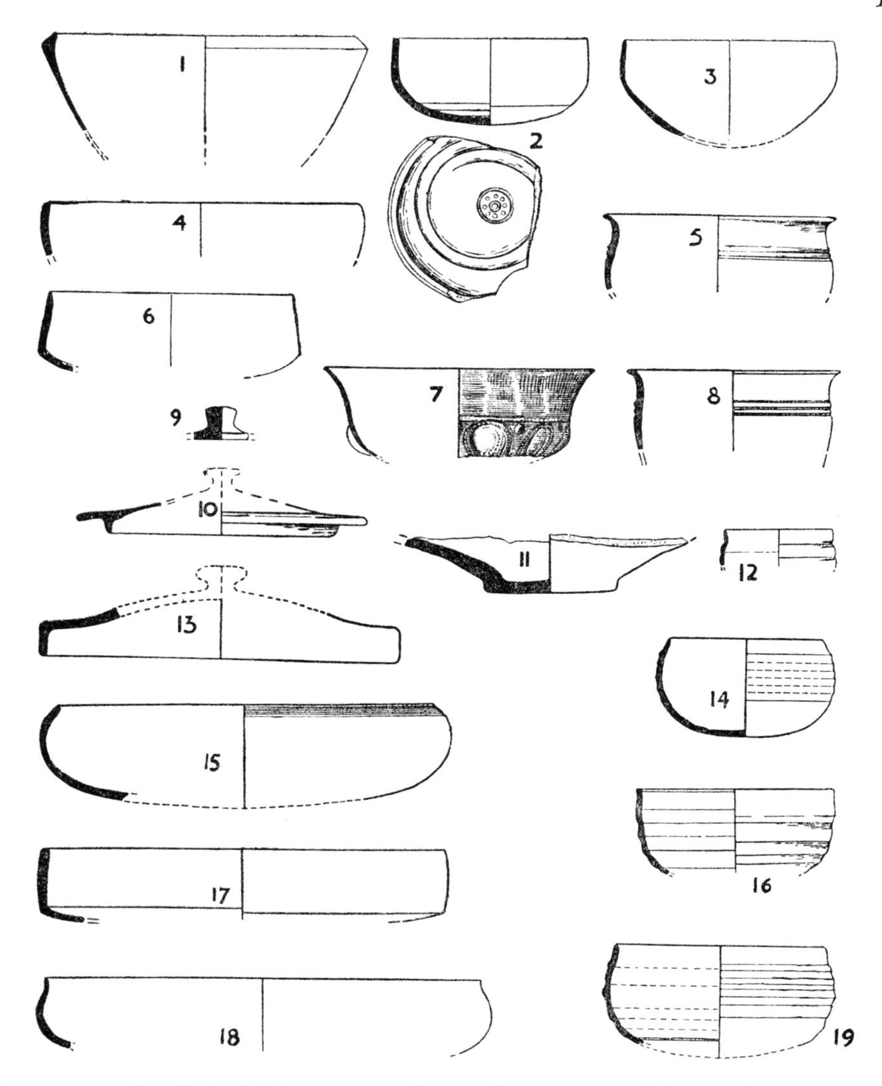

Fig. 2 Northern black polished ware: 1, 3, 5, 8, 10, 17, from Rupar; 2, 16, from Rājgīr; 4, 9, 12, 18, from Tripurī; 6, from Bahal; 7, from Taxila (Bhīr Mound); 11, 13, from Hastināpura; 14, 15, 19, from Ahichchhatrā. $\frac{1}{4}$

Briefly, in the following pages the schematic dates for the important Painted Grey Ware will be the 8th–5th centuries B.C.

2. *Northern Black Polished Ware (N.B.P. Ware)*. Many sites in northern and central India, occasionally as far south as Amaravatī, have produced this Iron Age ware, which is as distinctive in the subcontinent as is *terra sigillata* on European sites.[7] It is wheel-made and normally thin, with a highly lustrous surface ranging from grey or brown to black, and steel-like in quality. The paste is well levigated and is white to reddish. The bright gloss is not a glaze or lacquer. The process of manufacture is doubtful: it has been thought that, after being turned on the wheel, the pots were subjected to elaborate burnishing, and then coated with a finely levigated, highly ferruginous clay, and again burnished; and that they were then fired under reducing conditions to a temperature producing an incipient fusion of the slip, this accounting for their exceptional hardness and lustre. Recently, the laboratory of the British Museum has questioned the burnishing without, as yet, providing any complete alternative explanation. Its present verdict is that 'the unfired pots were dipped in a suspension of a ferruginous inorganic material, probably resembling a red earth; and that, after firing to a temperature of *c.* 800° C., the kiln was sealed so that the pots cooled in a reducing atmosphere. The mineralogical identity of the "red earth" has not been discovered, and the main problem, namely the precise nature of the surface layer, still remains unsolved.'

Fig. 3

The shapes are commonly bowls or convex-sided dishes, with a certain analogy—as, indeed, has the high quality of the fabric—to the P.G. pottery. The two may well represent the same tradition, with the addition of an improved or variant technique in the case of the N.B.P. Ware. The discovery of the new technique may be ascribed to the potters of the Ganges Basin, where the ware is particularly abundant. It may be suggested as an idle guess that the great popularity of the Ware was not altogether unconnected with its superficial resemblance to forged iron, which first appears in northern India shortly before N.B.P. Ware. Alternatively, it may reflect the liking of the Persians for a high metallic polish, as represented very notably in some of their masonry (p.174).

Fig. 2

The fabric has been dated on the basis of the prolonged excavations at the somewhat peripheral site of Taxila in the Punjab (West Pakistan), which yielded about twenty sherds. Of these, eighteen came from the earliest of the successive sites of the town, the Bhīr Mound, which was founded late in the 6th or early in the 5th century B.C. and is thought to have ended about 180 B.C. It was visited by Alexander the Great in 326 B.C., when the average level was about 6 or 7 feet below the present surface. It is noteworthy that sixteen of the Bhīr Mound sherds occurred at depths between 7 and 13 feet, only two being higher than 7 feet (one at 4 feet 10 inches, and one at 6 feet 2 inches). Since Taxila was not dug stratigraphically in the modern usage of the term, these depths are an unreliable guide, but, consistently with them, one of the two sherds found on the succeeding site of Taxila at Sirkap occurred at 18 feet below the surface, and should therefore be early in the history of that site, that is to say, in the first half of the 2nd century B.C. On this showing, the N.B.P. Ware may be ascribed to the 5th–2nd centuries B.C. The occasional survival of this high-grade fabric into later levels is to be expected; thus at Shishupalgarh in Orissa three N.B.P. shreds occurred above Rouletted Ware, which is not likely to be earlier than the beginning of the 1st century A.D. But much more evidence is required as to the initial date of the ware in the Ganges Basin, and the Taxila dating may not in this respect be representative. On recent observation I am indeed inclined to suspect that in the far North-west, at Chārsada near Peshāwar (where a dozen stratified sherds of this fabric were found in 1958), at Udegram in Swat (where Professor G. Tucci's expedition has found a sherd in a mileu attributed to the 3rd century B.C.), and even at Taxila itself, its arrival should mostly be equated with the spread of the Mauryan dominion from the Ganges to these parts after 323 B.C. In other words, I would provisionally ascribe the N.B.P. Ware of the north-westerly regions of the subcontinent to the period 320–150 B.C., without prejudice to the possibility of an appreciably earlier beginning in the Ganges Basin itself.

It is relevant to add that in the careful trial-trenches dug at Hastināpura in the Ganges valley over a hundred sherds of N.B.P. Ware were found in Period III, represented by 8 vertical feet of occupation-material. In the succeeding Period IV, which produced Mathurā coins ascribed to the 2nd century B.C., the ware was absent.

Fig. 3

3. *Rouletted Ware.* This ware was first recognized in 1945 at Arikamedu, near Pondicherry in South India, where it was found in association with Arretine ware imported from Italy in the early decades of the 1st century A.D.[8] In a more general sense this dating is confirmed at

Plate I

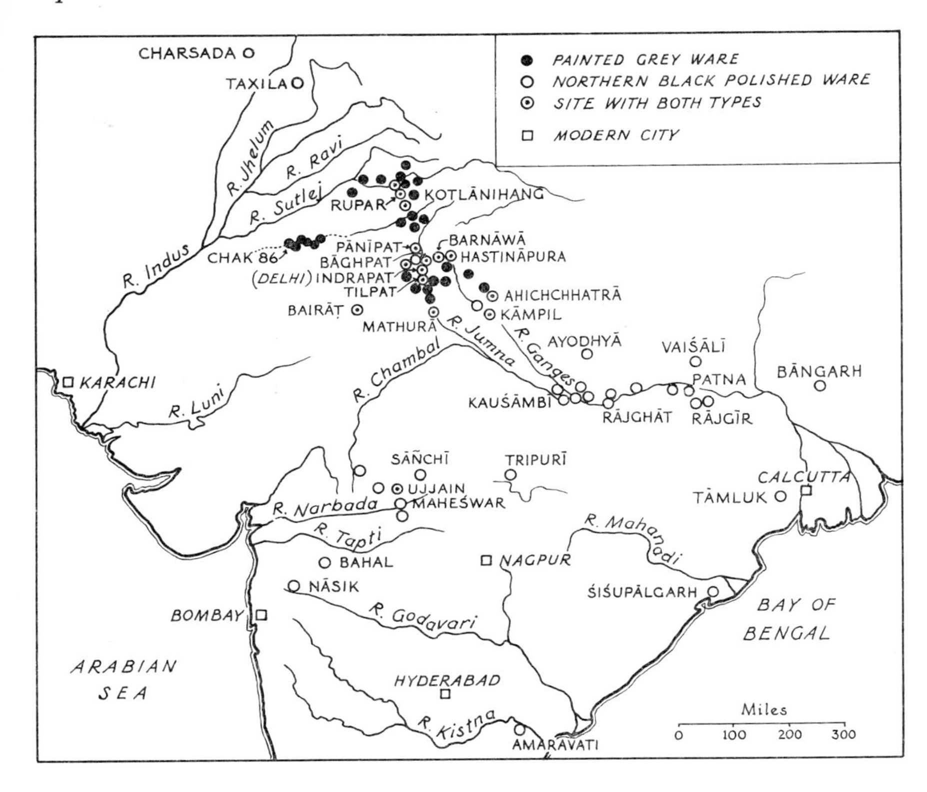

Fig. 3 Distribution of painted grey and northern black polished wares

Chandravalli in northern Mysore, where a denarius of Tiberius, dated A.D. 26–37, was found with closely derivative pottery and near actual rouletted sherds. The characteristic shape is a dish, sometimes more than 12 inches in diameter, with an incurved and beaked rim and two or three concentric rings of rouletted pattern on the flat interior base. This pattern is not an Indian feature and is certainly derived, like the associated Arretine, from the Mediterranean. The fabric is grey or black, has often a remarkably smooth surface, is usually thin, brittle and well-burnt, with almost a metallic ring. The better examples are doubtless imported;

cruder varieties seem to be local imitations. The ware is particularly characteristic of the South Indian areas reached by Roman trade in the 1st and 2nd centuries A.D. with an appropriate extension in the north-east to Tamluk, the ancient Tamralipti or Ptolemy's Tamalites, in Bengal,[9] and a stray sherd in the far north-west at Jhukar in Sind.[10]

This abundant and distinctive ware lies itself outside the range of the present book, but as the first clear datum in the protohistoric chronology of South India it serves as a terminus for some of the dating in our later chapters.

CHAPTER III

Stones

INDIAN STONE AGE TOOLS have been provisionally classified in three broad categories, chronological as well as typological: Series I and II representing the Lower and Upper Palaeolithic, and Series III marked by microlithic industries. In spite of its crude simplicity, this basic classification is useful in the present stage of research. Series II still lacks definition, but I and III, however interpreted, are readily recognizable brackets. This chapter is concerned mainly with Series I.

In India it is more than ordinarily difficult to set Man of the Old Stone Age, Palaeolithic Man, squarely upon his feet. That he abounded for a great many thousands of years is sufficiently evident from the unnumbered lumps of stone which he split and shaped and left for us in a variety of geological environments. But of the bones and branches which he may also have hewn in the fulfilment of his daily needs, practical or spiritual, of the skins and matting which may have adorned his person and his precinct, nothing has survived. Of his physical aspect we know nothing. His solitary memorial is an infinitude of stones.

His setting lies within the Pleistocene epoch of geology—the last prior to the Recent or Holocene in which we live—as defined by the presence of a distinctive fauna: Elephas, Equus and Bos. More particularly, the stone implements encountered in this chapter may be equated with the Middle Pleistocene and a schematic time-bracket of 400,000 to 100,000 years ago, though the terminal date for some of the industries may well be later. Broadly, they fall into three main categories.

1. Pebble-implements. These are more or less crudely sharpened pebbles, characteristically of quartzite, and frequently retaining a part of the cortex or crust of the pebble. Sometimes flakes are struck upwards from the edges of the flat platform of a pebble which has been cloven transversely by man or nature; the steep cutting-edge thus formed would enable the implement to be used as a chopper or scraper. Alternatively, a rounded or oval pebble may be shaped by the removal of flakes, normally on one side only to produce a scalloped cutting-edge or even a point. In the latter case, the sharpened pebble sometimes vaguely resembles a handaxe, and a genetic connection between pebble-handaxes and true handaxes in India has been postulated. Equally, the resemblance may be fortuitous or at most the result of interaction. Pebble industries in India are often referred to as 'Soan' (or 'Sohan') industries, from the Punjab river where they were first recorded.

2. *Flake-implements.* Two main series (with many varieties) have been recognized. The first is comparable with the Clactonian of Essex, in that the flake is struck off an unprepared block by means of a hammer or by striking a fixed anvil ('block-on-block' technique); the striking-platform of the flake shows no preparatory working and is set at a wide angle (110–125 degrees) from the ventral side of the flake, and there is a large semi-cone of percussion where the formative blow was struck. The second series approaches the French Levallois technique whereby a domical or 'tortoise' core is first trimmed by the removal of a series of small flakes from the stone block; then a large flake is detached sometimes by a blow on a small flat surface prepared at right-angles to the surface of the core. The detached flake shows converging flaking or fluting on the upper side and a flat primary surface on the under side, and is generally usable as a knife or scraper or spearhead without further trimming, though it may on occasion be submitted to some secondary working.

3. *Handaxes.* These are pear-shaped or oval implements, sometimes of considerable size, a foot or more in length, worked

to an edge on both sides of a core or occasionally a flake. The more primitive examples appear to have been made in a fashion similar to that of the Clactonian flakes; their French category is 'Abbevillian' (formerly 'Chellian'), but in India the term is liable to imply a greater measure of precision than the coarse material used there justifies. On the other hand the best Indian handaxes, showing, it seems, controlled flaking produced by the use of a bone or wooden mallet, may justifiably borrow the name 'Acheulian' from the more evolved French category. With the Acheulian handaxes are associated *cleavers*, oblong or rhomboidal in outline and with a wide chisel-edge, made by the same techniques. Levallois flakes partially overlapped the Acheulian handaxes but also outlasted them. Indian handaxes, with or without cleavers, are commonly known collectively as the 'Madras industry', from the region where they were first recognized, but the name bears no relation to the distribution of the type.

In 1863, R. Bruce Foote, of the Geological Survey of India, picked up a palaeolithic implement in a gravel-pit at Pallavaram, near Madras. From this early start began the intermittent study of the Old Stone Age of India, though it is a fair comment to add that that study is still in a rudimentary stage. Foote's own work was of fundamental value, but only in the last quarter-century has the subject received any further sustained attention from trained enquirers.[11] Here no complete survey or even summary can be attempted, but a few of the more notable palaeolithic sites in northern, central and southern India are selected to illustrate the current state of enquiry. If the result displays a somewhat sombre monotony, it is at least a sympathetic reflection of millennia of mental and social stagnation modified by reluctant technical variation and occasional slight advancement. In India, not less than in other parts of the world, the human race got off to a slow start.

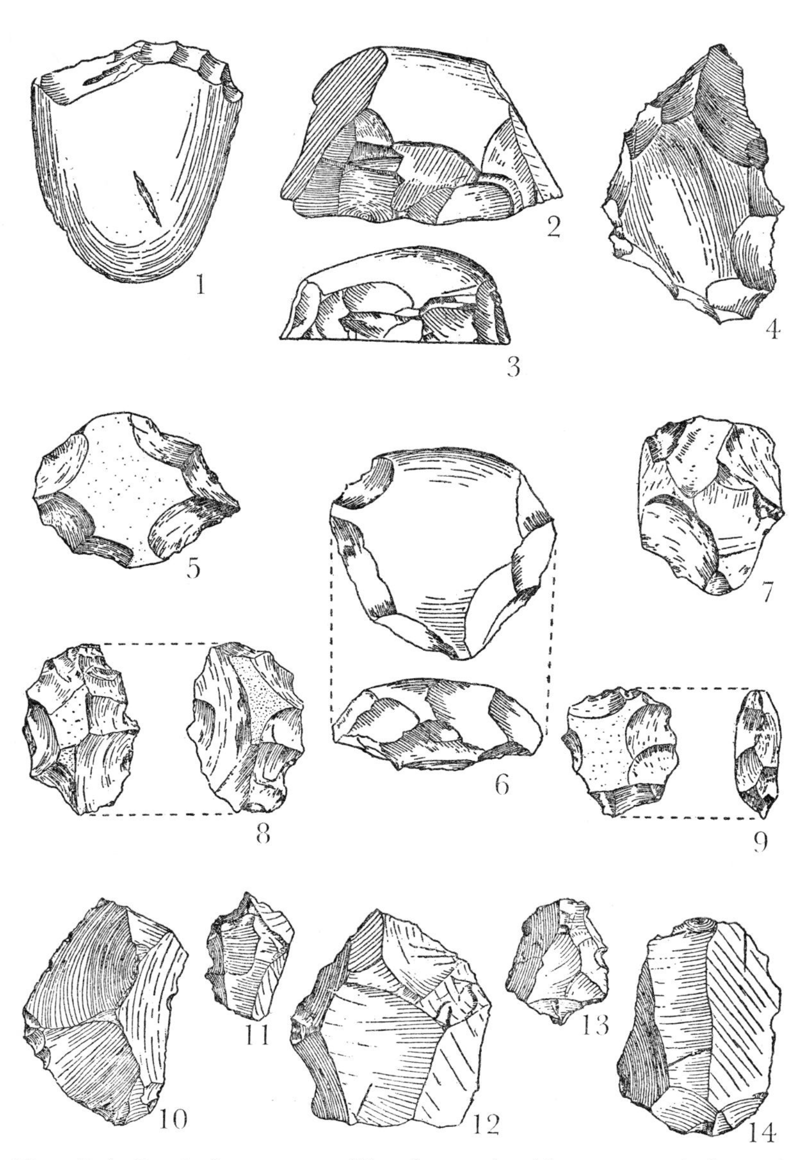

Fig. 4 Early Soan implements: 1–4, pebble tools; 5–9, discoidal cones; 10–14, 'Clactonian' flakes. $\frac{1}{4}$

NORTHERN INDIA

In northern India (Kashmir and the Punjab), as in Europe, the Pleistocene was an epoch of intermittent glaciation and, again as in Europe, four main advances of the ice have been recognized. It is likely but unproved that the Himālayan and the Alpine series approximate to one another in time, and may be equated in tropical India with pluvials or phases of extreme rainfall.

Towards the middle of the Pleistocene occurred the second of the four Himālayan glaciations, and the Boulder Conglomerate which represents it* has yielded the earliest tools of Stone Age India on sites in the sub-Himālayan valleys of the Indus and its tributary the Soan (or Sohan), in the so-called Potwar Area centred about Rawalpindi.[12] With the tools have been found bones of *Elephas namadicus*, which help incidentally to link these deposits with others on the Narbadā and Godāvarī of central India.

These early implements, which have been christened 'Pre-Soan', are worthy of their lowly position in the human scale. They are characteristically big flakes or split pebbles of quartzite, with large unfaceted striking-platforms mostly at angles of 100–125 degrees and with large, flat but well-marked cones of percussion. Their upper surface is usually unflaked, and there is no secondary working. Their primitive quality is enhanced by the native intractability of the material; furthermore, they are mostly very worn, and the edges are often battered either by use or by natural attrition. Many of them are recognizable as artifacts only by the trained eye, assisted by their association

* The sequence here followed is that of de Terra and Paterson. For a suggested variation, see F. E. Zeuner, *Dating the Past* (4th ed. London, 1958), pp. 274–7. The available evidence is admittedly inconclusive.

with more distinctive specimens, and it may be suspected that even the trained eye is not always impeccable.

Following the second glaciation was a prolonged interglacial phase—the Second Interglacial—during which the Boulder Conglomerate was partially eroded and redeposited as a covering on Terrace 1. In this Terrace two new industries make their first appearance: (i) the 'Early Soan', a pebble and flake industry which has been subdivided typologically but consists broadly of chopping and scraping tools; and (ii) a handaxe or 'Madras' industry consisting of more or less ovate tools worked on both faces. In both of the Soan groups occur worn and deeply patinated specimens, but their complete absence from the undisturbed Conglomerate suggests that they belong truly to various stages of the succeeding interglacial phase represented by Terrace 1.

Fig. 4

The flakes of the Early Soan include examples with plain high-angled Clactonian platforms, and others with faceted low-angled platforms recalling the early Levalloisian. Retouch is absent. The pebble choppers and scrapers are made in both the fashions described on p. 35. No fauna has been associated with this phase.

During the third of the four glaciations, Terrace 2 was formed in a process of aggradation represented by a basal gravel and a thick overlying deposit of loess or silt, known sometimes as the 'Potwar Loess'. Teeth of horse and dog (or wolf) have been extracted from this loess, but statements that camel and ox have also been found in it require confirmation.

The 'Late Soan' industry recovered from this Terrace is of two phases, equating with the two component strata. Phase A, from the basal gravel, is largely an extension of the pebble industry of the Early Soan, and is particularly characterized by rough oval pebbles with untouched butt along one side and flaking along the opposite side, though sometimes from each surface alternately, thus producing a wavy edge, straight or

Fig. 5

convex. Phase B, from the overlying loess, has produced recognizable workshop-sites with fresh tools, consisting mainly of flakes comparable with the Late Levalloisian of Europe, though including some pebble-choppers and cores as in Phase A. It was observed that there was an evolving tendency towards smaller and more finely made types. 'In the early stages [of the Soan industry] the flakes are crude. In the late Soan alongside the simple forms there are other flakes showing a development in technique, with much more regular primary flaking and often with faceted platforms.'

It is noteworthy that the Late Soan seems normally to be devoid of handaxes. This statement, however, needs modification if in fact the Soan site of Chauntra (20 miles south of Rawalpindi), which has produced a mixture of Madras and Soan pebble elements, is of the succeeding third interglacial age from Terrace 3. More evidence is required. From Terraces 4 and 5 no significant material has been recorded; in any event Terrace 5 is of post-Pleistocene age.

In recent years (1951–55) other 'Soan' distributions have been found in the Himālayan foothills of the Punjab: in the upper valley of the Sirsa, a tributary of the Sutlej, 30 miles west of Simla, and near Daulatpur in Hoshiarpur District 25 miles north of Jullundur. More important are B. B. Lal's observations in the upper valley of the Beas, with its tributary the Bāngangā, in the Kangra District 230 miles north-north-west of Delhi.[13] Four sites are named: Guler, Dehra, Dhaliara and Kangra itself. At Guler five river-terraces have been identified, though whether they are equivalent to the Kashmir-Potwar series has not been determined. Again, only the three higher (earlier) terraces produced implements, all of quartzite. Terrace 1 yielded unifacial choppers, a bifacial chopping-tool, and Clactonian flakes, but no handaxes. The workmanship is crude; the choppers consist of roughly sharpened pebbles, but the more evolved pebble-tool, approximating to a handaxe,

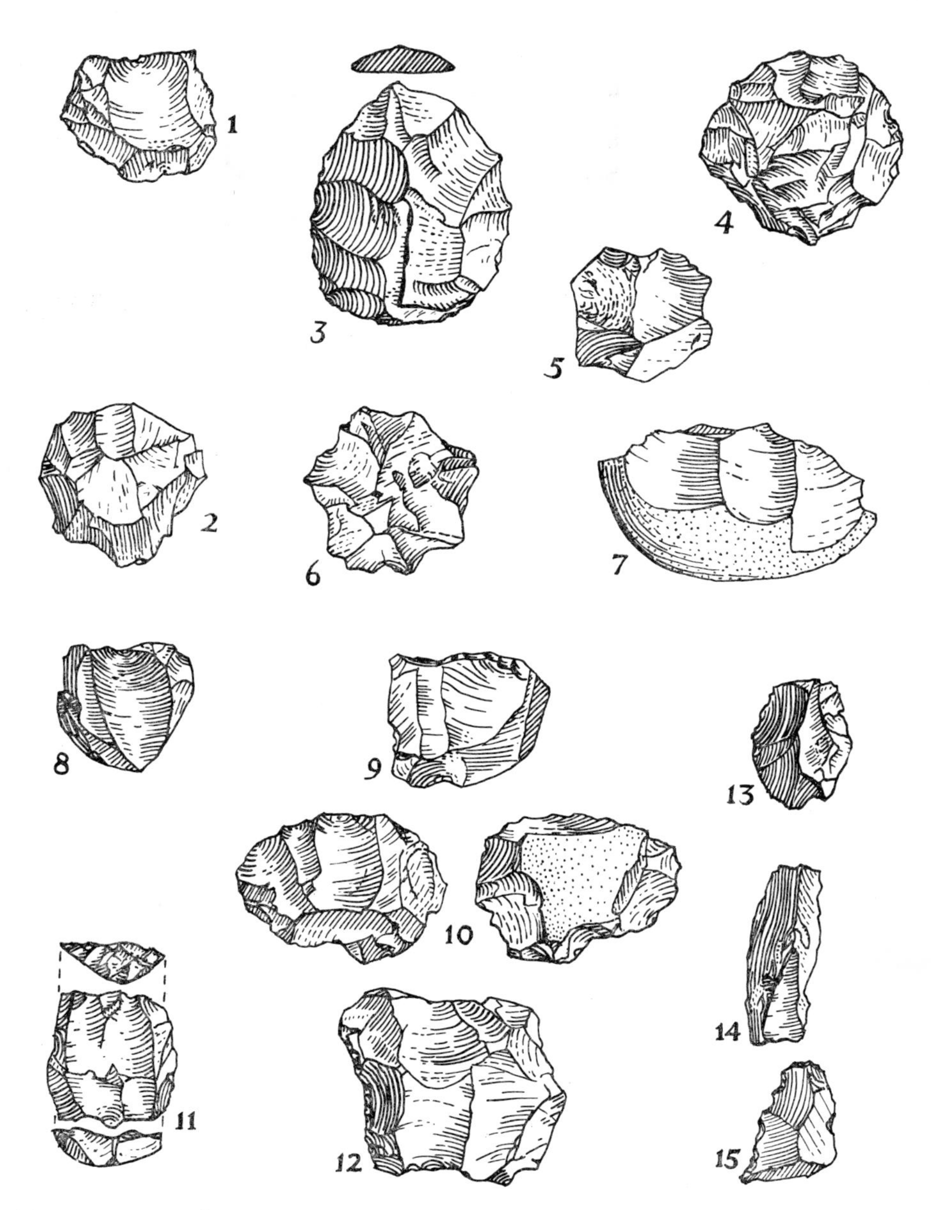

Fig. 5 Late Soan industry: 1–6, cores; 7, chopper; 8–12, cores; 13–15, Levalloisian flakes. $\frac{1}{4}$

is absent. From Terrace 2, more choppers were recovered, with a pebble-handaxe, Clactonian flakes, and two others which are reasonably described as proto-Levalloisian, with due allowance for the difficulty of the material. Both the pebble-handaxe and the proto-Levalloisian flakes seem to mark an advance upon the industry of Terrace 1. On Terrace 3 were at least seven unifacial choppers and two Clactonian flakes, and either from Terrace 2 or Terrace 3 came another proto-Levalloisian flake, a pebble-handaxe, and two bifacial implements which were, with some hesitation, regarded as genuine handaxes, distinguished perhaps with an excessive nicety as Abbevillian and Acheulian respectively. Both handaxes, if such they be, are rolled and worn. On the whole, the sequence from these three terraces is not in conflict with that from the Potwar area.

Farther south, in Rajasthan and Mālwā, a number of sites in the valleys of the Chambal river and its tributaries, particularly in Chitorgarh district, have produced Palaeolithic assemblages which seem to fall stratigraphically into two series.[14] The earlier of these, Series I, included handaxes and cleavers of the Madras industry in association with Clactonian flakes and choppers of the Soan industry. A later gravel contained Series II, characterized by Levallois flakes with prepared striking-platforms, and hollow and blade-scrapers, but devoid alike of choppers and handaxes. The occurrence of occasional flake-tools of Series II in deposits of Series I suggested to the explorers a more or less continuous occupation with changing needs and modes. Away to the east, the Jumna valley in the Banda district of Uttar Pradesh is reported to have produced a comparable tool-sequence in so far as handaxes were followed by Levallois flakes, but apparently without the admixture of Soan choppers.

CENTRAL INDIA

The next region towards the south where serious study of the Old Stone Age has been undertaken lies along the three main rivers which empty into the Gulf of Cambay—the Sabarmati, the Mahī and the Narbadā (or Narmadā)—and about the upper reaches of the Godāvarī, which nearly bisects the peninsula.[15] Eastward the area of investigation has been extended to the valleys of the Kaimūr Range south of Banaras. The whole of this transcontinental region shows an interesting overlap between the flake-and-pebble industries on the one hand and the handaxe-cleaver series on the other, with an emergent hint of later Palaeolithic groups of which the full significance is not yet adequately understood. Here too, if anywhere, is it likely that an equation or compromise between the pluvials of the tropics and the glaciations of the Himālayas may eventually be postulated;[16] but much further fieldwork, geological and archaeological, must precede this happy result. Indian research is already busy in the matter.

The great Narbadā valley[17] must have been a superb hunting-ground for Palaeolithic man, as it is for the modern explorer in his tracks. Its geological structure, so far as we are concerned, consists in the central reaches of two sedimentary deposits, a Lower and an Upper, comprising gravel capped with clay and sand; they overlie a thick deposit of laterite (see below) and are covered by the dark alluvial 'regur' or 'cotton soil' familiar to travellers in central and southern India. The junctions between these successive formations are well marked, and the Lower group, with extension into the gravels of the Upper group, has produced bones of a mid-Pleistocene fauna including *Bos namadicus*, *Elephas namadicus* and *Bubalus palaeindicus*. It may be recalled that *Elephas namadicus* has been found likewise in the Boulder Conglomerate which yielded the earliest

(Pre-Soan) flake implements of the sub-Himālayan Potwar area, and thus provides a useful palaeontological link between the two regions. It is appropriate that the earliest vestiges of Narbadā man are likewise contemporary with the formation of the Lower Narbadā group, and that they include an industry comparable with the Pre-Soan.

With the large flakes of Pre-Soan type, however, the Lower Narbadā group—unlike the Potwar Boulder Conglomerate—contains an appreciable handaxe industry, represented by heavily rolled Abbevillian implements and both rolled and unworn Acheulian tools. In the Upper group the handaxes seem to be less at home; they are predominantly rolled Acheulian and are thought to be confined to the basal gravel of the group. They may therefore be wholly or largely derivative. In any event, the characteristic industry of the Later group resembles the Late Soan, and consists of small discoidal cores, pebble cores, pebble choppers and beaked tools.

The interpretation of these resemblances and discrepancies between northern and central India is not easy. Nor is it facilitated by more recent observation in the Sabarmati valley.[18] There, in the main gravel, it is noted by Dr. Sankalia that crude pebble-implements occur alongside more finished types which include Acheulian handaxes of latish appearance. There are also numerous flakes, though rarely with the faceted striking-platform suggestive, as might be expected from the northern evidence, of a Levalloisian technique. Typologically, this complex assemblage could be divided into a sequence of cultures beginning with pre-Abbevillian, but there is no stratigraphical warrant for this and it must be assumed that the various types were approximately contemporary.

The problem is again illustrated but not solved in a tributary system of the river Son, the Singrauli basin, of Mirzapur District in the Kaimur Range south of Banaras.[19] Here a bed of redeposited Pleistocene gravel, covered by 5 feet of alluvial silt and humus and overlying a layer of sand upon a deep Boulder Conglomerate, has produced a series of quartzite implements which include about 43 per cent of handaxes and cleavers and about 15 per cent of pebble-and-core chopping-tools. There are also numerous flakes of which a fair proportion (some 26 per cent of the collection) may be described as proto-Levallois, or even unqualified Levallois, with faceted platforms. The pebble-tools recall the Early Soan 'chopper' industry and may be so classified. The bifacial handaxes are of Abbevillio-Acheulian or Madras types, some of them exhibiting all-over controlled flaking, with a more or less tongue-shaped point. The cleavers are straight-edged and round-butted, with oblique cutting-edge.

It should be emphasized that there was no apparent stratigraphic division between the pebble and the biface industries in this deposit. The pebble-tools were thought to be rather more worn than the bifaces, many of which were fresh in appearance; but this is the only hint of a differential chronology, and for the present the whole series must be regarded as approximately contemporary. No associated fauna is recorded.

SOUTH INDIA

South of the Narbadā, the pebble industry dwindles but does not completely vanish. Such at least is the evidence as it stands, with the proviso that, where handaxes or cleavers are present, there is a natural tendency to collect them at the expense of cruder pebble artifacts, and so to create a false bias. As things are, the most southerly site at which pebble-tools have been recognized in quantity is in Mayurbhanj in Orissa, where river-sections near Kamarpal have produced a mixed handaxe and pebble industry resembling the Early Soan but with the pebble-tools in a minority.[20] Farther south, pebble-tools occur only in small proportion, though other types or industries supplement and extend the Madras handaxes and cleavers which dominate the Peninsula. At first sight, a tenuous link between north and south is sustained by a distinctively mid-Pleistocene fauna. Thus at Nevasa on the Pravara river, tributary of the Godāvarī, between Ahmadnagar and Aurangābād, 150 miles east-north-east of Bombay, a hard cemented basal gravel (I), which is capped successively by two further gravels (II and III) and a thick layer of yellow-brown silt, has produced teeth of *Bos namadicus*;[21] and both *Elephas namadicus* and hippopotamus have been found in comparable gravels of the Godāvarī itself. As between the Soan and the Narbadā, a faunistic equation of this kind seems to make sense (p. 38), but it must be confessed that a similar equation between the Soan and the Pravara is at present less easy. Thus the basal Gravel I of the Pravara, which produced *Bos namadicus*, is said to have yielded a handaxe-cleaver industry of Early-Middle Acheulian type (using trap and dolerite); whereas the Boulder Conglomerate of the Soan, which produced *Elephas namadicus*, yielded only the crude 'Pre-Soan' industry. This apparent unconformity may represent a true technological variation between the two regions, or may be due rather to contemporary differences between the tropical and the submontane fauna; but it needs watching, and illustrates the perils of hasty equation.

On the Pravara, the Acheulian industry occurs also, though rarely, in Gravels II–III; in particular, an unrolled handaxe of chalcedony was found in Gravel II, 8 feet above the top of Gravel I, and a large pear-shaped handaxe of trap, flaked on both sides by fine step-technique and with subsequent retouch along the edge, one side weathered and the other side in mint condition, lay as high as the surface of Gravel III, under the final silt. But the normal industry of the upper two gravels was of another kind, consisting of scrapers, blades, cores, burins and points of agate, chert, chalcedony and jasper. Here is an

Fig. 6

acceptable Upper Palaeolithic craftsmanship of a sort at present inadequately represented in our Indian material, and further reference will be made to it in the next chapter.

Further south, in and near the Nallamalais Range of the Kurnool-Cuddapah districts north of Madras, a number of

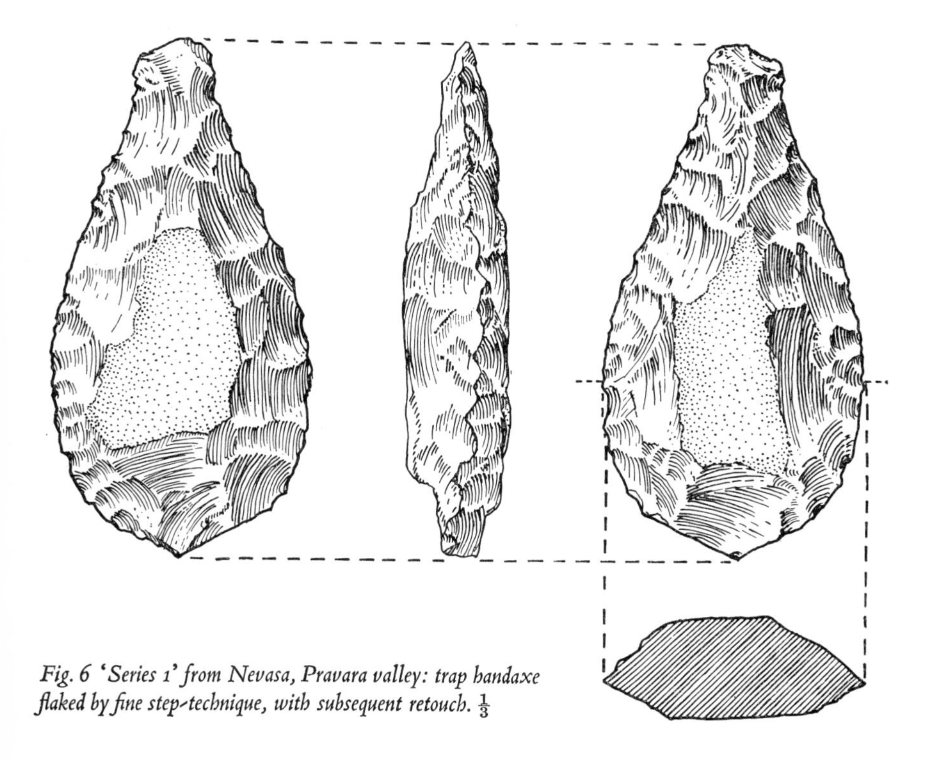

Fig. 6 'Series 1' from Nevasa, Pravara valley: trap handaxe flaked by fine step-technique, with subsequent retouch. $\frac{1}{3}$

sites have produced a large assemblage of implements which were analysed in 1930 in a classic paper by Cammiade and Burkitt.[22] The geological environment indicates a succession of prolonged pluvials and interpluvials, the basis being a reddish clayey mass of 'laterite', largely of hydrated alumina and iron-oxide, formed by the weathering of crystalline rocks under torrential rainfall alternating with dry seasons over a long stretch of time. It was on the weathered surface and in washed-down deposits of this laterite, when 'the swamps and forests of the laterite period gave place to large open plains' under supervening dry conditions, that human relics first appeared upon the scene. They consist largely of handaxes (classified as 'Series 1'), unrolled and stained by a largely-vanished capping of laterite. The implements are characteristically made from quartzite pebbles; they show the bold flaking and irregular edges which are encouraged by the coarse material and must not therefore be over-emphasized in a typological classification. *Fig. 9, 1* Amongst the handaxes is an occasional 'rostro-carinate', with flat ventral plane produced by the removal of a large flake, and a keel-like back formed by part of the original surface of the pebble—a type similarly associated with handaxes at Victoria West in South Africa and in the Oldowan of East Africa.[23]

Above the laterite-stained pebble-bed which produced the handaxes, a red clay laid down under renewed pluviation yielded flakes ('Series 2'), and other sites in the region are marked by flake-industries at an equivalent horizon. Handaxes are now the exception. Some of the flakes have prepared striking-platforms, others have not. Occasional examples may fairly be described as burins; one as 'a double-ended burin of a very Upper Palaeolithic appearance'. Whilst this post-handaxe series must represent (a part of) the later Palaeolithic of peninsular India, it is at the best a crude product, at a lower level of technical achievement than either the best handaxes and cleavers of 'Series 1', or the more slender backed-blades, planing-tools, end-scrapers, core-scrapers, and burins, made of materials of a more flinty nature, classified as 'Series 3'. The latter occurs on the surface of the red clay, and prepares the way for 'Series 4', which marks the topmost deposits and is generally microlithic in character (agate and quartzite). This belongs to the next chapter.

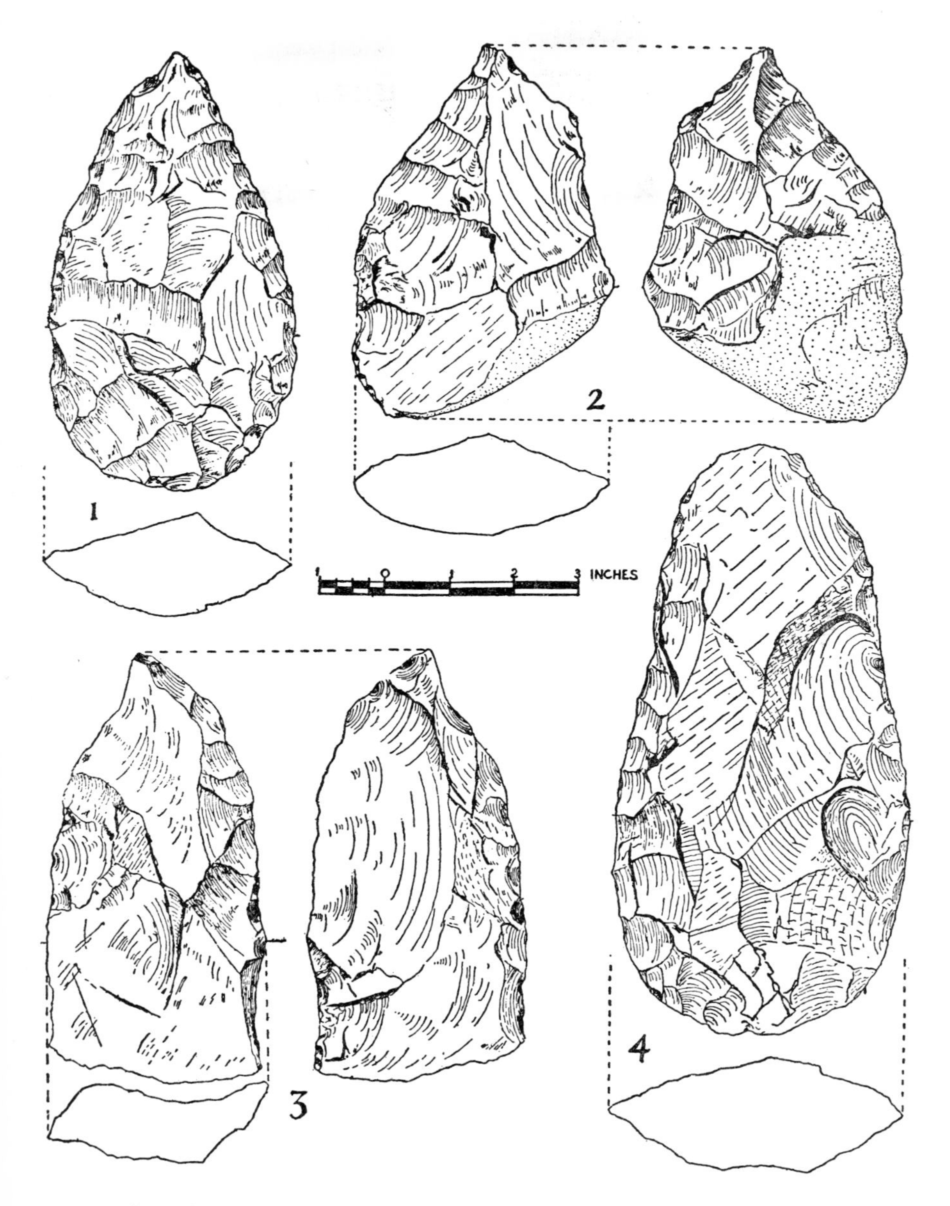

Fig. 7 Madras industry: 1, handaxe trimmed all over by controlled flaking; 2, similar, with pebble butt; 3, cleaver; 4, handaxe. All from Attirampakkam. $\frac{1}{2}$

Of the chronology of these industries, all that can be said at present is that not less than three pluvial episodes are seemingly identifiable since the first appearance of mankind in these parts, and the successive climatic phases were certainly of long duration. But it must again be affirmed that any attempt to equate these pluvials with the three glaciations associated with implements in the Potwar area of the north is premature on the evidence available.

A parallel series was identified by T. T. Paterson in and above the Red Hills near Madras, where four terrace surfaces were recognized.[12] Here a considerable layer of detrital or redeposited laterite overlay a well-developed Boulder Conglomerate; and the laterite was eroded to produce Terrace 1, on which were minor deposits of sand and gravel. This in turn was eroded to form Terrace 2, where thicker gravels were deposited and then covered by alluvium. Three groups of implements are associated with this sequence at a number of sites.

At Vadamadurai Tank, north-west of Madras, the Boulder Conglomerate at the base of this sequence produced handaxes and cores of the first group, which, on grounds of typology and patination, falls in turn into an earlier and a later series. The earlier series includes very crude Abbevillian handaxes with thick pebble butts and much remaining cortex; the flaking denotes a 'stone' technique producing large irregular flake-scars. The cores belonging to this series were large, also with rough irregular flaking. Both handaxes and cores bore a very deep whitish crust. The later series is less heavily patinated and is typologically more advanced. It is marked by handaxes of Early Acheulian type, showing the beginnings of a step-flaking technique, though large free flaking is still commonly used. The cores are mostly discoidal, with fairly regular alternate flaking.

The overlying laterite gravel had stained to a characteristic red colour the implements of the second group. This comprises neater and more regularly shaped (ovate and pear-shaped) handaxes of Middle Acheulian type showing considerably more step-flaking, together with flakes which have only primary flaking and unfaceted platforms.

The third group has no laterite-staining and but little patination. The handaxes may be classified as Upper Acheulian, and include both ovates with small, fairly flat step-flaking, and

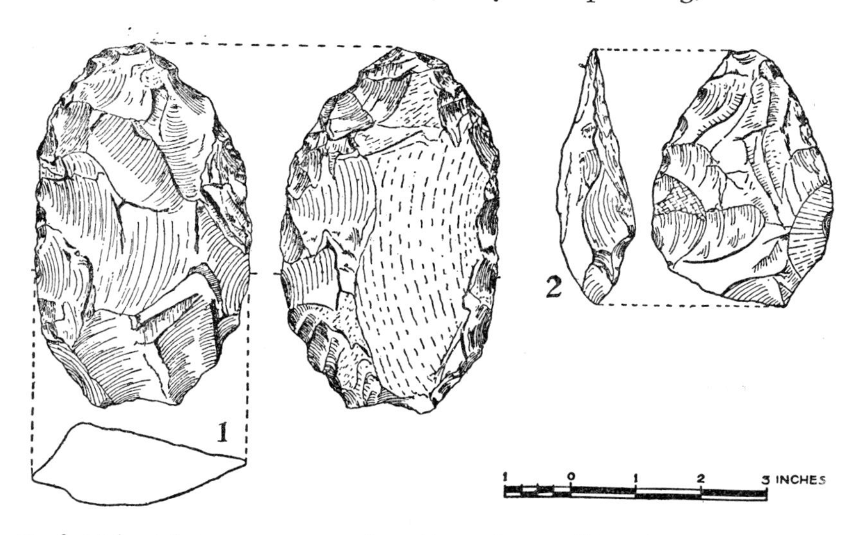

Fig. 8 Madras industry: 1, ovate; 2, cordate with secondary step-flaking along margin. Both from Attirampakkam

long pointed forms with thick pebble butts and large, neat free-flaking. The cores are discoidal; the flakes still have unfaceted platforms, but a few have been retouched for possible use as side-scrapers. One cleaver is present. This third group belongs to the gravels of Terrace 1.

Attirampakkam near Madras is an important site which demands further work. Professor Zeuner informs me that the early series here, consisting of pebble-tools, flakes and handaxes, is pre-laterite. Then came a laterite-weathering phase,

Figs. 7–8 during which the decomposition of the earlier implements proceeded. This was followed by the denudation of the laterite deposit, and the sediments thus formed in the valleys contain an Acheulian industry with a strong flake-component. The so-called Attirampakkam 5 series (late Acheulian) is fresh and is found in the lowest or latest terrace.

In recent years fresh fieldwork has been carried out in the vicinity of Giddalur, District Kurnool.[24] The Series 1 and 2 of the Cammiade-Burkitt analysis have again been recognized, and within them a gradation from earlier and rougher to later and more evolved has been partially established on the basis of the degree of rolling present in the individual specimens. Thus the Abbevillio-Acheulian handaxes and associated rostro-carinates of Victoria West type, made out of pebbles which often preserve cortical patches, are liable to exhibit a fair measure of rolling. *Fig. 9* With them are associated Clactonian flakes and cores, likewise rolled, and flake-made handaxes. The more advanced Acheulian ovates and handaxes, ranging from narrow, elongated specimens to wide, almost discoidal forms, are generally fresher in appearance; but no clear geological stratification is described. Cleavers are abundant, and flakes with prepared platforms, of Levallois type, occur though in a small minority. One or two scrapers, including a double-ended scraper with 'nibbled' retouch, recall Upper Palaeolithic industries of the West, but typologically the two Series may be described generally as of a Mid-Palaeolithic facies. Frequent cross-references to African analogies are convincing, though the significance of these comparisons is matter for discussion. Here the problem in relation to the Indian Palaeolithic as a whole, can only be indicated as a background to further research.

Setting aside for the moment the blade-and-scraper groups such as the 'Upper Pravara' which may prove to be the nucleus of a widespread Upper Palaeolithic, we are left with three

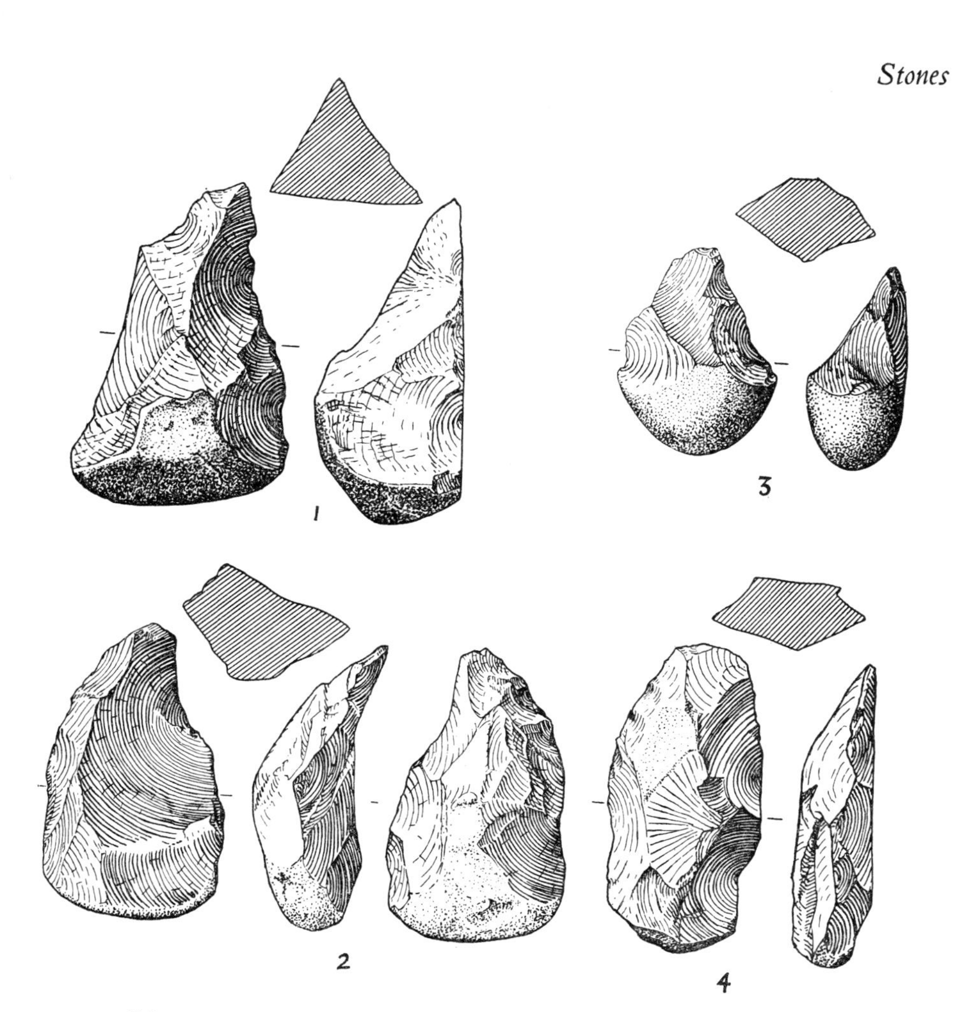

Fig. 9 Giddalur I: 1, quartzite rostro-carinate; 2–4, quartzite pebble-tools and handaxe. $\frac{1}{5}$

main Early-Mid Palaeolithic series: A, the large-flake Pre-Soan industries; B, the pebble points and choppers represented pre-eminently by the main Soan succession; and C, the Madras handaxes and cleavers. Of these, Series A stands for the time-being in isolation. The Boulder Conglomerate in

Fig. 10

which it occurs has been equated tentatively with the Boulder Conglomerate of the Madras Red Hills which has yielded pebble-tools of the 'pebble-handaxe' type along with biface core tools and flakes;[25] but the equation lacks all evidence, and cannot be used as an indication that pebble-tools appear earlier in south India than in the north. It must be accepted that pebble-choppers are significantly dominant in the north (the Punjab), although on a number of sites handaxes occur with them as a subordinate element. In central India the position is reversed; the handaxes are now in the ascendant, and south of the Narbadā and Orissa the pebble-choppers are in a small minority.

The first impression conveyed by this differential distribution is that the two series are essentially separate and complementary, with dispersal centres respectively in the north and in the south. This may be the correct answer; the seeming separateness of the series is slightly reinforced by the fact that the handaxes which accompany pebble-choppers in the Early Soan are wholly or largely absent from the Late Soan, which is otherwise its logical sequel, and a comparable sequence recurs in the Narbadā valley. Here it may be that a changing environment or population is the answer; but, even so, the seeming ease with which the two main elements of the Early Soan or the Lower Narbadā group slide apart is at least consistent with a divided tradition. Again, in the Sabarmati valley evolved Acheulian handaxes have been observed alongside a crude pebble and flake industry with which they have no obvious affinity. A somewhat similar disharmony is apparent in the Series 2 of the Nallamalais Range in south India, where the splendid handaxes of Series 1 are largely replaced by a crude pebble and flake industry which is not readily explained by the normal processes of devolution, though again a changing environment (of which we know very little) may be a cause. Certainly the possibility of independent origins for the pebble-

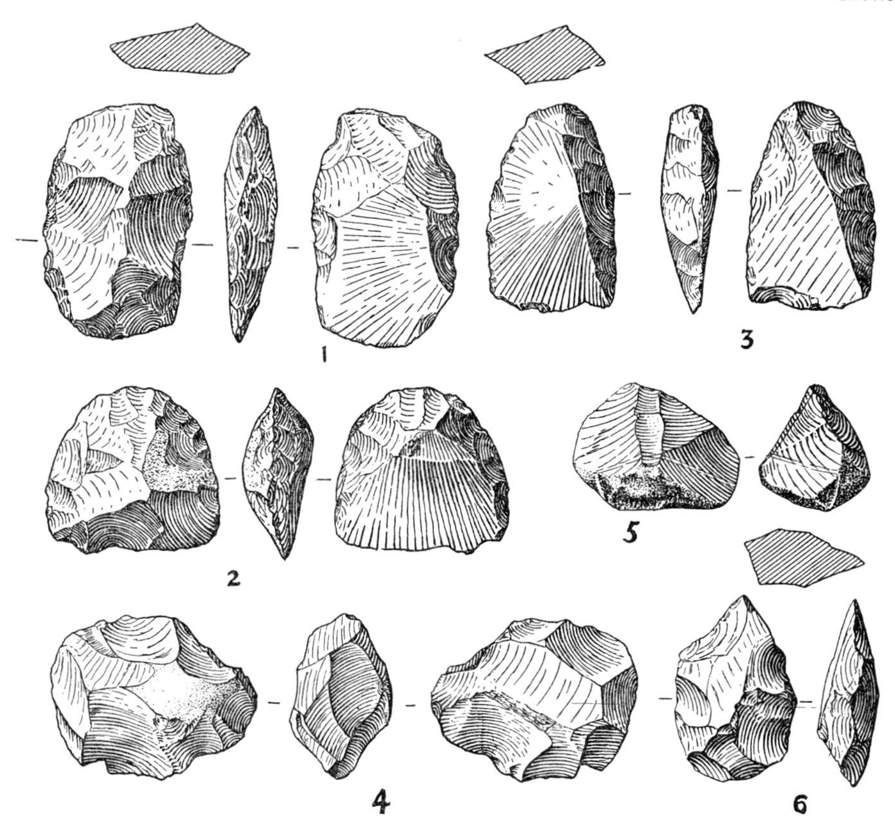

Fig. 10 Giddalur I: 1–3, cleavers; 4, discoidal 'Clactonian' core; 5, pebble-chopper; 6, small handaxe showing removal of alternate flakes on opposite sides. $\frac{1}{3}$

choppers and the handaxes must be kept open, and receives some support from wider geographic considerations. Before considering these, however, we must glance at the parallel situation in Africa.[23]

There the Victoria West (Cape Province) rostro-carinates have already been cited as analogies to the rostro-carinates of the Madras industry. But the similarities between the Indian

Fig. 9,1

and the African Palaeolithic are both more extensive and perhaps more significant than isolated resemblances suggest. Both in East and in South Africa the earliest Stone Age industry consists of pebbles from which one or two flakes have been struck to produce an irregular cutting edge. The industry is ascribable to the Lower Pleistocene, but it was of long duration and an alleged East African manifestation, known as the Kafuan from the river Kafu in Uganda, has been thought to exhibit a modest evolution. Here however a word of warning, applicable alike to India and to Africa, must be interpolated. The most primitive of human industries, whether in Europe, Africa or elsewhere, are necessarily liable to approximate to natural forms; and conversely, natural forms are sometimes liable to pass for primitive human artifacts. Various factors such as the quantitive occurrence of these 'artifacts' in a given deposit, and their occurrence or non-occurrence with human bones or other vestiges, help to shape a final judgement, but a subjective element is likely to remain. And so it is that the Kafuan series is not universally accepted as a human industry at all, and must be used with caution as a supporting analogue to Indian industries, whilst these in turn, in their more rudimentary forms, should only be accepted with the greatest circumspection. I have, in fact, little doubt that already in India more chipped pebbles have been received as artifacts than are, or should be, dreamt of in our archaeology.

We are on surer ground in East Africa with Leakey's 'Oldowan' pebble-industry, which is ascribed to the lower part of the Middle Pleistocene but may be somewhat earlier. Here crude choppers made by the removal of flakes in two directions along one side of the pebble seem to merge logically into very simple pebble-handaxes flaked in three or four directions so that two jagged cutting edges intersect in a point at one end. Subsequently, as at Victoria West, some of the implements display rostro-carinate characters, with the flat ventral surface and keeled dorsal surface described above. These characters combine with those of the bi-convex handaxes, and finally a mature Acheulian type, based on cores or large flakes, is achieved. It is possible here to regard the whole process from pebble to Acheulian handaxe as organic and evolutionary. With the Acheulian handaxes, other elements of more disputable ancestry—straight-edged cleavers, tortoise cores and Levalloisian flakes—complete the conventional assemblage. But it is not unimportant to add that simpler pebble-tools remained in use long after the handaxe complex was fully developed.

If from this orderly picture we return to the Indian problem, the thought occurs that there, too, the pebble-chopper and handaxe industries *may* not be unrelated. Pebbles sharpened bilaterally like great clumsy pencils have suggested the name 'pebble-handaxes' (above p. 35), and they may in turn, with the supplementary use of large flakes as cores, have contributed directly to the development of the Abbevillio-Acheulian types. The Acheulian cleaver, as in Africa, is more difficult to fit into any such evolutionary scheme, but may itself be in origin a Clactonian flake with secondary dressing. A real if partial affinity *may* in fact subsist between some facets of the pebble (and flake?) industries and of the great handaxe complex; whether by mere interaction or by genuine kinship is another matter.

There remains, however, the overriding factor of geographical distribution. This has been discussed in general terms by Hallam Movius,[26] who is inclined to write off the near-handaxes of Java and Malaya for technical reasons as an independent development and to exclude both the Acheulian handaxe and the Levalloisian flake entirely from the Far East.* This leaves the pebble—or chopper—industries in dominant possession there, in contrast to India, Western Asia, Africa,

* Professor Zeuner, on the other hand, would include the Javan and Malayan handaxes in the main series.

and central, southern and western Europe, in all of which Acheulian handaxes and flake implements manufactured by the prepared striking-platform and tortoise-core technique are at home. But, as we have seen, the handaxe distribution is not exclusive. In North, East and South Africa, as in many parts of India, there is a basic or background pebble-chopper industry, the uncontaminated survival of which in the Far East may be due to the (alleged) failure of alien handaxe-elements to penetrate farther eastward than India. In other words, the differential distribution of choppers and handaxes on the wider map may seem to favour a cultural duality as the explanation of their differential distribution on the smaller map of the Indian subcontinent. If this inference be correct, Africa becomes the obvious centre of primary dispersal for the handaxe complex, and we are confronted with the diffusion of ideas on a vast scale.

Fig. 11

Here two points emerge, both of which will be encountered in later contexts. The first is the recurrently unitary aspect of the cultures fringing the Indian Ocean. We are accustomed to the recurrent interrelationship of the lands framing the Mediterranean; we may equally accustom ourselves to a cultural community between East Africa, Arabia and India, whether in prehistoric or historic times. Today, the interests of the East African Coast are vested in Indians and Arabs no less than in Africans and Europeans. Further back, the principal medieval mosque on the island of Kilwa, off the coast of Tanganyika, reflects the great mosque of Gulbarga in the Deccan. The medieval history of that same coast is a story of Arab trade and domination. Then and later, Chinese wares flowed around this great periphery. Earlier than all these, the *Periplus* tells us how in the 1st century A.D. traders linked East Africa with Egypt, Arabia and India. Like the Mediterranean, the Indian Ocean is an essentially unitary 'culture-pool', if so insignificant a name may be stretched to so immense

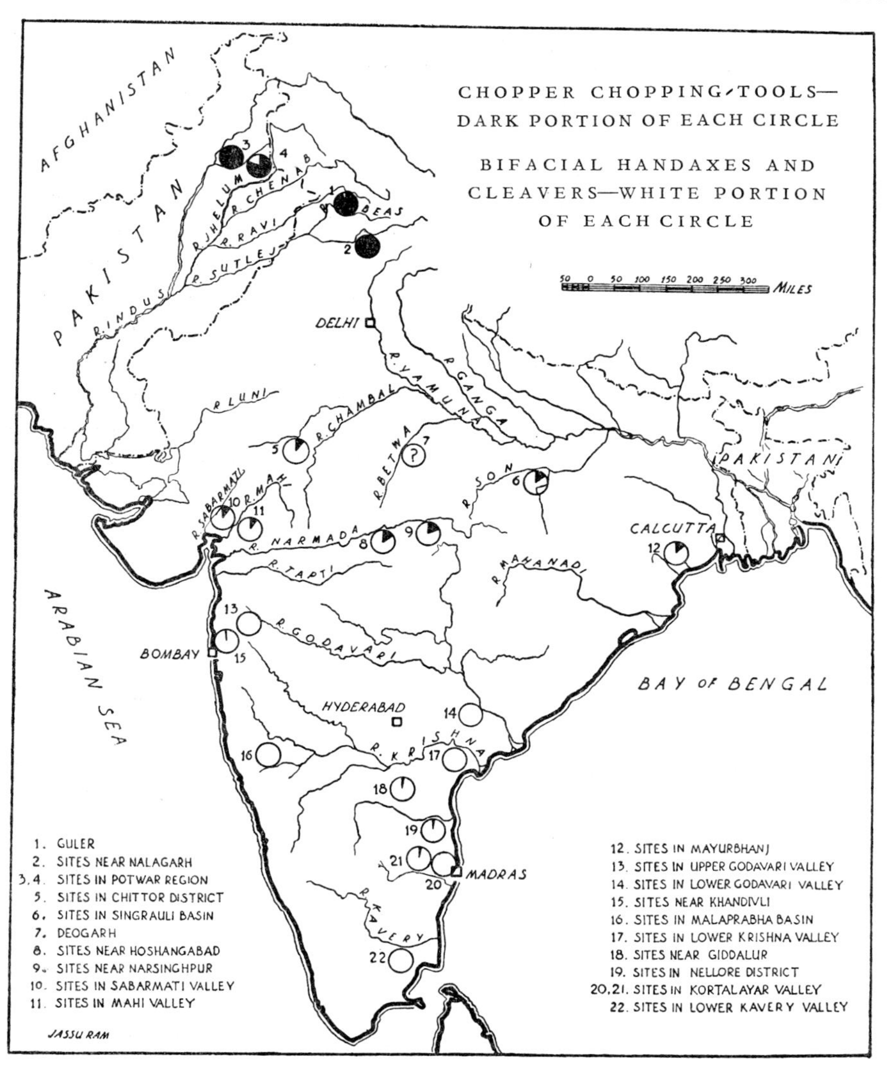

Fig. 11 Comparative occurrence of 'chopper chopping-tools', bifacial handaxes and cleavers

a compass; and it was already a unitary culture-pool, it seems, far back in the Middle Pleistocene.

The other point is this. The transference of industries, or even cultures, from one part of the world to another does not necessarily imply mass-migration. It does not take a thousand men to carry an idea, particularly a revolutionary idea. Indeed, I sometimes think that ideas have wings and fertilize like casual butterflies. There is at least no need to imagine African hand-axe-battalions marching north and east and imposing a new colonialism upon backward pebble-using natives. If one thing is more certain than another, it is that the time-intervals represented by these various industrial modes were astonishingly lengthy, and that for thousands or even hundreds of thousands of years cultural change must have been scarcely perceptible. Changes, when they came, may have been relatively sudden, whether actuated by violent alterations of environment, by disease or other accident, or by the even less predictable impact of human genius. There is no simple answer, nor ever will be.

Finally, let us glance back over this chapter as a whole. By and large, it must be admitted that the story of Old Stone Age man in India is at present monotonous, inhuman stuff. We have no solitary tooth of his, upon which we can exercise our humane imaginations, still less a skull wherein we can enclose that intelligence which was content, age after age, to batter quartzite pebbles into some crudely utile shape. It may be that sometime before 1881 we came nearer to a little knowledge of his likeness if a human cranium discovered by W. Theobald in what may have been a Pleistocene bone-bed in central India was truly of that geologic age.[27] But the skull was subsequently lost in the museum of the Asiatic Society of Bengal, and we can only wait, with a proper impatience, for Indian palaeontology to get to work anew.

Nor need the answer, when found, be a simple one. It is more than likely that, in the Middle Pleistocene, India was populated by human or sub-human beings of very various types, perhaps both more and less advanced than the *pithecan-thropi* or ape-men, of doubtful speech and diverse aspect, who have been recognized elsewhere in Asia. It is not impossible that these heterogeneous types, partially contemporary with one another, shared in the industries which we have described. Meanwhile, in fairness to our proto-Indians of the Old Stone Age, let it be said again that we know almost nothing about them. Their brains, many of them, were probably no less ample than ours, and their thoughts may have been only a little more inconsequential. We like to imagine them as squatting along the river-banks in the neighbourhood of suitable out-crops, shaping, with prodigal expenditure of material, endless masses of stone with which to slay and dismember endless processions of animals in the unwary moment of the morning or evening draught. But in sooth we do not even know the intent which lay behind this industrious manipulation of flakes and pebbles. What, for example, was the real function of those weighty handaxes, sometimes a foot in length, which were so skilfully sharpened on both sides alike by carefully con-trolled blows? It has been suggested that the handaxe was 'an excellent instrument for digging up roots, grubs, and other food from the ground': truffles with a handaxe. On the other hand, at that astonishing site at Olorgesailie, near Nairobi in Kenya, tens of thousands of handaxes are associated with animal-bones split to extract the marrow and skulls smashed to extract the brains. Handaxe man was certainly an indifferent vegetarian; and the answer doubtless is that this tool, made by the million, was in fact an all-purposes tool, whether actually held in some vast encompassing handgrip or mounted for use in some fashion lost to us. We do not even know whether the abstract creature whom we have called 'Handaxe man' had articulate speech.

An ingenious Dutch psychiatrist suggests that handaxes were made symmetrical for ambidexterous users, whereas the emergent flake-industries were connected with nascent right-handedness; and that this right-handedness was in turn linked with the development of speech-centres on the left side of the brain.[28] That may be sound physiology but it is perhaps not very good archaeology since flakes occur as early as handaxes. It may of course be that men with the gift of articulate speech co-existed with others, grunting *mlechchhas*, who lacked it. We simply do not know.

Even the inferred bias towards river-banks may well be wrong. The picture is as likely as not to be unbalanced by the fact that river-cuttings are of their nature particularly liable to expose the buried strata on which these remote peoples had their being. No doubt, however, it is near enough to the truth. The story of these folk is a part—in years, a very long part—of the story of India; the careful and onerous investigation of their industries and environment is a primary task for Indian and Pakistani archaeology; but, for all our skill, they are doomed to remain, these pioneers, little more than 'Handaxe folk' or 'Pebble-chopper-chopping folk', little more than archaeological labels which thinly disguise the poverty of our understanding.

Chapter IV

More Stones

THE PRINCIPAL INDUSTRIES described in the last chapter may have begun about 400,000 years ago and may have ended—to use an abrupt term for what was certainly a very long and ragged process—something under 100,000, perhaps nearer 50,000, years ago, with survivals, as in South Africa, down to relatively recent times. So far, our handaxes and pebble-choppers have offered little hint of succession or replacement, and to this sequel we must now turn, though without great hope of definition. The example of Africa shows how much can be achieved by a single generation of scientific field-workers, and India is equipping herself for a similar advance. Meanwhile the present somewhat dubious position may be summarized under two questions. First, what evidence is there for a distinctive Upper Palaeolithic phase in India, as in Africa and Europe? And, secondly, is there in India, again as elsewhere, a recognizable Mesolithic between the Old Stone Age and the New—if indeed there be a New Stone Age at all? This question involves, *inter alia*, the problem of the microlithic or small-stone industries which occur profusely in parts of the subcontinent and stoutly resist easy classification.

First, then, the Upper Palaeolithic. In the north, as already noted (p. 40), there was a tendency in the Late Soan towards finer flake-implements, apparently without handaxes. This trend is appropriate to the Upper Palaeolithic but needs much further investigation; for example, Terrace 4 of the Soan series is at present an uncertain quantity, and surface sites of small flakes and pebble-tools on the Sil (tributary of the Soan) near Pindi Gheb and at Dhok Pathan nearby are without stratigraphical context. Like the flakes, the pebble-tools are smaller than the average Soan type, and include a new form, a kind of awl made on a small oval pebble flaked on both sides at one end to make a sharp point. Associated flakes are similar to Late Soan: a few are retouched, and one is a steep scraper with fine trimming. Faceting of the platform is rare. 'The age of this series', adds Paterson, 'is uncertain, but, to judge from typology and the state of preservation, it is undoubtedly fairly late and must be at the earliest contemporary with the Late Soan, possibly later, perhaps even of the fourth glacial age.'[29] In the Jhelum valley of Kashmir, de Terra and Paterson found 'great numbers of artificially flaked stones, among which were flakes and cores reminiscent of palaeolithic technique' including the Levalloisian; 'but in all these places it was certain that the flakes are associated with pottery-bearing layers of either neolithic or historic date'.

That has not carried us very far—or, rather, it has carried us too far—and the three terraces which have been noted in the Beās and Bāngangā valleys, with their consistent assemblage of choppers and handaxes (p. 40), likewise take us at present no further in this problem. But in central India the evidence begins to clear. In the last chapter attention was drawn to a remarkable disc and blade industry described by Sankalia from the upper gravels of the Pravara, tributary of the Godāvāri.[30] This industry apparently overlies the bulk of the Acheulian handaxes which, with rare survivals just sufficient to suggest a cultural overlap, are, if the account is correctly interpreted, concentrated in Gravel I, the lowest, of the geological succession (above, p. 46). It does not fit easily into the current categories, and may provisionally be known as the 'Upper Pravara' until its position and affinities are more amply established. Its materials are agate, chert, chalcedony and jasper, and its forms constitute a miscellany of scrapers, blades and cores. The cores, to some of which the somewhat loose term 'Clactonian' is applied, include also very non-Clactonian examples worked all over by pressure-technique, with

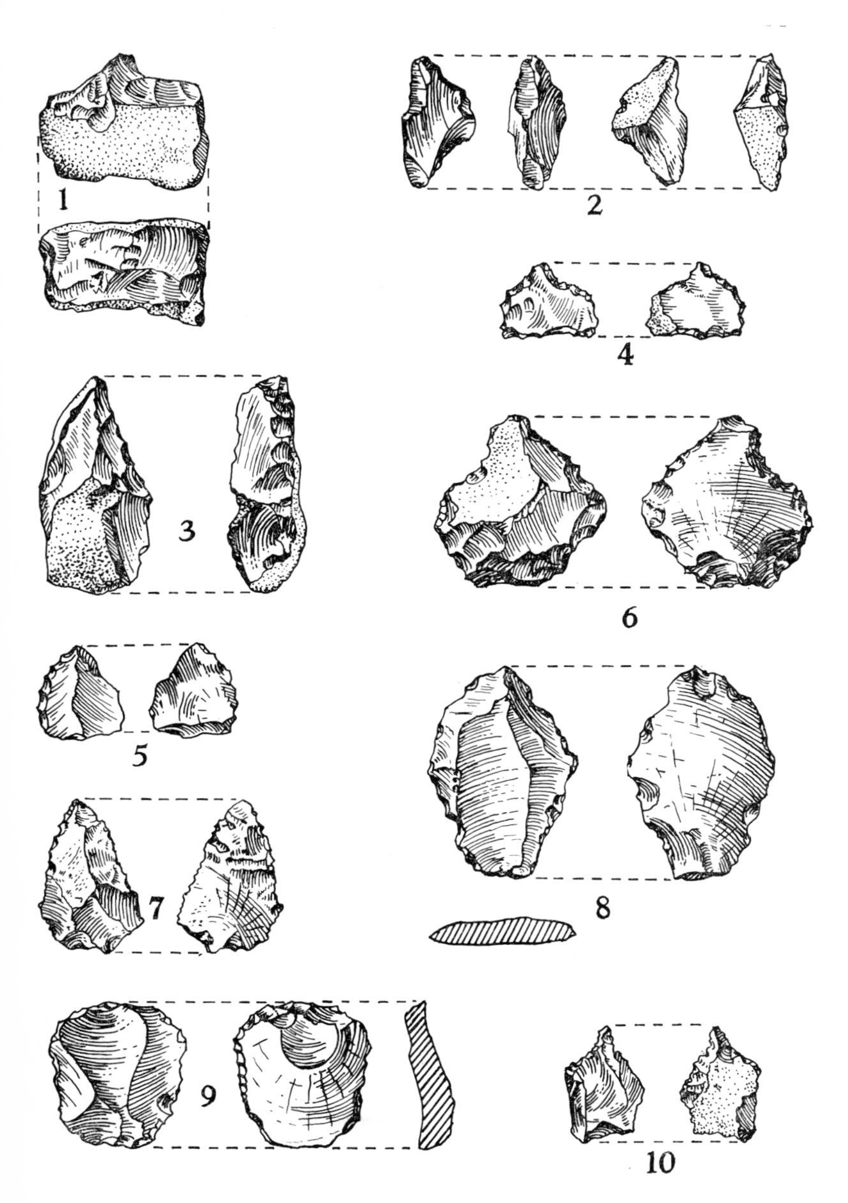

Fig. 12 'Series 2' from Nevasa, Pravara valley: 1, chert burin; 2, chert double-ended burin; 3, agate point; 4, chalcedony point; 5, quartz point; 6, pointed chert flake; 7, pointed chalcedony flake; 8, leaf-shaped chert flake; 9, chert scraper; 10, chalcedony awl. $\frac{1}{2}$

irregular wavy edge. Amongst the blades a type about an inch long with blunted back and retouched edge merges into an end-scraper in examples with more emphatic flaking; but there are also half-round scrapers and side-scrapers with extensive retouch, and indeed the blade-scraper series exhibits a wide range and an evolved tradition. A few flakes show Levallois characters with faceted striking-platform and some retouching round the edges. Two or three implements with beaked point may be described as burins—a relatively rare type in India.

Figs. 12–13

Microlithic elements occurred in the overlying silt, above a considerable intervening deposit devoid of artifacts; but the Upper Pravara as a whole showed no specifically microlithic trend, and a vaguely Aurignacian facies can be claimed for it without emphasis. It shows some analogy with earlier phases of the Kenya Capsian or Aurignacian, and may in fact be the forerunner of an equivalent Indian development. It is at least sufficient to encourage further search for a true Upper Palaeolithic phase in the Indian succession.

A comparable hint of an Upper Palaeolithic horizon was detected by Commander K. R. U. Todd in a clay- and gravel-pit at Khaṇḍivli, 21 miles north of Bombay,[31] though here again an admirable piece of pioneer-work awaits consolidation and development. Upon the native rock, a deposit of bluish-brown clay, the Lower Clay, 3 to 50 inches thick contained rough tools and flakes 'somewhat recalling a Clacton industry' but occasionally showing more than one period of flaking. This industry approximates in kind to the pre-Soan. On the surface of the Lower Clay occurred another somewhat similar industry comprising scrapers, cores and choppers, sometimes in mint condition, with 'an early form of rostrate hand-axe'. Overlying the Lower Clay was the Lower Gravel, 1–6 feet thick, containing numerous implements of Abbevillian and Clactonian types in varying states of preservation. On the surface of the gravel were Clactonian flakes and Acheulian

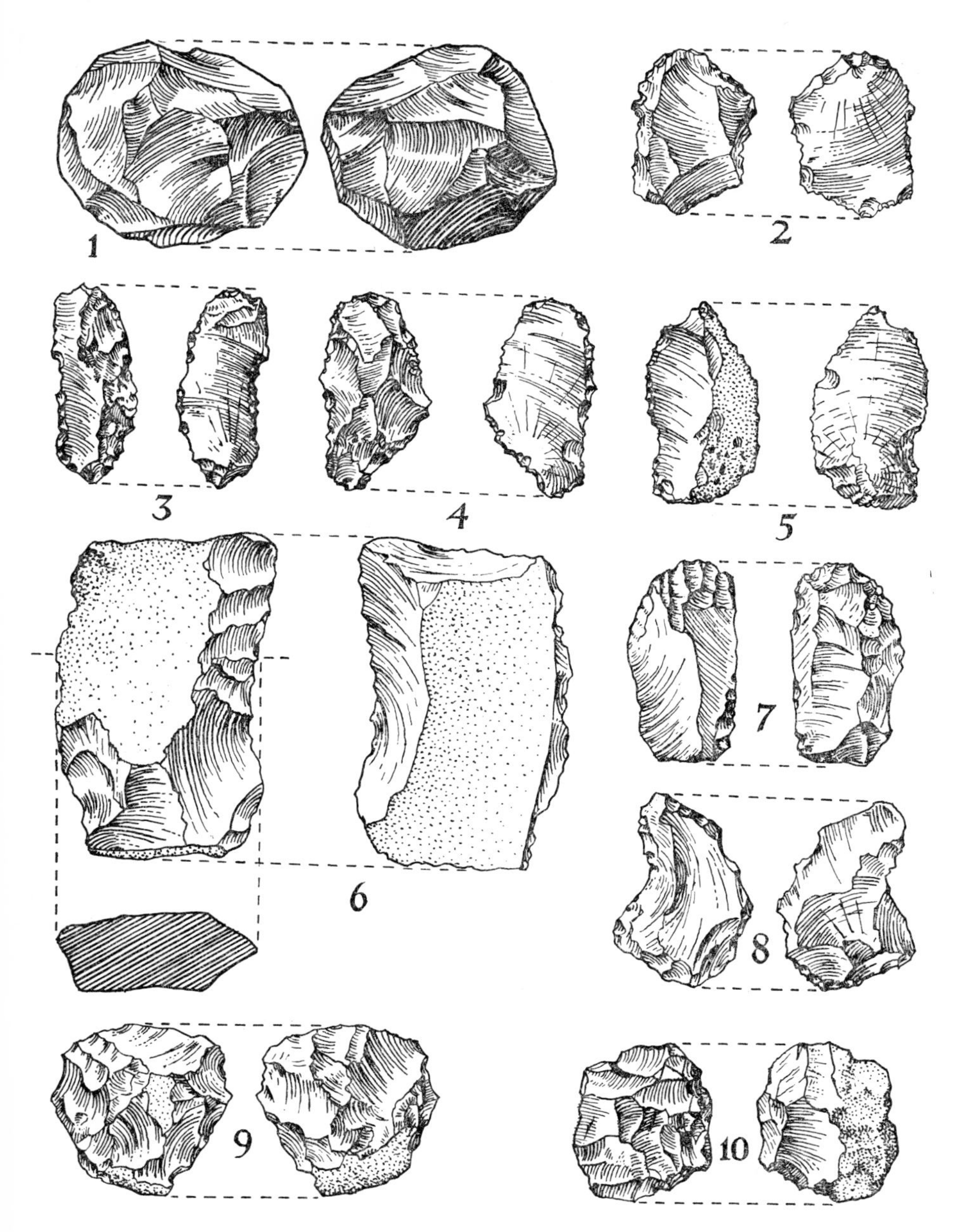

Fig. 13 'Series 2' from Nevasa, Pravara valley: 1, chert discoid; 2, chalcedony flake with prepared striking-platform; 3–5, chalcedony blades with blunted back and edge partly retouched; 6, tabular side-scraper, chert; 7–8, chalcedony end-scrapers; 9–10, chalcedony discoids. $\frac{1}{2}$

handaxes in mint condition, with a number of unclassified flake-implements 'probably Acheulian in culture'. So far, all is reasonably plain sailing. In the present context it is the relationship of these lower layers to their successors that matters.

Above the Lower Gravel was alternatively a further layer of clay known as the Middle Clay, or a sandy stratum representing probably the laterization of the upper part of the Lower Gravel. These deposits were themselves devoid of implements, but on their surface was a blade industry, including cores, blades and scrapers, with a few small handaxes made on flakes. On top of the sand or Middle Clay lay the Upper Gravel, about 3 feet deep, on which was found a working-floor with a blade and burin industry accompanied by little heaps of waste flakes of indurated shale. Over all were 18 inches of Upper Clay containing a more developed blade and burin industry, including polyhedral and angle burins and one of parrot-beak type. In and on the surface appeared the inevitable microlithic industry of these parts (see below, and Chapter 7).

In this series, both the Lower and the Middle Clays may represent periods of pluviation, whilst the gravels may indicate phases of a semi-arid character,* but to equate the pluviations with the standard glaciations is, in the present state of knowledge, mere guesswork. At a venture, the Lower Clay might be matched with the penultimate glaciation, and, if so, is congenially associated with its pre-Soan-Abbevillian industries whilst the Middle Clay may correspond to the last glaciation, which would thus be brought into a familiar terminal relationship with a blade, burin and scraper industry of a roughly Upper Palaeolithic facies. Beyond that oracular statement, even guesswork falters.

In the south of India a partially equivalent Upper Palaeolithic seems to emerge as Series 3 of the Cammiade-Burkitt

* Todd thought that the Lower Gravel was laid down under pluvial conditions, but this is perhaps less likely than the view here suggested.

succession. In the Nandikanama Pass north of Madras (p. 48), on the surface of a red alluvial clay which is in turn sealed by red sandy soil—both layers which should be subsequent to the gravels containing the handaxe- and flake-industries of Series 1 and 2—have been found a number of knife-blades of black (Lydian?) stone showing fine blunting down the backs, together with core-scrapers and burins mostly of the gouge type. Small crescents or 'lunates', however, of a normal microlithic type also occur in the Series, and, if in place, suggest that the industry may be too late to constitute an immediate follow-up of the Mid-Pleistocene Series, 1 and 2. On the other hand, Series 3 has an affinity with the so-called Capsian of Kenya, where lunates also occur with backed-blades, burins and end-scrapers. Incidentally, two radiocarbon dates for the partially comparable Upper Capsian of North Africa give *c.* 6500 and 5000 B.C.,[32] and, if the Indian dating should prove to be of the same order or even somewhat earlier, an appreciable gap between Series 2 and 3 becomes virtually certain.

In brief, the Upper Pravara and possibly the Khanḍivli groups are for the moment the only industries in India for which an organically intermediate position can be claimed with reasonable probability between the Acheulian-Levalloisian groups of the late Middle Pleistocene and the evolved microlithic 'spread' to which we must now turn.

The small-stone (microlithic) industries of Europe, Africa, western Asia and India present, like the handaxes before them, a standard example of the problems of diffusion over a wide map. Their considerable degree of specialization and a vague but not entirely negligible approximation in their dating (as it seems) do indeed suggest some sort of cultural nexus in their distribution; but progress in the understanding of this remarkable possibility is dependent upon a closer analysis of the existing material and the acquisition of new. There is slight but accumulating evidence that Arabia formed a cultural, as indeed it forms a geographical, extension of the Sahara zone, and so may have constituted a central link between northern Africa and western Asia on the one hand and India on the other (cf. p. 58).

There are many places in India, such as the banks of the Narbadā, where the most casual collector can readily fill his pockets with these small flakes and implements. Their material—often chalcedony, agate, or other semi-precious stones—catches the eye, and their minute size stimulates curiosity and acquisitiveness. Many of them are undoubtedly the remains of composite tools, of which wood or bone formed a part; for example, arrow-shafts with barbs of small sharp flakes such as lunates, inset and gummed near the point on opposite sides of the shaft. Most of them, on the other hand, can only be described as 'industrial waste'.

Fig. 16

The familiar lunates—crescent-shaped flakes from $\frac{3}{4}$ inch to $1\frac{1}{2}$ inches in length, with the natural edge of the flake as the cord and steep retouching to blunt the rear arc, to take the pressure of the thumb or to inset in wood or bone—are the most constant denominator of microlithic industries, whether in Africa or India. Splayed lunates may have been used as transverse arrowheads. Trapezoidal forms occur occasionally but are rare; and points which can fairly be likened to the numerous burins of north Africa and western Europe are very exceptional indeed, unless 'borers' are included. Triangles merge into angular lunates and scarcely deserve separate classification. Disc scrapers are relatively abundant but are not particularly characteristic of the microlithic complex. On the whole, the Indian microlithic groups make an indifferent showing beside those of Africa, Palestine and Europe. Attempts to subdivide them into categories such as 'non-geometric' and 'geometric' are a move in the right direction but are premature in the present state of the evidence. As elsewhere, a very large

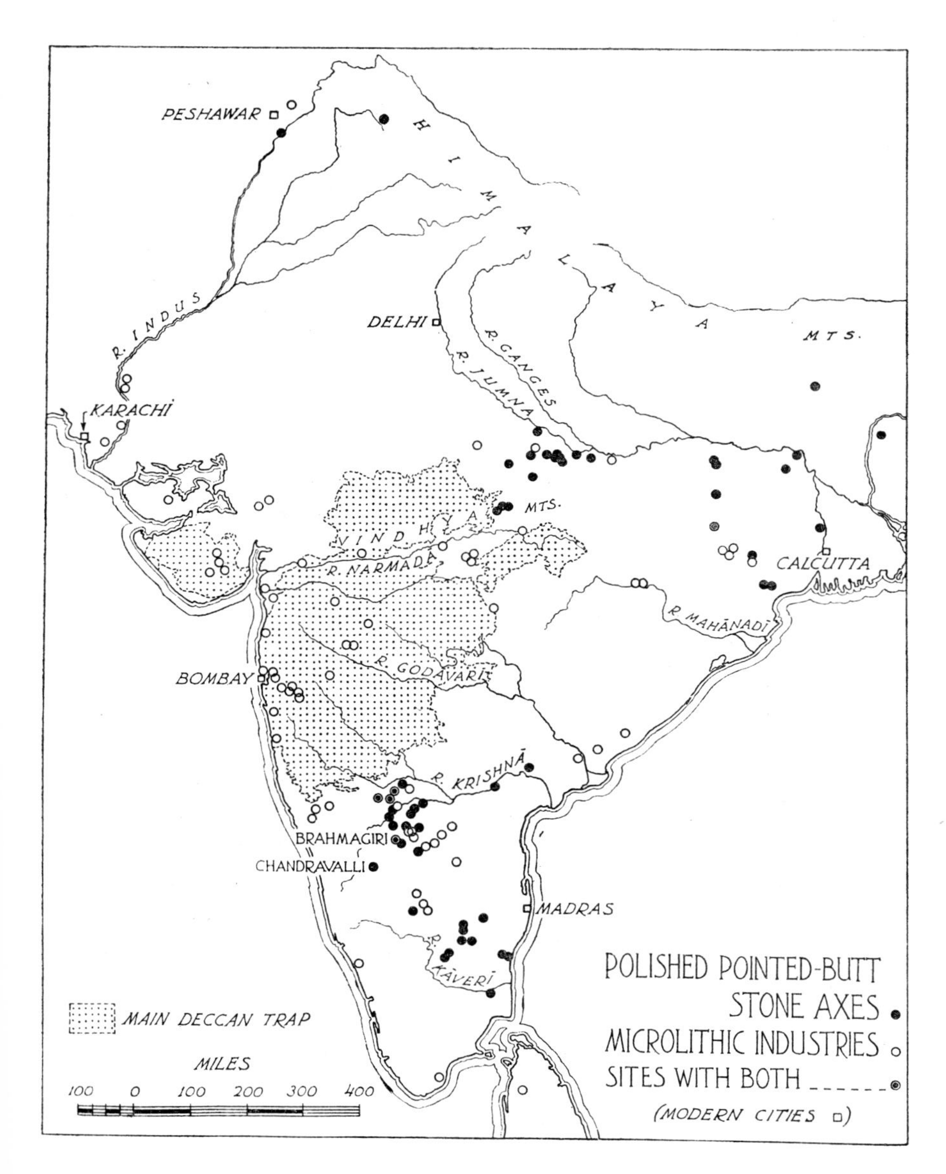

Fig. 14 Distribution of stone axes and microlithic industries

proportion of the material consists merely of primary flakes, which in a few instances suggest use but are mostly waste.

Fig. 14 On the map, the concentrations of microlithic sites are in central and southern India, with extensions up the west coast to the lower Indus. The Punjab and the northern plains are almost blank, though whether this is significant or rather due to inadequate exploration or to the covering of appropriate sites by aggradation cannot be affirmed. A similar doubt arises from the seeming absence of microliths from north-east India—East Bengal, Orissa and Assam. But the negation receives support from the fact that south-east Asia as a whole has failed, so far, to produce any microlithic industry truly comparable with that of India south of the Vindhyas.

The dating of these Indian industries is at present full of doubt. Provisionally, a line of division may be drawn between (earlier) microlithic industries which are not clearly associated with pottery and (later) ones which are. True, the incidence of pottery is likely to be a variable and even accidental datum. In recent years a number of Late Stone Age cultures devoid of pottery have been identified sporadically in Asia: at Kila Gul Mohammed near Quetta in Baluchistan, at Jarmo in the foothills of northern Iraq east of the Tigris, at Jericho in Jordan, and farther west in Cyprus. At Jarmo radiocarbon tests give a date about 4700 B.C. or earlier. At Jericho similar tests indicate that the pre-pottery Neolithic was flourishing both before and after 6000 B.C. The Baluch example produced a radiocarbon date of about 3350 B.C. Broadly, it may be affirmed that there is no reason, as knowledge stands, to assume the existence of good kiln-baked pottery anywhere in the world much before 4000 B.C., or in India before 3000 B.C. Some at least of the pottery found with microliths in India is of the Bronze or even the Iron Age, i.e. well within the 1st millennium B.C. Indeed it is a fair generalization that, in the Deccan and probably also in peninsular India, the Iron Age, which began there not earlier than the 5th century B.C. and in some places appreciably later, is an alien structure founded directly upon a microlithic and chalcolithic substratum (see Chapter 7).

Until recently, a classic instance of the variable relationship of pottery to microliths was supplied by Sankalia's well-known site in Gujarāt, at Langhnāj. There a considerable depth of dry wind-blown sand accumulated anciently, but, at an average depth of four feet from the present surface, the accumulation was interrupted by a faint layer of humus, indicating temporarily damper conditions. In the lower part of the sand above the humus, microliths were associated with potsherds of 'Neolithic' age or later. The humus land-surface itself and the sand below it were long thought to be completely devoid of pottery; but further examination of these layers in 1952 and 1954 is said to have produced 'very small quantities of extremely comminuted pieces of coarse, handmade and ill-fired pottery'.[33] The few fragments found were exceedingly tiny, and, if they are truly *in situ* and have not merely percolated through the very flimsy humus-layer, it would be interesting to know whether we are here confronted with true pottery or rather with baked basket-linings such as have been noted in the Upper Kenya Capsian. The buried humus layer produced vast numbers of microliths (including a majority of primary flakes) of quartz, jasper and chert. With them were sandstone slabs flattened on one side and used for grinding; and mineralized human skeletons of 'modern' dolichocephalic type, found in a crouched position below the humus, are assumed to be related burials. The fauna included Indian rhinoceros, hog-deer, axis deer, nilgai antelope, black-buck, bovines, mongoose, pig, horse, dog or wolf, tortoise and fish, but not, in the latest review of the material, any hint of domestication. Nor do the grinding-stones necessarily reflect agriculture, since they may equally have been used for wild grasses and spices. In any case, it seems likely that the economy of the settlement was dominantly that of the hunter. It should be added that, in the sand below the main occupation-level was found a part of the shoulder-blade of *Rhinoceros unicornis* bearing at least eight artificial pits on one side and suggesting use as an anvil in the fabrication of microliths.

The general picture is that of a community squatting on the dry sandy soil during a period of moderate rainfall, and occupied in the manufacture of small blades of which many may be supposed to have been set in bone or wood as composite tools. The small pebbles available for this purpose may have been collected in the Sabarmati river, some eighteen miles away. The community lived mainly on the products of the chase, but they supplemented their meat with prepared grasses or herbs, which nature may have provided without artificial aid. Pottery in the accepted sense was either absent or, if sparsely present, was of the crudest sort.

The stone industry from this land-surface included a great quantity of waste, due to the uncertain and irregular flaking of the material used. Fluted cores show that many of the blades broke off half-way down the core, but are small monuments of human persistency. Some cores were made from thick flakes, a practice noted elsewhere in central India. Of a hundred implements properly so-called (as distinct from mere flakes), the commonest is the lunate, backed along the arc either from one side or both. Irregular specimens, bulging nearer one end, may be described as points. These may have been used as arrowheads. For the rest, the series includes a few rather crude scrapers, and an oblique-ended point which might almost be described as a burin; but as a whole the industry is a poor one, with few specialized forms.

No significant difference is noted between the microliths on the ancient land-surface and those found (in far smaller numbers) with potsherds in the overlying sand. Again, the vast majority of the specimens from this upper layer are no more

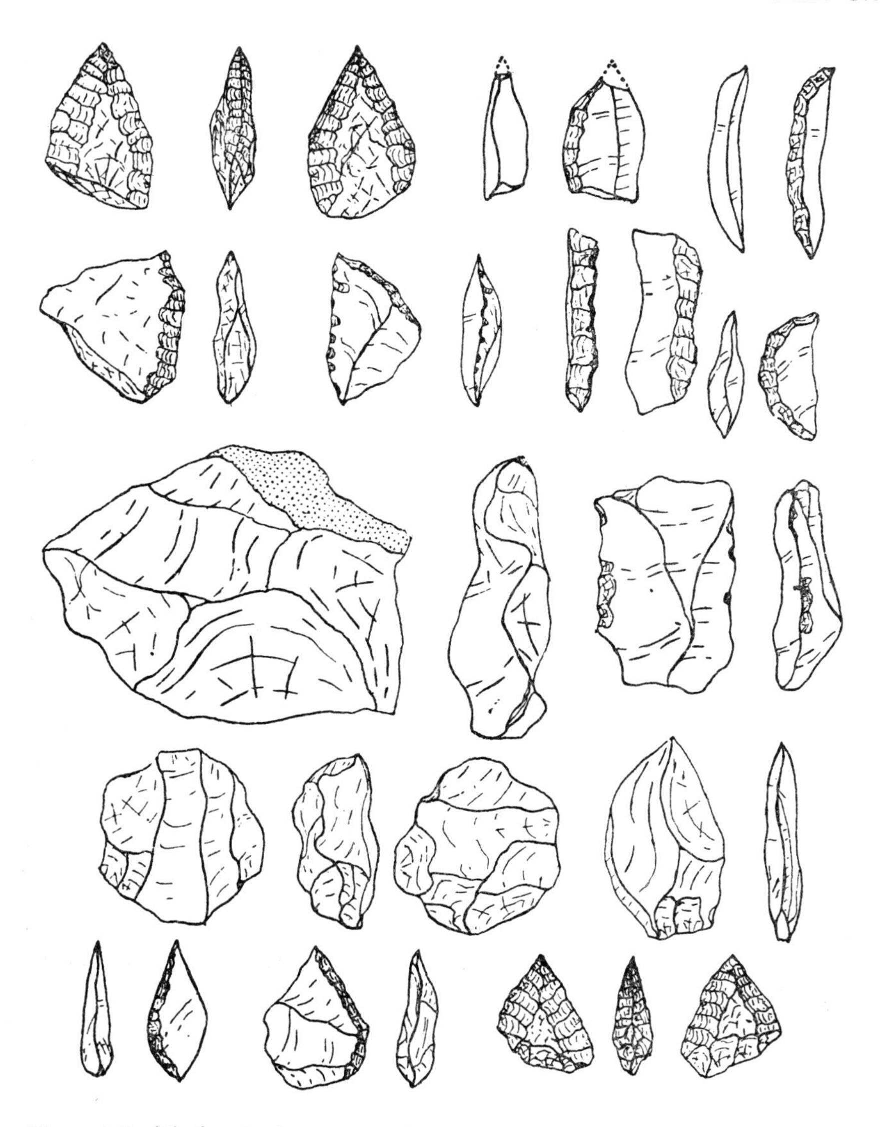

Fig. 15 Microliths from Ṭeri *sites, Tinnevelly district. Nearly* $\frac{1}{1}$

than minute primary flakes. The associated sherds, though of far better quality than the scraps from the lower levels, have not been dated more closely than 'Neolithic-Iron Age'.

A similar vagueness often attaches to sherds found elsewhere with microlithic industries, and the only value which can be derived from the association is the implication that no very remote age is ascribable to the industries in question: be it repeated that most of them are probably not earlier than the 1st millennium B.C. True, in East Africa crude pottery, or something very like it (above, p. 73), occurs in the Upper Kenya Capsian which is basically Upper Palaeolithic but includes an appreciable microlithic element, particularly lunates from $\frac{3}{4}$ to 1 inch in length. This industry has not yet been closely dated, though a North African analogy of about 6500–5000 B.C. has already been cited (p. 69). The Capsian is followed in Africa south of the Sahara by more wholeheartedly microlithic groups, of which the earlier Wilton has been compared with the latest of the four Cammiade-Burkitt series from South India—a profuse surface-mélange of pigmy tools including lunates, backed knife-blades, triangles, and core-scrapers. Similar microlithic assemblages, equally undated have been collected widely in the Mahī and Godāvarī valleys, the Vindhya Hills and elsewhere in the centre and the south, but only in two instances have they, at the time of writing, been associated with an informative stratigraphy devoid of pottery.

The first is at Rangpur in Kāthiāwāḍ where, beneath material related to the Indus Civilization, was a layer containing crude microliths of jasper and agate without pottery. The layer has not yet been adequately investigated, and all that can be said is that on this site microliths were in use not later than the latter half of the 2nd millennium B.C. The second instance is in the Tinnevelly District of the southern part of Madras State. Here the coastal plain is characterized by extensive sand-dunes or *ṭeris*, whence the sites associated with them

Fig. 15

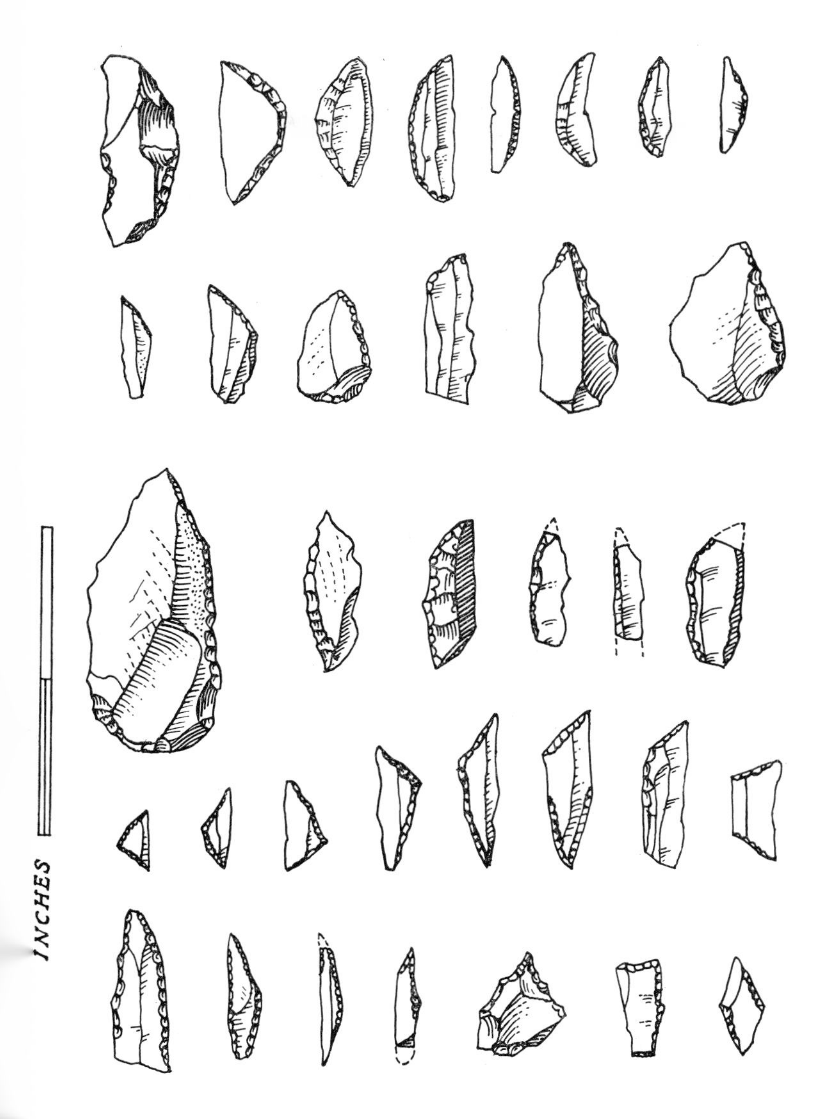

ig. 16 Microliths from Yerangal, Bombay

are known as Ṭeri sites. The sands are connected with fossil-beaches of calcareous sands largely of organic origin. Farther inland several morphological steps representing successive lagoon-floors of a greater age have been observed. On these various steps, A, B and C horizons have formed, but in many places the loose A horizon has been blown away, so that on the surface of the cemented B horizon is now encountered a concentration of industries originally deposited on or in A. In the aggregate, the industries must extend back to a very appreciable antiquity. They have been studied by Professor Zeuner and Mrs. Allchin.[35]

These stratified Ṭeri industries contain lunates, transverse arrowheads, bifacial points showing pressure-flaking, backed blades, unifacial and bifacial discoids, a microburin, end- and side-scrapers, and an occasional pebble chopping-tool of greater size. The tools are of quartz and variously coloured cherts. On certain sites, association with black-and-red sherds of urnfield or megalith type and of the last three or four centuries B.C. is ascribed to the blowing away of the A horizon and the consequent re-deposition of the sherds at the lower level. There is little doubt that, as a whole, the Tinnevelly Ṭeri industry represents a pre-pottery or at least a non-pottery phase. The pressure-flaked bifacial implements are elsewhere absent from India but recur in Ceylon.

We seem to have here the vestiges of a hunting or fishing people settled or temporarily encamped in the vicinity of an old coast-line 20–30 feet higher than today, sometime before the advent of polished stone axes (rare in any event so far south) and the pottery-using Chalcolithic. The phrase 'Mesolithic Period' is still too nebulous in India for definitive use, but it would appear likely that, under the impact possibly of micro-lithic elements received via Arabia (p. 70), in the Peninsula as in Africa a microlithic trend in the Upper Palaeolithic was subsequently so emphasized as to represent a distinctive stage in the Stone Age sequence. The general absence of a true flint or obsidian deprived the Indian tool-maker of the apt materials which encouraged his opposite numbers in Africa and Europe to perfect the fabrication of these minute implements, and, with occasional exceptions, it must be confessed that the Indian

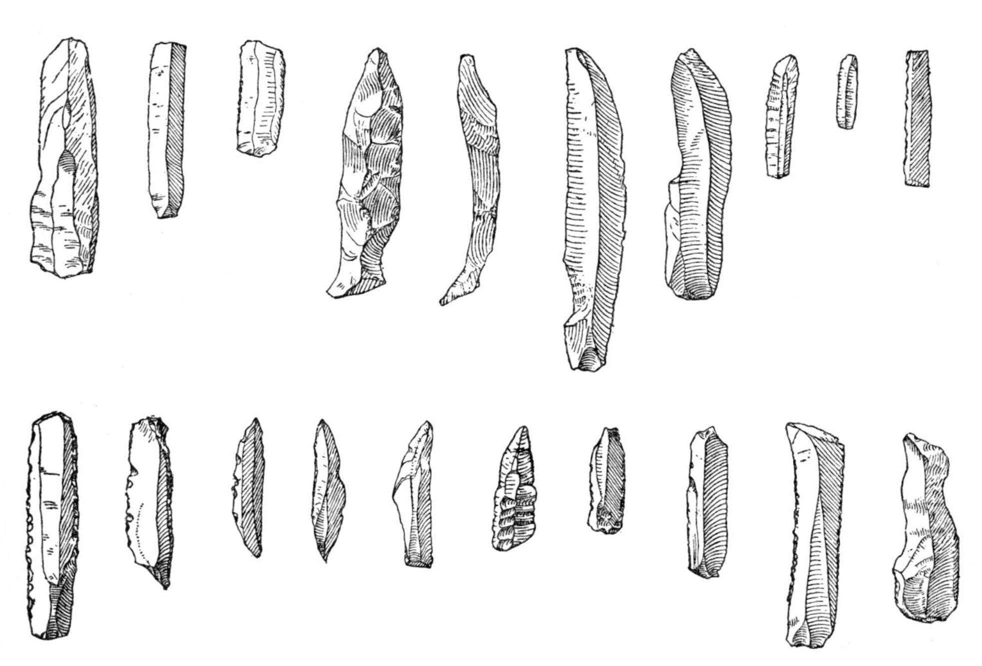

Fig. 17 Microliths from Brahmagiri. $\frac{1}{1}$

micro-industries rarely rise above the second-rate. K. R. U. Todd, however, who had an extensive knowledge of Indian microliths particularly in the Bombay area,[31] came to the interesting conclusion that 'the [west] coastal microliths as a whole appear, from their form, patination and state of preservation, to be definitely of earlier date than the pygmies from the

Fig. 16

inland sites at Jubbulpore and the Vindhya Hills. Further, they include many forms not recorded in the inland sites, which seem to consist of lunates, blades and cores only.' If this observation is confirmed—and it is consistent with the scarcity of microliths farther east though a crude non-pottery industry has recently been recognized near Durgapur in West Bengal—it may be interpreted as a further pointer towards a western, and therefore south-west Asian or north-east African, source for the Indian series, and will once more illustrate our 'Indian Ocean culture-pool' (see above, p. 58).

Fig. 17

Certainly at the end of the story, in and before the 3rd century B.C., the technical level was a low one. The pre-Iron Age culture at the inland site of Brahmagiri, which was of this period,[36] was fairly extensively sampled and produced only a crude flake-industry with a microlithic bias—small backed-knives, serrated blades, one crested flake, a beaked burin (?), side-scrapers, and an inferior lunate. These poor implements were associated with polished stone axes and occasional copper and bronze, and would seem to represent the microlithic tradition at its last gasp.

The relationship of the Chalcolithic and iron-using cultures of central India with microlithic industries will be further considered in Chapter 7.

At present the term 'Neolithic' or 'New Stone Age' does not make much sense in India. Unless some of the microlithic cultures be so classified, no integral Neolithic culture has yet been isolated there. Blade-industries with a microlithic trend existed, as we have already seen, both before and after the introduction of metals. It is less certain that polished stone implements preceded some slight knowledge of copper or bronze. Before turning to them, however, something more must be said of the flakes and blades which culminated in the Chalcolithic cultures of northern and central India.

Both at Sukkur and at Rohri, situated on opposite banks of the lower Indus in Sind, have been found core- and flake-industries showing a typological affinity with the Chalcolithic series but associated neither with pottery nor with metal.[37] This might be explained by the evident fact that the sites were primarily workshops. On the other hand, there is also some geological reason for supposing that they antedate the Indus Chalcolithic, in that the hill-top soil associated with them disappears on the slopes under a covering of silt left by an Indus flooding at a considerably higher level than today and *a fortiori* higher than in Indus-Civilization times. (In the early days of Mohenjo-daro the flood-plain of the lower Indus was at least twenty feet lower than today.) This has suggested but does not prove that the Sukkur-Rohri industries may be earlier than, and ancestral to, the Chalcolothic cores and flakes of the Indus valley, though not necessarily at any very great interval of time.

Their material is derived from the Eocene limestone of the locality and is as true a flint as can be found in the subcontinent. The cores, flakes and implements occur on hill-tops, either on or close to the surface, and include both unpatinated examples and others showing degrees of patination which have been thought, without emphasis, to indicate a time-scale. Amongst much waste, the Sukkur series comprises broad and narrow blades, all somewhat crude and thick, with rare retouching down one or both sides and sometimes with a natural 'back' or cortex; flakes either with lengthwise or with convergent primary flaking; a few 'plane' scrapers with steep trimming; a few conical cores showing long, narrow, shallow flake-scars, like the cores typical of the Indus Civilization; and occasional axe-like cores bearing a superficial resemblance to Acheulian handaxes but differing from them in technique as in date. The Rohri sites produce large quantities of blade-cores, mostly conical, and a multitude of crude and irregular blades which may be regarded as 'export rejects'. It is sufficiently evident from the careful preparation shown by some of the cores that blades of good quality were also made, comparable more nearly with the better examples from the Civilization. These better blades were presumably dispersed by trade.

The great Civilization which flourished in the Indus valley and southwards to the Gulf of Cambay at the end of the 3rd millennium will be discussed in the next chapter, but here it may be observed that the common knife with which this Civilization widely supplemented its bronze tools was a long, parallel-sided blade of chert. Similar blades are found in some of the Baluch hill-communities which existed before or alongside the Civilization. The blades were rarely retouched; Colonel D. H. Gordon has noted that, of 1,758 examined at the two principal Indus sites, only 104 showed any secondary working; a few of these had been worked down both sides to form a point, some are backed, and some are notched at the base for binding to a handle. The peculiarly brilliant gloss produced on the edge by the cutting of corn has occasionally been detected. Some of the nuclei or cores were also polished and had probably been used as burnishers on metal. No characteristic microlithic forms are present. On the other hand, there are a few large (sometimes huge) square-sectioned 'axes' which may have been either hoes or tree-cutters.

Parallel-sided chert blades of normal Indus type have been found as far south as southern Kāthiāwāḍ, at the Indus sites of Lothal and Rangpur. It may be therefore that there is a cultural kinship between these blades and those which have in recent years been recovered from a considerable series of Chalcolithic sites in central India (northern and central Deccan): Tripurī, Nagda, Maheshwar, Nāvḍā Ṭolī, Prakāsh, Bahāl, Nevāsā, Jorwe, Nāsik, and Maski. At these sites the Chalcolithic phase, though not closely dated, is clearly post-Indus, and

1200–500 or 400 B.C. is probably a fair guide.* Nor, in spite of the occasional affinity of their flake-industry with that of the north, can it be described as significantly 'Indus'; it has, as already pointed out, a strongly microlithic bias (doubtless emphasized by the limitations of the raw material available) and includes lunates and occasionally other microlithic forms, although the published ascription of the over-all term 'microlithic' to an industry such as that at Maski, where chert blades up to 5¼ inches long are included,[38] is not to be commended. Further reference will be made in Chapter 7 to these central Indian cultures; meanwhile it may be suspected that the Maski blades, like those of Kāthiāwāḍ, represent an intrusion from the blade-industries of north-western India into the essentially microlithic cultures of the Deccan.

Finally, something must be said about the ground or polished stone axes and adzes which are amongst the most characteristic stone artifacts of India. In some regions of the Deccan or the Peninsula they can be picked up almost casually on a country walk. The sequel normally is that their find-spot is quickly forgotten, and the museums of India and Great Britain contain innumerable unidentified examples. Something like eighty localities can, however, be put on the map, and it is clear that, apart from a thin scatter in the north-west (sometimes out of context), the distribution lies south-east of a line drawn from Bombay to Kanpur (Cawnpore) on the middle Ganges and extends at least as far south as the Kāverī river. In other words, the axes belong essentially to eastern and southern India, but are absent from the extreme south and from Ceylon.

Fig. 14

On the basis of form they have been tentatively divided into three groups, each subdivided into four sub-groups. Within

* Since this was written, Dr. Sankalia has informed me that a C14 analysis of burnt wheat from a late chalcolithic stratum of Nāvḍā Ṭolī by the University of Pennsylvania has given the date 1336 B.C. ± 125.

the narrow limits of the present summary I do not propose to discuss the individual types or possible variations in their distribution. This has been attempted in part by Subbarao, Worman and Allchin,[38] but except in the Bellary region little exact information is forthcoming. Here it will suffice to differentiate the two underlying techniques. Technique 1 consists of (a) the rough hammer-shaping of the stone—commonly dioritic trap or basalt—followed by (b) the further reduction of unwanted excrescences by means of a 'fabricator' (rather like a stone finger) and sometimes by pecking, and (c) a final grinding and polishing of the cutting edge and often over half or less than half of the surface of the tool. The resulting transverse section is ovoid, trapezoidal or sub-triangular. Technique 2 consists of (a) the removal of flakes from faces and sides of the core so that an implement with almost flat faces and rectangular section is produced, and (b) in general the smooth polishing, with occasional pecking, of the whole or most of the surfaces. The commonest type in Technique 1 is an axe or, rarely, adze with a bluntly pointed (sometimes rounded) butt; the most distinctive type in Technique 2 is the tanged or shouldered adze or hoe.

Plate 2

The pointed-butt axes were first put into a stratigraphical context in 1947 at Brahmagiri in northern Mysore, thirty miles south of Bellary. There, on an ancient town-site, the latest of a clear sequence of three main cultures was dated by its rouletted and russet-coated painted ("Āndhra") wares (p. 31) to the 1st century A.D. Below and overlapping it was an elaborately iron-using 'megalith' culture (p. 162) which is unlikely to have arrived there much before the 3rd century B.C. In turn, overlapping and underlying this megalith culture was a Chalcolithic culture with two subdivisions, marked by abundant pointed-butt axes, crude microliths, rough pottery and rare scraps of copper and bronze. The overlaps in each case imply a partial contemporaneity between the new culture and the old, but equally in each case there was no organic cultural transi-tion. We are dealing with three essentially distinct cultures of which the lowest is characterized by the axes and ended, as a cultural substratum, soon after 200 B.C. In other words, our stone axes with their copper-bronze accompaniment endured in the southern Deccan for something like three centuries after the use of iron had been established farther north. The con-trast is not remarkable; there are much later analogies for an emphatically differential development in India.

The Brahmagiri axe culture or cultures extended down-wards through 8 or 9 vertical feet of occupation-material—not mere dump, much of it, but the legitimate accumula-tion of floors, hearths and structures over a very appreciable period. What this means in terms of time is anyone's guess. Five centuries are probably not a fantastic over-estimate, and about 700 B.C. is offered as a provisional and schematic date for the beginning of this particular settlement.

The Brahmagiri evidence is not alone. It is matched by that obtained by Dr. Subbarao at Sanganakallu, close to Bellary, where there was an axe-culture accumulation 4½ feet deep (a considerable depth on this hill-top site) before the megalithic culture arrived upon the scene. Again the axes were associated with microlithic flakes, and again an overlap was observed between the two main cultures.

Other evidence supports the active survival of pointed-butt or comparable axes into the latter half of the 1st millennium B.C.: for example, at Sonepur in the Gaya district of Bihār they occurred with good Northern Black Polished Ware (p. 30) and iron in a stratified series.[40] But the occasional presence of an isolated stone axe (for example, at Taxila) in a late occupation is not necessarily significant chronologically or geographically, since these distinctive objects are liable to have been picked up as curiosities or even used for cult-pur-poses at any period down to the present day. They can still be seen in South India as offerings or symbols at village shrines. Only when they are present in quantity or are associated with factory-flakes or with other objects of the same cultural stage can they fairly be regarded as utile tools. Whilst they may well have survived in this capacity in backwaters of the Deccan or the Peninsula to an appreciably later date, there is at present no clear evidence of their fabrication after the end of the 3rd century B.C. or thereabouts.

At the other limit of the time-scale, there is no proof that these axes preceded the working of copper or bronze. True, a negative of this kind is difficult to establish since, at the best, metal was scarce amongst the axe-using communities. But, as we have seen, it was known to the axe-culture of Brahmagiri. Similarly, in the lowest post-palaeolithic phase* at Nevāsā in the Upper Godāvarī-Pravara basin polished pointed-butt axes and hammer-stones were accompanied by two chisels, a needle, a spear and four beads, all of copper or bronze, together with the microlithic (chalcedony) industry of lunates, triangles and backed blades which we are learning to associate with the axes.[41] The pottery included distinctive spouted vessels with flaring rims, painted with geometrical and other designs in black on a fine re-slipped surface and comparable with the wares from other chalcolithic sites (Nasik, Jorwe, Nāvḍā Ṭolī) in the northern Deccan. The absolute chronology of these sites has not yet been determined; but on some of them the Chalcolithic was succeeded by an Iron Age culture of the latter half of the 1st millennium B.C., and the general context is consistent with the evidence from Brahmagiri. Short of proof, it is likely that most of the polished pointed-butt and similar stone axes of India were made between 1000 and 200 B.C., with a preference for the latter half of that period.

Before the origin of the Indian axes is considered, something must be said of a more individual type of implement which

* Separated from the palaeolithic phases by deposits of clay and silt.

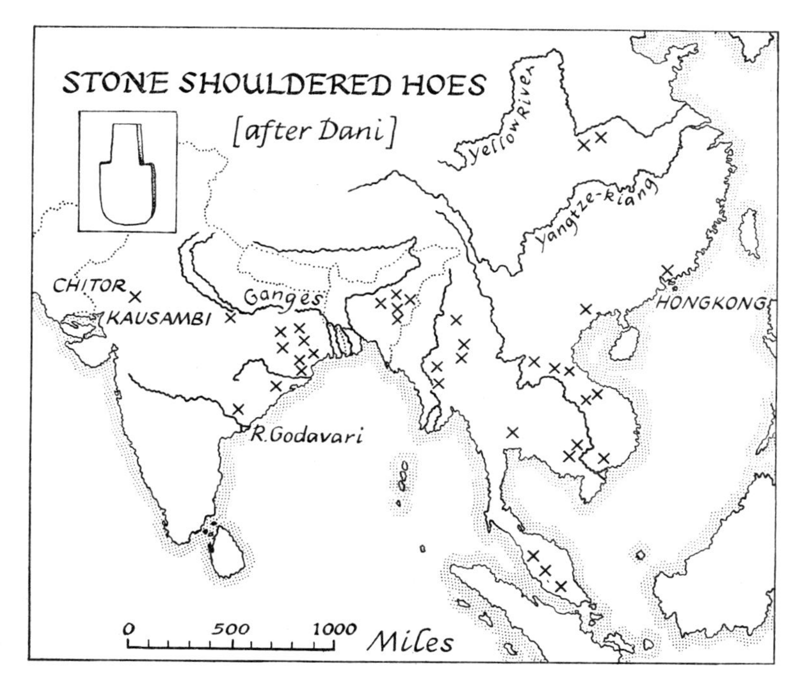

Fig. 18 Distribution of stone shouldered hoes

partially coincides with them in distribution. The tanged and shouldered hoe or adze, with angular or sloping shoulders, often carefully polished and with a single-chamfered edge in one of the broad planes, is a well-known though not a common type in certain parts of eastern India, as far south as the lower Godāvarī. The material is commonly chert or schist. In Assam the form occurs freely except in the Sadiya frontier area; but examples from the Gāro and Khāsī Hills are rough and irregular and suggest provincial imitations. Though rare in Bengal (an example has recently been found in Midnapur district) they reappear near the Bengal-South Bihār border in

Plate 3

the Santal Parganas, Mānbhūm and Dhālbūm, and farther south in Mayurbhanj and elsewhere in Orissa. To the west, stray specimens have been found in the Banda district of southern U.P. and within the fortifications of Kaushāmbī (p. 128), and one is alleged to have come from as far afield as Chitor in Rājasthān. Generally, however, the eastern bias of the type is clear enough.

Beyond India, Burma has produced good examples, and the type, highly finished or in the rough, is widely characteristic of south-east Asia. It is recorded from Malaya; in Indo-China it is included both in the so-called Bac-Sonian culture north of Hanoï and in the more southerly Somrong Sen culture of Cambodia and Annam. In no instance has an example been found by a competent excavator, but there seems little doubt that the users of the shouldered hoe were also potters and occasionally employed bronze or copper.[42] In Tongking, allegedly associated remains were of the Han period (202 B.C.–A.D. 220). Farther north usually crude shouldered hoes occur sporadically over a wide stretch of China from Hong Kong to Hunnan and the Yangtse valley of Szechwan.[43] More doubtfully, they are reported from Manchuria and Japan. The type has been related, very speculatively, to bronze shouldered axes of the Yin dynasty (about 1300–1028 B.C.) in An-yang, south-west of Tientsin.[44] Certainly the more highly finished rectangular examples suggest a metal prototype, and it has been suspected that the stone was in some instances cut with a metal wire, a technique which still obtains in India.[45] The evidence as a whole points to a Chinese parentage for the shouldered hoe, with an origin perhaps in the earlier half of the 1st millennium B.C. and a southerly trend through the Chinese lowlands to Laos and Burma. When it arrived in India is at present unknown; no example has there been found in any significant association, although the Tongking evidence, if verified, might favour a date in the latter half of the

Fig. 18

millennium, i.e. somewhat later than the first of the polished axes. To link its arrival with that of Austroasiatic languages from south-eastern Asia, as has been attempted, is mere guesswork.

To return now to the polished axes of India is in some measure to retrace the same ground. It can be stated without argument that these essentially east-Indian types were not derived, at any rate directly, from western Asia.[46] On the other hand, they occur in Burma, although casual collecting has made it impossible to plot find-spots adequately on the map. More vaguely still, Laos has produced both axes and shouldered adzes. In Malaya pecked and partially smoothed axes, comparable with those from India though more round-butted, are a recognized type. In Tongking they were used by communities which were still, it seems, largely in the hunting stage, without systematic food-production, and a technical sequence with an increasing use of stone-polishing has been postulated though not proved. Farther north, they occur in Honan and Shantung, and it has been observed that some of the North Chinese examples of pecked axes correspond even more closely with certain of those of India than do the examples from Indo-China. The patchy state of present knowledge, and not least the absence of clear dating, prevents any close correlation of the Chinese and the Indian evidence; but, geographically, routes up the Yangtze river (for example), past Szechwan in the direction of Hunnan and the Burma passes seem possible for the axes, though scarcely for the shouldered hoes, which, unlike the axes, are absent from Yunnan. Alternatively, coastal routes to Indo-China are feasible lines of access to Burma, Assam and Bengal. At least the evidence is ample enough to suggest, if less forcibly than in the case of the shouldered hoes, an eastern origin for our Indian series, with a bias in favour of central China. Even so, the major exploitation of the round-butted or, more characteristically, point-butted axe occurred on Indian soil.

Fig. 14

There remains the most important question of all: what, in terms of living man, man upon the landscape, is the implication of the whole of this stone-axe phase? Of the skeletal types of Brahmagiri and elsewhere nothing can be said until the loitering Anthropological Department of India produces its long-overdue reports. Meanwhile, we know not the shape of any one of these wielders of the stone axe. But what can be inferred of their way of life?

First, it can be affirmed that the great accumulation at Brahmagiri reflects an essentially static, food-producing population, which had lived in timber huts, some at least rectilinear on plan and reinforced by basic dry-stone walls. The surrounding countryside under natural conditions would be jungle, but their abundant stone axes would enable the villagers to make clearings for farming, probably with the assistance of fire.

In this context, Dr. C. von Fürer-Haimendorf has suggested the living analogy of the Reddis, who maintain today an atavistic mode of life in the hills flanking the Godāvarī gorge of the Deccan. They stand midway between semi-nomadic food-gatherers and settled peasantry, occupying hamlets of no great substance, and they supplement wild plants and tubers by raising crops and breeding animals. 'Their agricultural methods are extremely primitive: they clear and burn the jungle and then sow sorghum, small millets and pulses in the ashes, partly by broadcasting and partly by dibbling with the help of a digging-stick. No hoe is used. . . . Neolithic man in possession of a polished celt may well have practised a similar form of agriculture.'[47] If anything, the Brahmagiri axe-people would appear to have been more advanced and static (or less decadent and harassed) than the Reddis; it may be suspected that they had already learned to supplement 'slash-and-burn' agriculture with some knowledge of crop-rotation. But the general picture of a limited agriculture based on jungle-clearance within the range of nuclear settlements is a convincing one, and gives a needed actuality to the somewhat tedious vestiges now recover-able from the soil. To this it may be added that a number of 'cinder-mounds' situated mostly between Bellary and Hospet have been identified by Professor Zeuner as ancient accumulations of cattle-dung, and in and about one of them I collected a dozen or more pointed-butt axes in the space of half an hour. In 1938 Sir Leonard Woolley had a similar experience; at the Kupgal near Bellary he 'picked up, on and around a cinder-mound, two or three celts of basalt trap'; and as long ago as 1872 R. Bruce Foot found a 'celt' in a cinder-mound between Bellary and Gadag. The suggestion is that of a pastoral community in our axe period. We may fairly regard our axe-people as herdsmen anchored by a rudimentary agriculture.

In summary, about 1000 B.C. or a little later, groups of simple farmers, not perhaps originally very numerous, infiltrated into the hill-jungles of north-eastern and eastern India, coming from the direction of Burma if not beyond. They were equipped with stone industries of Neolithic types familiar archaeologically as far afield as northern China; there already, however, the axe-makers may have had some knowledge of bronze, which is recorded historically to have been in use in the North well before 1000 B.C. In south-east Asia, as far as Malaya, the same stone equipment is liable to appear with or without associated metal, which may not be earlier there than the 4th or 3rd century B.C. Meanwhile stone axes, followed, as it seems, by the shouldered hoes, found their way into India *via* Burma; but to associate their arrival either with Austro-asiatic languages or with megaliths is to exceed the evidence. None of these stone implements has yet in India been associated stratigraphically with a megalith.

In central India it would seem that the stone axes were superimposed upon, or commingled with, the microlithic flake-industries which were already rooted in the centre and south of the subcontinent. In central India at least it is unlikely that, to any major extent, the microlith-folk were still altogether ignorant of agriculture and stock-keeping, which had been well understood in the north and north-west for many centuries. To them, in the forested valleys, the new jungle-clearing axes may have been economically a useful accession. Whether from remote China the stone axe or adze was accompanied by a memory of copper and bronze is more problematical. This knowledge may rather have been contributed afresh by the Chalcolithic cultures of India. So it may be that, after all, the bringers of the stone axes were in a truly Neolithic stage of culture when they first entered the subcontinent. If so, here at last is a momentary Indian Neolithic of a conventional kind. But archaeology has not yet confirmed this. Systematic evidence from Burma or Assam would be crucial.

CHAPTER V

The Indus Civilization

THE WORD ‘CHALCOLITHIC’ occurred in the last chapter and will recur in its successors. It is a term which has been widely and not always very discriminately used by writers on Indian archaeology; applied alternatively to essentially stone-using communities to which copper or bronze are rare luxuries, or, less aptly, to copper- and bronze-using communities which retain a substantial though subordinate stone equipment. It may be accepted as an ugly utility-term; an alternative label, ‘Protometallic’, is scarcely more elegant or exact.

Of the Chalcolithic phase in the Baluch hills and the Indus valley much has been written in accessible form,[48] and the barest summary must here suffice. In general terms, the situation is as follows, with the reminder that all dates prior to the latter half of the 3rd millennium (and many after it) are very insecure.

In the 4th and 3rd millennia, if not before, the sullen borderland where the Iranian plateau drops tumultuously to the Indus plain sheltered a hive of hidden tribal and village societies, appropriately cellular but sharing a common standard of living and technology. In their recondite valleys they were diversely reaching the cultural optimum which their rugged milieu permitted. Their pottery, modified from region to region and age to age, was by 3000 B.C. of good quality, wheel-turned and well-baked, often thin and attractively painted with geometrical or semi-realistic motifs which betrayed both their own individuality and their cultural kinship with the societies of the great plateau behind them. They made stone implements amongst which simple chert blades predominated, and a little copper or bronze was beginning to come their way for use or ornament. Occasional contact between one community and another and with the outside world is manifest, but for the most part the tribes or regions, though not necessarily devoid of a nomadic element, were self-contained on the basis of the local crops which they learned to irrigate by the concentration of flood-water (with or without masonry dams),[49] and the small flocks and herds which the children tended on the neighbouring slopes. Further integration, whether political or cultural, was barred by environment.

Just so far, it may be claimed that the potential of these upland groups was not unlike that of early Greece, with its small hill-divided and independent states. There, however, the encompassing sea provided a sufficient measure of mutual contact to create, if not unity, at least an inter-territorial sentiment of Greek civilization and nationhood as against the outer 'barbarians' of alien speech and tradition. In the massif of Baluchistan, save at its southernmost end, this vitalizing link was missing. Instead, however, there lay along its flank the great plain of the Indus and its tributary or adjacent rivers, a plain at that time largely jungle-covered but serving, with its broad waterways, in some sense as an inland sea and as a passable means of lateral communication. Those two factors—the terminal ocean and the flanking plain—were together formative in the sudden emergence of the next cultural phase, that of the Indus Civilization, probably a little before 2500 B.C.

It is now widely familiar that, since 1921, has been laid bare in and near the Indus valley some part of the most extensive civilization of the pre-classical world. With metropolitan centres, each more than three miles in circumference, at Harappā in the Punjab and Mohenjo-daro in Sind, it stretched from Rūpar at the foot of the Simla hills to Sutkagen-dor near the shores of the Arabian Sea, a distance of 1,000 miles. But that is not all. Exploration during the past ten years has extended the reach of this vast civilization eastwards to Ukhlina, 19 miles west of Meerut in the Jumna basin, and southwards into Kāthiāwāḍ (Rangpur, Lothal, Somnāth, the Hālār

Fig. 19

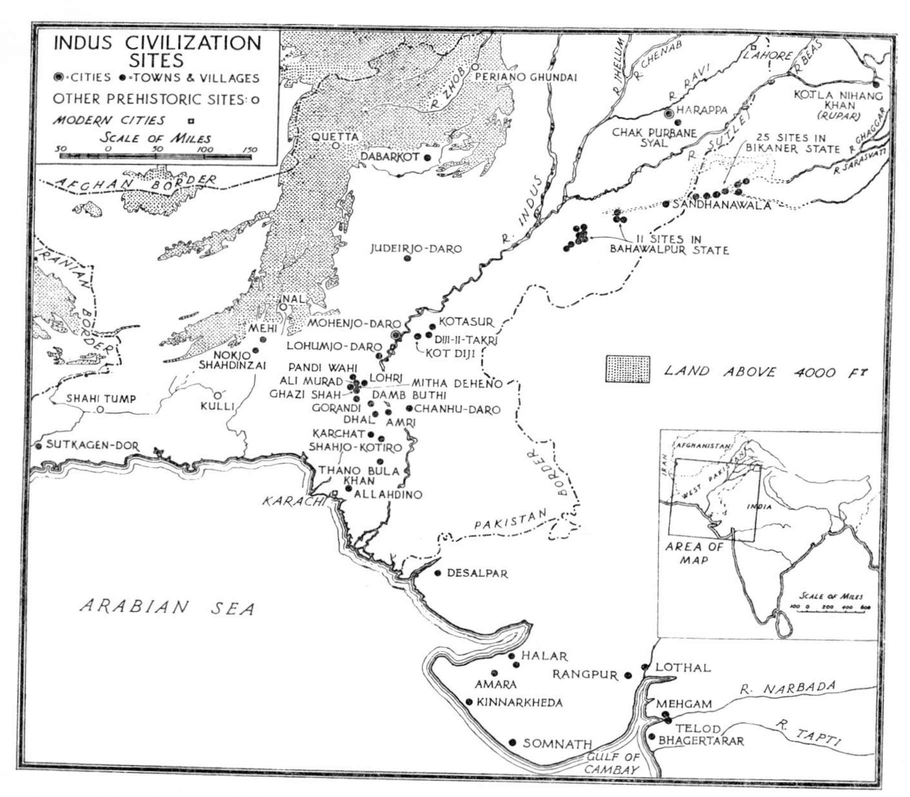

Fig. 19. (Not shown: Ukhlina, W. of Meerut, and Rosadi, central Kāthiāwāḍ)

district), and beyond, to the shore of the Gulf of Cambay near the estuaries of the Narbadā and the Tapti. There, 500 miles south-east of Mohenjo-daro, at three sites, Mehgam and Telod and Bhagertarar, potsherds of the Indus Civilization were found in 1957, and there for the present is the Civilization's southernmost limit.[50] These southern extensions on or near the shores of the Arabian Sea have altered the shape of the Civilization as previously envisaged; they immensely enlarge

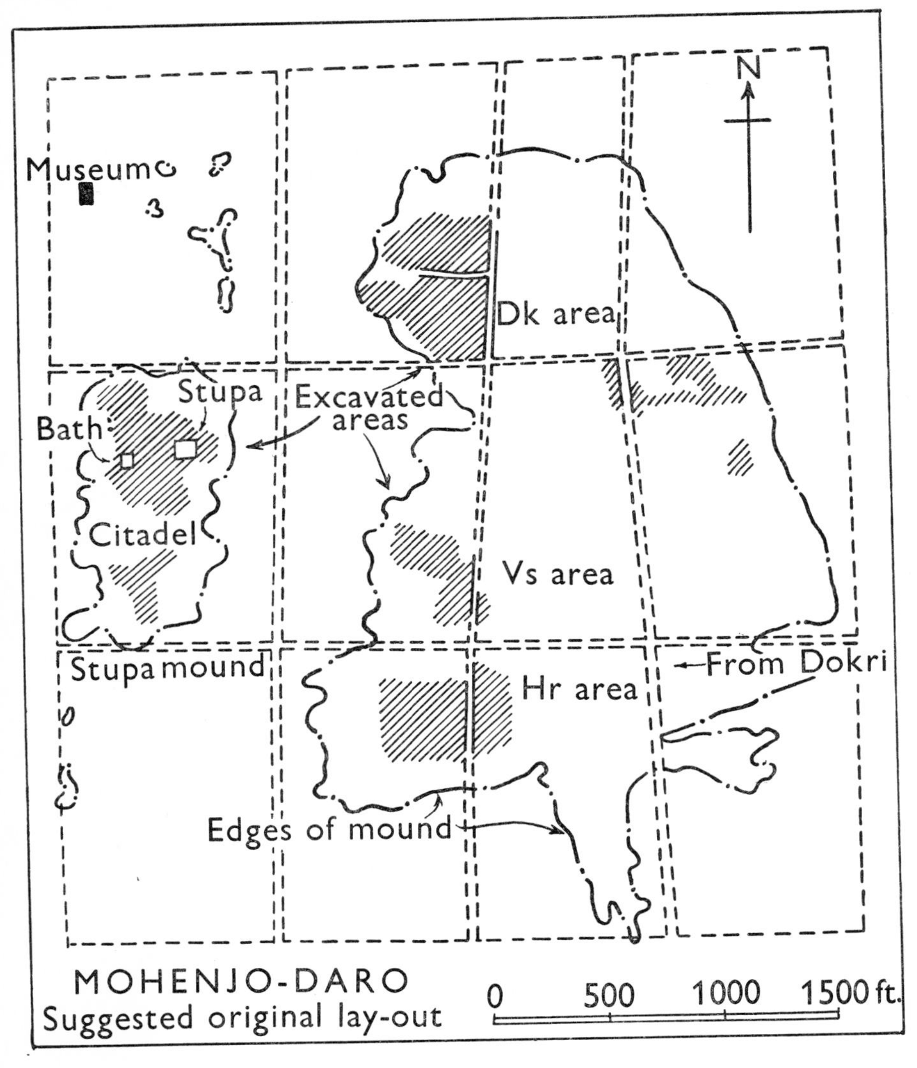
N
Museum
Dk area
Stupa
Excavated
areas
Bath
Citadel
Vs area
Stupa mound
Hr area
From Dokri
Edges of mound
MOHENJO-DARO
Suggested original lay-out
0
500
1000
1500 ft.

Fig. 20

the coastwise aspect of the problem of origins and contact, and in the new context these must be briefly reconsidered.

But first the principal characters of the Civilization may be recalled. Both at Harappā and, more clearly, at Mohenjo-daro excavation has revealed the general shape of the great cities in their prime and decadence. At the earliest period known to us, they were already rigorously planned in regular rectangular blocks, each measuring about 400 by 200 yards, divided from one another by broad main streets, and containing methodically drained lanes and buildings. So far as present evidence goes, they possessed no general system of urban fortification, though there is the possibility that at Mohenjo-daro an ancient embankment designed to restrain the Indus floods may be of this period. The recent report that Lothal in Kāthiāwāḍ, a similarly regimented coastal township of the same Civilization, had been protected after a flood-disaster by an embankment upwards of eight feet high is incorrect.[51] On the other hand, both Harappā and Mohenjo-daro were dominated by an embattled acropolis or citadel, occupying a marginal block and built up with mud and mud-brick to a height of forty or fifty feet above the featureless plain with a revetment of baked brick. Upon this acropolis were ritual buildings and places of assembly. That at Mohenjo-daro also carried the State Granary, which must have been the economic focus of the régime; at Harappā, less known to us, equivalent or supplementary granaries were marshalled on the lower ground between the acropolis and the river. From its acropolis we may suppose that each city was regarded by rulers who may on general probability have had priestly attributes but, as their well-ordered towns and evolved dwellings imply, were essentially secular in outlook; sufficiently benevolent or far-sighted, at the least, to nurture an uncommonly high general standard of living,* and at the same time sufficiently authoritative

Fig. 20

Figs. 8, 9

Fig. 21

Plates 6, 7

Plate 5

Plate 4

Fig. 22

* Large numbers of substantial courtyard-houses imply a wide distribution of wealth and a prosperous middle class during the best period of Mohenjo-daro.

to ensure that this general standard was long maintained. In this sense the contrast with Pharaonic Egypt, where, under a totalitarian god-bound administration, civic life in any liberal usage of the phrase scarcely existed, is manifest, To the nearer analogy of Mesopotamia we shall turn in a moment.

What wider function the two outstanding cities fulfilled is more speculative.* They are 400 miles apart, and between them, opposite the Sulaiman Range and the Bugti Country, the Indus valley is constricted, so that each city may be said to dominate a partially defined and unitary province. The overriding facts remain, however, that they are situated upon the same river-system, and are culturally identical. That identity extends throughout the immense territory—nearly half a million square miles—wherein the Indus Civilization has now been recognized. It is tempting to infer something like an imperial status for so uniform a civilization, perhaps with the metropolitan duality which was later to mark the Kushān, Arab and Mogul régimes in northern India and seems indeed to be endemic in that spacious land. If at any rate the underlying inference is correct, as it may be, then the Indus Civilization exemplifies the vastest political experiment before the advent of the Roman Empire.

But whatever the political implications, the cultural unity of the Civilization is itself a sufficiently imposing phenomenon,

---

The 'extreme concentration of economic power' which has been ascribed to the early civilizations of Egypt and Asia (e.g. by V. G. Childe, *The Prehistory of European Society*, p. 160) is true of the former but not altogether of the latter, at any rate in the 3rd millennium.

* For a moment recently their hegemony seemed to be threatened by the first reports of a large Indus site known as Judeirjo-daro, a mile west of the Quetta road 18 miles north of Jacobabad. This newly identified group of mounds (which I have seen) is of great interest since it is untouched and apparently early in the Indus series, but the total length of the assemblage is scarcely more than 500 yards. Judeirjo-daro is thus a sizeable Indus town but no rival to the two great cities.

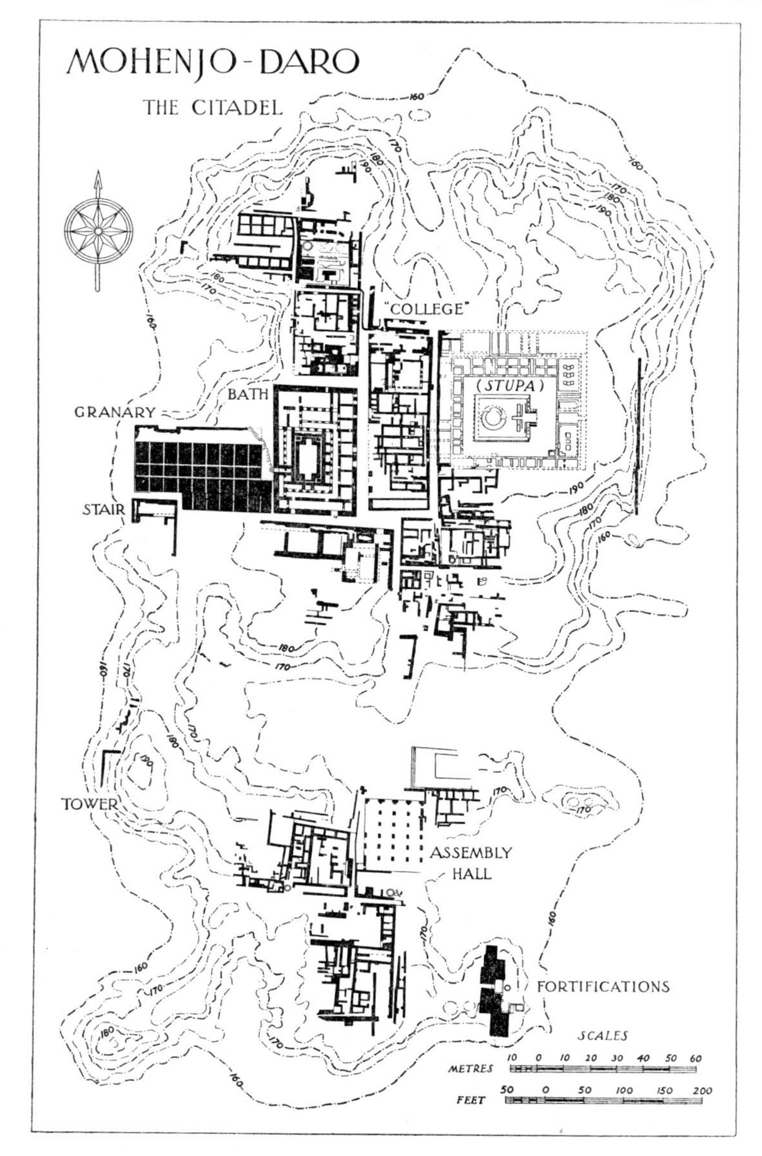
MOHENJO-DARO
THE CITADEL
"COLLEGE"
(STUPA)
BATH
GRANARY
STAIR
TOWER
ASSEMBLY
HALL
FORTIFICATIONS
SCALES
METRES
10 0 10 20 30 40 50 60
FEET
50 0 50 100 150 200

Fig. 21

and the problem of its origins, as of its ultimate fate, commands attention.

How far was the Indus Civilization a product of the *genius loci*? How far, if at all, was it indebted to outside influence? One's thoughts, encouraged by the new coastal bias of the Indus distribution, turn naturally to Mesopotamia as a source. Certainly Mesopotamian civilization was a going concern several centuries before the earliest date to which we can ascribe that of the Indus. Certainly, too, there is much in what we know of the Mesopotamian urban way of life that matches our Indus evidence: the suggestion of middle-class well-being, of effective civic consciousness, to which the Mesopotamian records give a definition that is absent from the Indus evidence. The indication is that the citizen in the streets of Mohenjo-daro must have had much the same sort of interests as his contemporaries in the streets of Sumerian Ur. Of the two cities, indeed, Mohenjo-daro with its admirable public sanitation and its comprehensive planning suggests an even more evolved civic intelligence. True, we cannot there point to an artistry that might rival the elaborate polychromy of the Mesopotamian temples or the dramatic extravagance of Sir Leonard Woolley's 'Royal Tombs'. But then we have as yet found nowhere in the Indus valley the corresponding tombs of the ruling class, and cannot guess what awaits us when chance shall deliver them to us, if, as may be suspected, they somewhere exist. Nor can we guess the quality of the vanished Indus woodwork, though the skill of later Indian wood-carvers suffices to remind us of the possible magnitude of our loss. We can find some consolation in the superb carving of miniature animal forms on the famous steatite seals of the Indus, and reflect that to these at least Mesopotamia can offer no native equivalent.

Plate 18

In brief, analogies between the two civilizations are of a general kind and cannot be pushed into detail. Even general

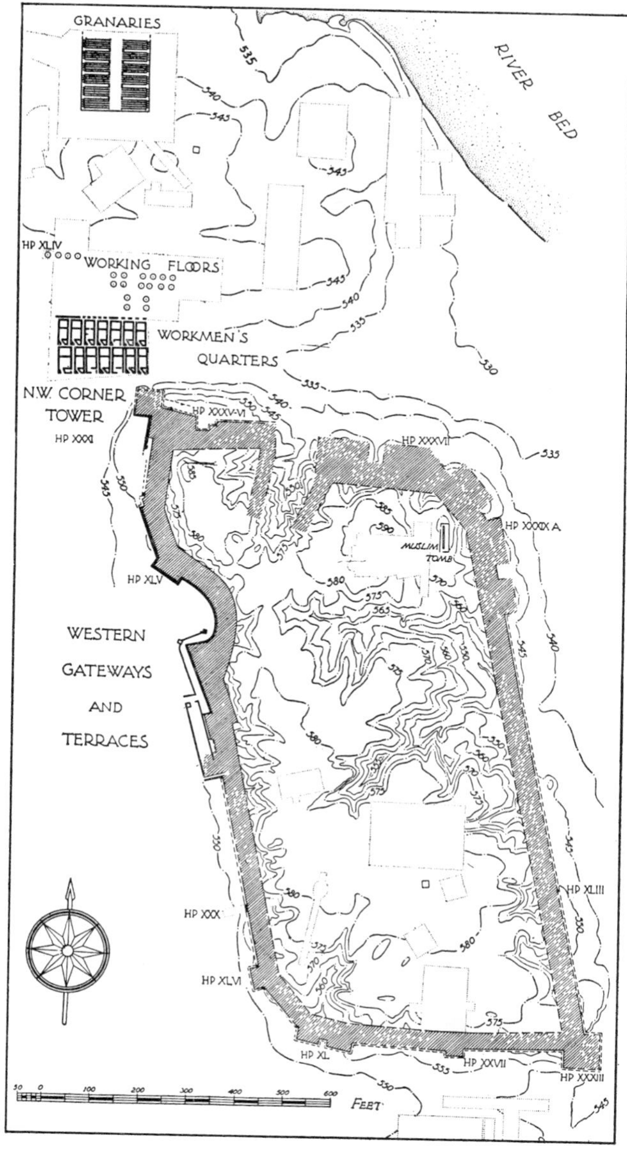

Fig. 22 Harappā: the citadel

,y fails in an important respect if the inferred political of the Indus Civilization approximates to fact, as against asic trend in Mesopotamia towards nucleation in city-; though even here, in the 24th century B.C., when com-ial contacts show that the Indus Civilization was in its prime, an imperialistic régime had emerged in Akkad and may have influenced, or even been influenced by, contemporary political development on the Indus. But if we stick to material evidence the differences are emphatic enough. Neither in its ceramic industry nor in its tools and armoury does the Indus Civilization suggest a remotely foreign origin. Its pottery, though specifically individual, is as generically akin to that of some of the village communities in or below the Baluch hills as to that of Sumer. The thin, rather feeble knives and spears and the flat axes, of copper or bronze poor in tin, run counter to the types prevailing in Iran or Mesopotamia. The unread Indus script is unlike any other in the ancient world. The baked bricks of which the two largest and several of the smaller Indus towns were mostly built (doubtless in response to a relatively rainy climate), though not without precedent in early Mesopotamia, are exceptional there. The normal Mesopotamian building-material was unbaked brick or plain mud.

Plate 19

Fig. 23

Plate 21

Fig. 24

Now this last consideration does in fact raise an interesting issue at Mohenjo-daro. The two earliest buildings at present known on the acropolis, the State Granary and the first of a succession of peripheral towers near the south-east corner, are built of baked brick but were reinforced superficially and internally with timbers in a mode natural to mud-brick structures, but alien to baked-brick construction. Inevitably in the Indus climate these timbers quickly decayed, causing local collapses of the brickwork and necessitating brick reinforcement. The lesson was learned and the experiment was not (so far as we know) repeated; but its occurrence in the early phase suggests that the master-builder concerned had been a foreigner

Fig. 21

Plate 7

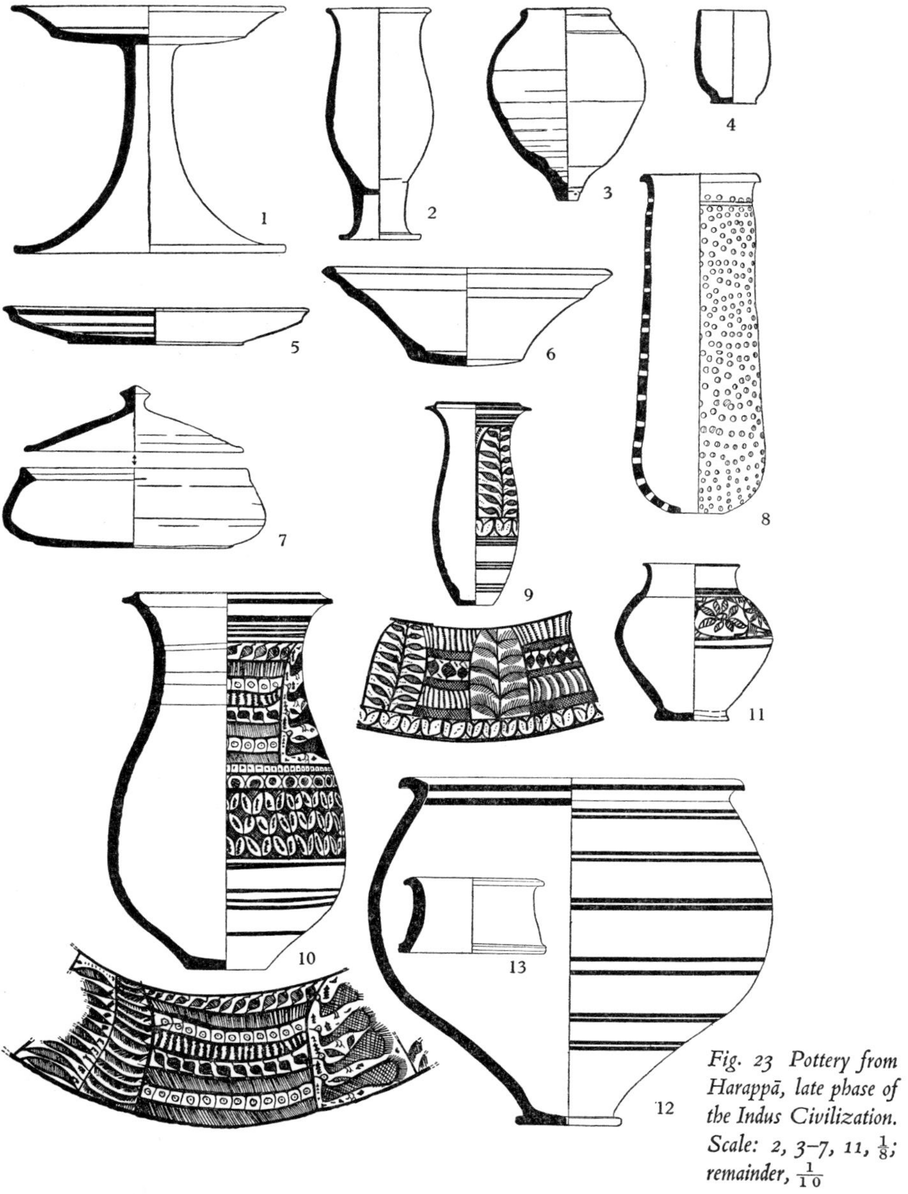

Fig. 23 Pottery from Harappā, late phase of the Indus Civilization. Scale: 2, 3–7, 11, $\frac{1}{8}$; remainder, $\frac{1}{10}$

accustomed to methods appropriate to a drier climate and inexperienced in Indus conditions. Here if anywhere we have a hint of direct intrusion from abroad. Of its wider implication, if any, nothing can be affirmed without much further excavation.

If, apart from this reservation, we now review the comparison between the two civilizations as a whole, it is fair to recognize a general affinity with recurring and important differences in detail which are at least sufficient to set aside any likelihood of immediate or wholesale colonization of the Indus region from Sumer. For the physical structure of the Indus Civilization we must look to more local sources and causes. But that is not to rob Mesopotamia of a close responsibility in the matter. Mesopotamia, and none other, retains her world-priority, not to the 'invention' of town-life (in which at present Jericho in Jordan is far in the lead), but to the production of a mature and literate civilization, with organized accounts and archives: in other words, to the essential *idea* of civilization. Thanks to Mesopotamia, by the end of the 4th millennium the *idea* of civilization was in the air of the Middle East; and, as I have remarked before, ideas have wings. Archaeology, in its proper pursuit of material evidence, is liable to understress the intangibles which may have been, and in some circumstances certainly were, the true agents of diffusion, penetrating more surely and significantly than pence and potsherds. So from Mesopotamia, by easy land-routes, the idea of civilization penetrated shortly to Egypt, where the ideas of writing and of certain architectural modes were adopted and adapted in a local idiom. From Mesopotamia, we may be sure, the mature idea of civilization, always including that of writing, later reached the Indian coast and the Indus valley by an easy sea-route and perhaps by land, to be adapted there to local taste and circumstance. The alternative postulate, that in each of three lands so accessible to one another the immensely complex idea of an evolved civilization should, within the narrow

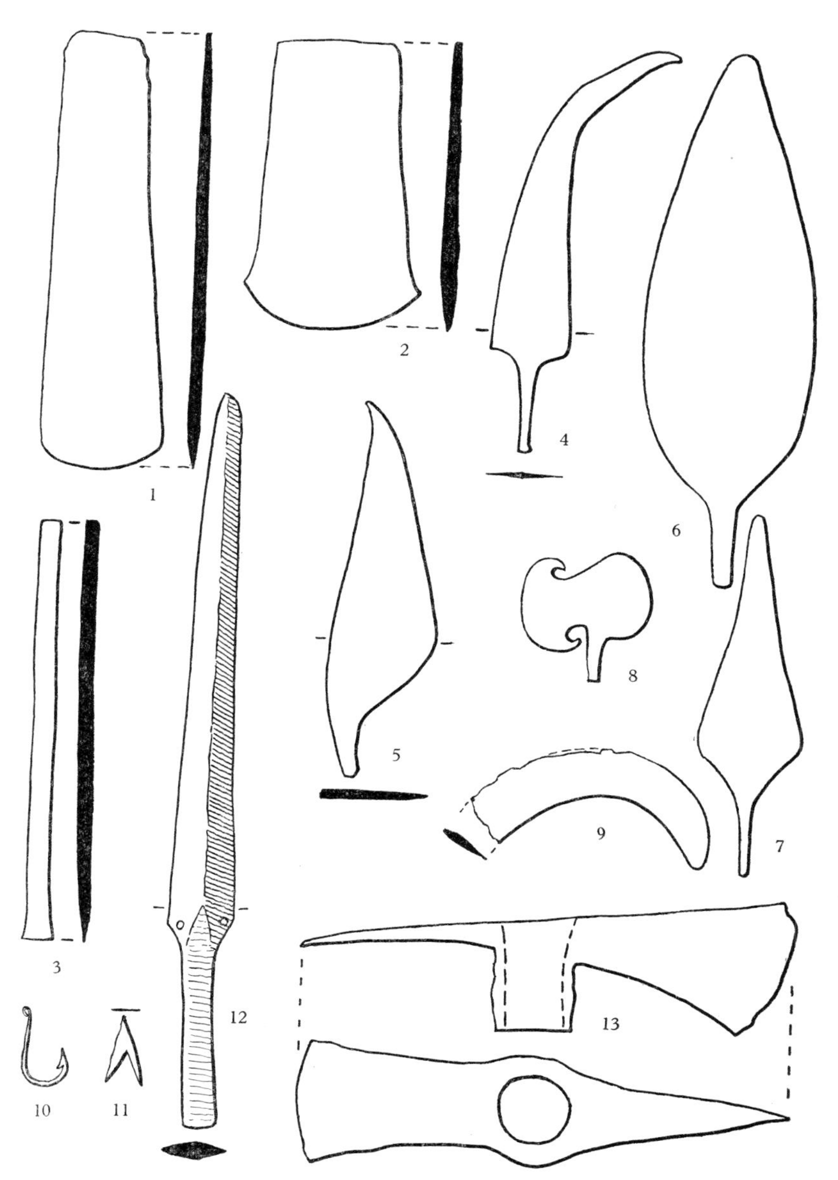

Fig. 24 Mohenjo-daro: implements of bronze and copper. $\frac{1}{4}$

space of some five or six centuries, have emerged spontaneously and without cross-reference, is too absurd to merit argument.

In this connection it is no doubt significant that the later (19th century B.C.) town-plan of Ur, mostly laid out in orderly rectilinear fashion, incorporated devious and casual main streets, obvious survivals from an amorphous small-town beginning, just as in New York the ancient suburban Broadway trundles carelessly across the modern grid-plan.[52] In other words, Ur evolved from 4th-millennium village to 3rd-millennium city, learning as it went; whereas the later foundation, Mohenjo-daro, came into being (as it seems) in full awareness of the evolved civic idea—an idea which it can only have received from an adult Mesopotamia.

But it stands equally to reason that an idea can only take root in prepared and congenial soil. By the middle of the 3rd millennium, something very important was happening in the Indus valley, and happening probably at great speed. Then or rather earlier, certain of the little communities in the Baluch foothills were emboldened to experiment. Who the first leaders were who led their people, however hesitantly, down to the wide and jungle-ridden plain we shall never know, nor why they ventured; but they were bold men, pioneers in the fullest sense, no mere ejects from the highland zone. Some, perhaps many of them, led forlorn hopes and perished. Imperfect though our knowledge be, we know enough to recognize here and there on the Indus plain the débris of villages or small towns which antedate the full-blown civilization and were superseded by it. For example, at Kot Diji, fifteen miles south of Khairpur and twenty-five miles east of Mohenjo-daro, excavation in 1955–7 revealed a town of pre-Indus date with a strongly walled citadel armed with rectangular towers of stone and mud-brick. About 2400 B.C. (the central figure, as Dr. F. A. Khan tells me, of a C 14 dating by the University of Pennsylvania of some of the latest pre-Indus material) this town was covered with a burnt deposit upon which was built an unfortified settlement of Indus Civilization type. The pottery of the pre-Indus town was partially comparable with that found under the Harappā fortifications in 1946, but already included, by borrowing or anticipation, some Harappān elements.[53]

Seemingly the attempted colonization of the valley continued intermittently, failure succeeding failure, until at last a leader, more determined and far-sighted and fortunate than the rest, won through. To appreciate his qualities and those of his associates and successors, it is necessary to glance a little more closely at his problems.

Amongst the favourable factors confronting him was, of course, the great river-system itself, flanked by wide expanses of fertile alluvium which was renewed by the annual flood. Its broad jungles and intermittent marshes were indeed infested with elephant, tiger, buffalo, rhinoceros and crocodile, familiar to us from their exquisite representations on the Indus seals. But the rivers themselves were full of fish that are still the livelihood of whole floating villages and were both netted and hooked by the Indus people,[54] in whose script they became one of the most recurrent symbols. Those same rivers were arterial routes to the sea and the Persian Gulf on the one hand and to the timber-producing Himālayas on the other. Along them, and along the trackways which would shortly flank and feed them, metals and gemstones foreign to their alluvium could be brought by long-range traffic. And by the same token intellectual interchange, a currency in ideas, now became feasible with unprecedented ease and scope. In contrast to the upland valley with its scanty soil, uncertain water-supply, and close horizon, the prospect was a spacious one indeed.

But there was a debit side to this account. The annual snow-melt flood fertilizes but, unrestrained, is also an angry destroyer. The extensive irrigation demanded by a large city of the plain involves tireless planning and co-ordination, and readily succumbs to indifferent control. Fevers are endemic to marsh and jungle. The arterial waterways which may carry trade may equally carry invasion. The benefits offered on so formidable a scale by an environment at the same time so vast, so exuberant, and so menacing are dependent, and *dependent from the outset*, upon the power of man to master and constrain. The situation was one which can have brooked no pusillanimity, no piecemeal compromise. A society strong in heart, disciplined, numerous and imaginatively led grasped the problem and, we may be sure, simultaneously solved it; else it had perished. Here if anywhere may we fairly discern in human affairs an example of that swift adaptation and progression which biologists know as 'explosive evolution'.

From this explosively successful beginning, from the lightning subjugation of the huge valley and the adjacent coast, the Indus citizens seem to have drawn the penalty of early success: a complacency, even a self-satisfaction, which impeded further effort. Our admittedly incomplete knowledge does not suggest any trend towards new social or aesthetic horizons. The Indus Civilization settled down for perhaps a thousand years to the exploitation of its environment with an equanimity disturbed only by unceasing struggle with its essential but implacable rivers. With the aid of some sort of irrigation-system, which is now deeply buried by post-Indus aggradation but may, in principle, be assumed, it grew food-crops and cotton; it kept considerable herds; and, as a scatter of Indus seals and other trifles in the Mesopotamian cities shows, it traded with its neighbours of the Persian Gulf from the 800 miles of coastline which we must now allot to it. And here it may be that certain cuneiform texts of Old Babylonia help to fill out the picture.

Inscribed clay tablets from the city of Ur, which served as the principal port-of-entry into Mesopotamia in the time of the Dynasty of Larsa (*c.* 1950 B.C.), show that sailors returning at that time from Telmun or Dilmun—that is, with little doubt, the island of Bahrain in the Persian Gulf—offered a share of their cargoes at the temple of the goddess Ningal. Gold, silver, much copper, lapis lazuli in lumps, stone beads, ivory combs and ornaments and inlays, eye-paint, certain kinds of wood, and perhaps pearls ('fish-eyes') are mentioned.[55] But in this period Telmun was merely an intermediate market at which the Ur shippers bartered their stocks for goods brought to the island from 'Makkan' and 'Meluhha', two places of which the identity is conjectural. This practice had not always prevailed. In the time of Sargon of Akkad (*c.* 2350 B.C.) we hear of ships from or destined for Meluhha, Makkan and Telmun as moored in the harbour outside the capital. Some at least of the trade with these places was then direct, using Telmun doubtless for revictualling purposes rather than as a commercial intermediary. Later, under the 3rd Dynasty of Ur (*c.* 2100 B.C.), we find that trade was still sustained with Makkan and Telmun, but that Meluhha was now out of direct reach, although copper, stone, wood, ivory objects and certain breeds of animals were still somehow obtained from there. Later again, under the Dynasty of Larsa, Telmun monopolizes the role of middleman; and sometime between the fall of the Larsa Dynasty and the decline of the Hammurabi Dynasty (*c.* 1700 B.C.) Telmun lost contact with the mining centres of Makkan and its ancillary sources. The implication of this record of dwindling trade is that Telmun, Makkan and Meluhha lay at successively greater distances from Mesopotamia; and if to this inference be added the association of the ultimate Meluhha with ivory, wood and copper, its identification with the Indus Civilization (with its forests and elephants and its sources of copper in Rājasthān) becomes probable. It matches, too, with the archaeological evidence. Ivory-working was an Indus craft; one of the victims of the last massacre at Mohenjo-daro, for instance, was attempting to carry away an elephant's tusk when he was cut down. And the main stream of Indus relics recovered from identified strata in the Mesopotamian cities dates from the Sargonid period of direct contact with Meluhha, with a diminishing trickle into the Larsa period of indirect contact. With that maritime enterprise which characterized ancient Indian trade in many ages, we may imagine cargoes of woods and metals and ivory—and why not also apes and peacocks, both familiar to the Indus artist?—setting sail from the Indus ports in the heyday of the Civilization; and in the sequel, with the long-drawn-out decline which, as will be seen, is evident in later civic standards, it is easy to visualize a corresponding decline in the scope and volume of overseas traffic. Inference from the records and the material evidence are at one.

Consistent too are the results of the excavations recently carried out by Dr. P. V. Glob's Danish expedition on the island of Telmun or Bahrain itself.[56] The principal ancient settlement on Bahrain was at the northern end of the island, at Ras al Qala'a, where particularly good springs are available. The excavations there exhibit a town of the competent but rather crude kind which might be expected from its function merely as a mart and servicing-station. A few links with Mesopotamia and with the Indus have been identified, notably circular steatite seals with grooved and pierced bosses at the back, variants of an Indus pattern. Since only five of these seals have been found in fairly extensive excavation at Bahrain, they are perhaps unlikely to be local. They bear animal and other designs—short-horned bull with head twisted slightly to one side, a square grid, a manger (?)—reminiscent of Indus seal-motifs but not identical with normal mid-Indus types, amongst which the circular seal is itself exceptional. They approximate more nearly to circular steatite seals found occasionally at Ur and elsewhere in Mesopotamia:[57] there the general type is equally alien and intrusive, and since five or more of the seals bear the distinctively Indus script there is no doubt as to the origin of some of their users. Thus as a whole the Ur-Bahrain series can be ascribed neither to the great inland cities of the Indus, such as Mohenjo-daro, nor yet to Sumerian invention. Rather must we associate them in some more general fashion with the coastal entrepôts which we are beginning to identify between the Gulf of Cambay and the head of the Persian Gulf. To distinguish them from the Indus seals proper, as we know them, I propose to name them the 'Persian Gulf seals'.

How did the Indus Civilization end? Certainly, at the centre it declined and fell, as has already been hinted, though how universal its decline and how precipitous its fall cannot at present be affirmed in general terms. It is to be anticipated that so far-flung a society decayed differentially and found death or reincarnation in varying forms from region to region. But at Mohenjo-daro at least the picture is clear enough: decline was long-drawn-out and progressive, the final fall catastrophic.

First, the decline. Everywhere in the later levels of Mohenjo-daro the excavators have found an increasing deterioration in standards of building and living. Walling and flooring tended to become more ramshackle, older buildings were subdivided, even domestic courtyards, the focus of the household, were partitioned in untidy fashion. And that this process was prolonged may be illustrated by a single example. Adjoining the northern end of the Great Granary on the side of the acropolis, the main building-level is over twenty feet below the present level of the plain, and a dozen feet below the present dry-weather water-table. In digging down to it in 1950, I passed through a continuous succession of buildings, all subsequent to the construction of the acropolis-mound and the immense brick podium of the flanking granary. The lower buildings, so far as explored, were still of tolerably good build but the upper walls, enclosing small rooms, were of increasingly shoddy aspect. The highest of them, founded upon a mass of débris, were right at the top of the podium, at least forty feet above the lowest established level of the mound. Interpreted in terms of time, this vast accumulation must be supposed to represent the lapse of several centuries.

In any interpretation of this process, however, two considerations are important. The first is the annual impact of the Indus flood which raises the flooded area and simultaneously raises the water-table. Today, the Mohenjo-daro landscape is only preserved from disastrous inundation by large annual expenditure on a series of protective banks or bunds. So, no doubt, from the outset considerable engineering was already needed when the new city rose upon its far lower flood-plain. Even so, the swollen river broke through from time to time; its alluvium has been identified at intervals in deep sections, and houses were raised to safer heights, sometimes with the help of mud-brick platforms.* Any relaxation in the supervision of the bunds, any accidental weakness in their structure, any exceptional volume in the spring torrent, must have been immediately fatal. And a population harassed by this recurring enemy may well have tired a little, as human societies under continuous stress are apt to do. A convergence of causes may be thought to have induced an increasingly rapid decline.

The other factor is this. Millions of well-baked bricks went to the building and rebuilding of Mohenjo-daro. Millions of tons of firewood went to the baking of them. With all allowance for the arrival of floating timber from the upper reaches, this implies a widespread deforestation of the surrounding region. This in turn, though partially compensated by growing crops, must have checked the transpiration of moisture and reduced the rainfall. If at the same time energy and discipline

* A similar procedure has been recognized at Lothal, on the coastal plain of Kāthiāwāḍ.—*I.A.* 1955–56, p. 6.

were flagging, and irrigation-channels and bunds inadequately maintained, the total deterioration must have been appreciable. Desert was encroaching on the sown. In rough terms, Mohenjo-daro was *wearing out its landscape*, whether by excessive zeal or by excessive indolence. Over the years it was dying long before the final blow.

That final blow has often enough been described. It is represented by groups of skeletons—men, women and children, some bearing axe- or sword-cuts—which have been found lying on the topmost level in the sprawled or contorted positions in which they fell. They had been left there by raiders who had no further use for the city which they had stormed. In that moment Mohenjo-daro was dead.

Plate 23

Now what is the historical meaning of all this? We do not know but I have made a guess. The Indus Civilization is commonly and, I think, rightly regarded as non-Aryan in character.[58] There is some material evidence that it was still in action within the first half of the 2nd millennium B.C.; and it is widely accepted that somewhere about the middle of that millennium occurred the Aryan invasion which is reflected in the earliest literature of India, the hymns of the *Ṛigveda*. In these hymns the invasion constantly assumes the form of an onslaught upon the walled cities of the aborigines, and the only fortifications of approximate date known to us are those of the citadels of Harappā and Mohenjo-daro and at certain of the smaller contemporary towns. It is tempting to relate the two circumstances to one another and to recognize in the destroyers of Mohenjo-daro, indifferent to the city which they had sacked, some of these heroic but barbarian nomads, to whom city-life was alien. It is not indeed impossible that the name of Harappā itself is concealed in the Hari-Yūpīyā which is mentioned in the *Ṛigveda* as the scene of a battle. But at present these thoughts are no more than conjectures; picturesque, perhaps probable, but not proven. It must not be forgotten that Mohenjo-daro is the only place where clear material evidence of final massacre is at present forthcoming.

What was the immediate sequel to the Indus Civilization? North Indian history first assumes definition in the time of the Buddha, about 500 B.C. If we infer provisionally that in the central Indus region the Civilization ended within a century or so of 1500 B.C., there remain a thousand years with no surer written content than that provided by the great Indian epics, which have reached us as a romantic amalgam of many ages. Happily, however, Indian archaeologists have recently been at work upon this Dark Age both in the north and in the west, and dawn is on the horizon.

In due course we shall encounter in the northern plains an Indian Bronze-Age ceramic of cardinal importance known as the Painted Grey Ware, a highly distinctive fabric to which the schematic dates 1000–500 B.C. have been provisionally given, though 800–500 B.C. would be safer. This ware has been found on a number of sites (notably Rupar) which have also produced Indus Valley relics, and in every case the Grey Ware overlay the Indus material with a clear intervening gap. Here in the north, therefore, we are left with the period 1500–1000 or 800 B.C. (more or less) to fill, and, as the task is still actively in hand, no detailed discussion is appropriate to the present review.

Briefly, the present position is this. On a number of Indus sites, superimposed vestiges of later cultures have been observed. At Harappā itself remains of jerry-built houses of re-used brick have been found built into the débris overlying the Indus city, and the intruders buried their dead in alien fashions and in or with good but largely alien pottery, in a cemetery known to archaeology as 'Cemetery H'. This Cemetery H culture has at present been identified on only two other sites (in Bahāwalpur), and little is known of it save that it would appear to have post-dated the Indus Civilization by an appreciable interval. Again at Chanhu-daro, some eighty miles south of Mohenjo-daro, a shoddy late Indus phase was succeeded by a squatter-culture of lower grade, named the 'Jhukar' culture from another site in Sind. The Jhukar squatters made coarser pottery than their Indus predecessors, and used round button-seals, commonly bearing radiate or compartmental patterns reminiscent of 2nd-millennium types in northern Iran and the Caucasus. There would appear to have been an approximation of age between the end of the Indus Civilization here and the arrival of the squatters, though actual continuity is not implied. After an interval, more squatters (the 'Jhangar' people) replaced the Jhukars. The whole succession is undated and leaves us little wiser, but is sufficient to show a continuing cultural deterioration in this region after the end of the Civilization, and to suggest recurrent links with Iran and the Caucasus. This suggestion may be sustained into the latter part of the 2nd millennium by burial-cairns at Moghul Ghundai in the Zhob valley of northern Baluchistan, from which a tripod jar, horse-bells, rings and bangles have been thought to recall similar objects from 'Cemetery B' at Sialk in central Iran, dated to 1000 B.C. or thereabouts. On the other hand, there is some evidence that these cairns may in fact be appreciably later.[59] Again, to the bracket 1200–1000 B.C. and to a western origin Heine-Geldern would ascribe both the celebrated bronze dagger of about the 12th century B.C. found at Fort Munro in the Sulaiman Range west of the Indus, and a copper trunnion-axe from the Kurram valley on the Afghan border.[60] These and other scattered objects, of indubitably western (Iranian or Caucasian) type but often of disputed date, are at least sufficient to suggest infiltration into north-western India in the centuries closely following the end of the Indus Civilization, and may be associated by the temerarious with the Aryan movement from Iran and Afghanistan into the Punjab. But proof is distant.

Fig. 25

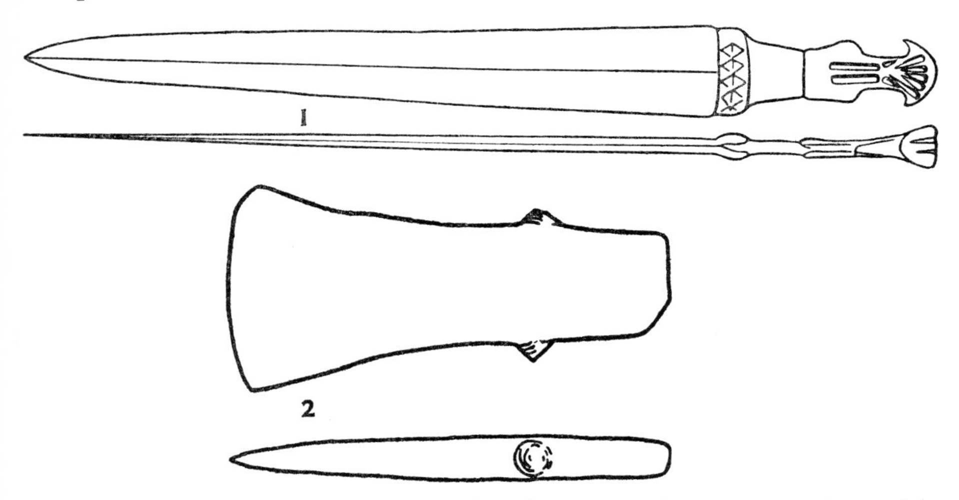

Fig. 25 1, bronze dagger from Fort Munro, in the Sulaiman Range. $\frac{1}{4}$. *2, copper trunnion-axe from the Shahlozan valley, Kurram. Nearly* $\frac{1}{2}$

If, however, it is clear enough that sporadic destruction and low-grade replacement marked the end of the Indus Civilization in its central region, it does not follow that the same fate attended the more southerly cities in Kāthiāwāḍ, which probably lay beyond the Aryan impact. The evidence there is indeed of a contrary kind. Thus at Rangpur excavation revealed a basic microlithic industry without pottery, succeeded by a Chalcolithic culture containing Indus Civilization elements, which was in turn followed by a culture described as 'late Chalcolithic' with red and buff pottery suggesting an organic development from the previous phase. The late phase also contained, in its top level, sherds of Black-and-red Ware which had 'a technical similarity with the "megalithic" pottery of southern India'. This Black-and-red Ware, of which more will be said, is not normally earlier than 1000 B.C. and is often much later; but it certainly occurs, in small quantities, with late Indus Valley material at Lothal, which is only thirty miles north-east of Rangpur, and a similar association has now been observed at Rosadi in mid-Kāthiāwāḍ. It is becoming increasingly clear that the more southerly towns of the Indus Civilization endured for an appreciable time after the fall of Mohenjo-daro, and that the general similarity of the early Black-and-red sherds of Rangpur and Lothal to the pottery of the southern megaliths of a later age is specific and significant. Meanwhile, the important conclusion is that here, in Kāthiāwāḍ, the Indus culture was not obliterated but was transmuted into successor-cultures which adapted Indus ceramic forms and evolved eventually, with other wares, a fine lustrous red pottery painted sometimes with schematized caprids in the old chalcolithic tradition.

For the rest, it will suffice to add that the distinctive Painted Grey Ware, which in the north marks the lower bracket of our Dark Age (1000 B.C. or somewhat later), was preceded at Hastināpura in the upper Ganges valley by a settlement which used crude ochre-coloured pottery and copper implements. An interval elapsed between the two occupations, so that the ochre pottery should carry us back well into the hiatus there. Again, this is at present merely a pointer without substantive value; but in one way and another, and particularly in the western coastlands, Indian archaeology is beginning to close in upon its Dark Age from both ends, and the gap may well have vanished by the time that these words appear in print.

CHAPTER VI

The Ganges Civilization

FROM THE INDUS BASIN with its spreading coastline we turn eastwards to the *doāb* or two-river country of the holy waters of Hindustan, the Yamunā or Jumna and the Gangā or Ganges. The actual distance from the Sutlej, of the Indus system, to the Jumna at the foot of the Simla hills is less than eighty miles, but anciently the two valleys were a world apart. Here was a true partition between the submontane Punjab and the Great Plains of northern India. Hereabouts only a little more than 100 miles intervenes between the vast Thar or Indian Desert, which stretches towards the Arabian Sea, and those same Himālayan hills; and it was through this jungle-filled corridor that the invader from the mountains of the north-west had to force his way. The corridor was further narrowed, indeed almost closed, fifty-five miles north of Delhi, where the upper waters of the (former) river Ghaggar approached to within a narrow margin of the Jumna. Squarely in the midst of this shallow divide stands the town of Pānīpat which has on at least three occasions been the scene of a decisive battle.[61] Today the mound which rises in the midst of the little town is sixty feet high, and its crumbling sides exude the débris of close upon 3000 years.[62]

The archaeology of the Ganges valley is in its infancy, and correlation between its material cultures on the one hand and linguistic or literary factors on the other may wisely be deferred. The composite individuality which, from an early date, distinguished this region from the Punjab on the west and Bengal on the east requires much further evidence and analysis for its proper understanding. No part of India has been changed more drastically by the encroachment of tillage on jungle, and the first act of the historical imagination must be to replant 'the

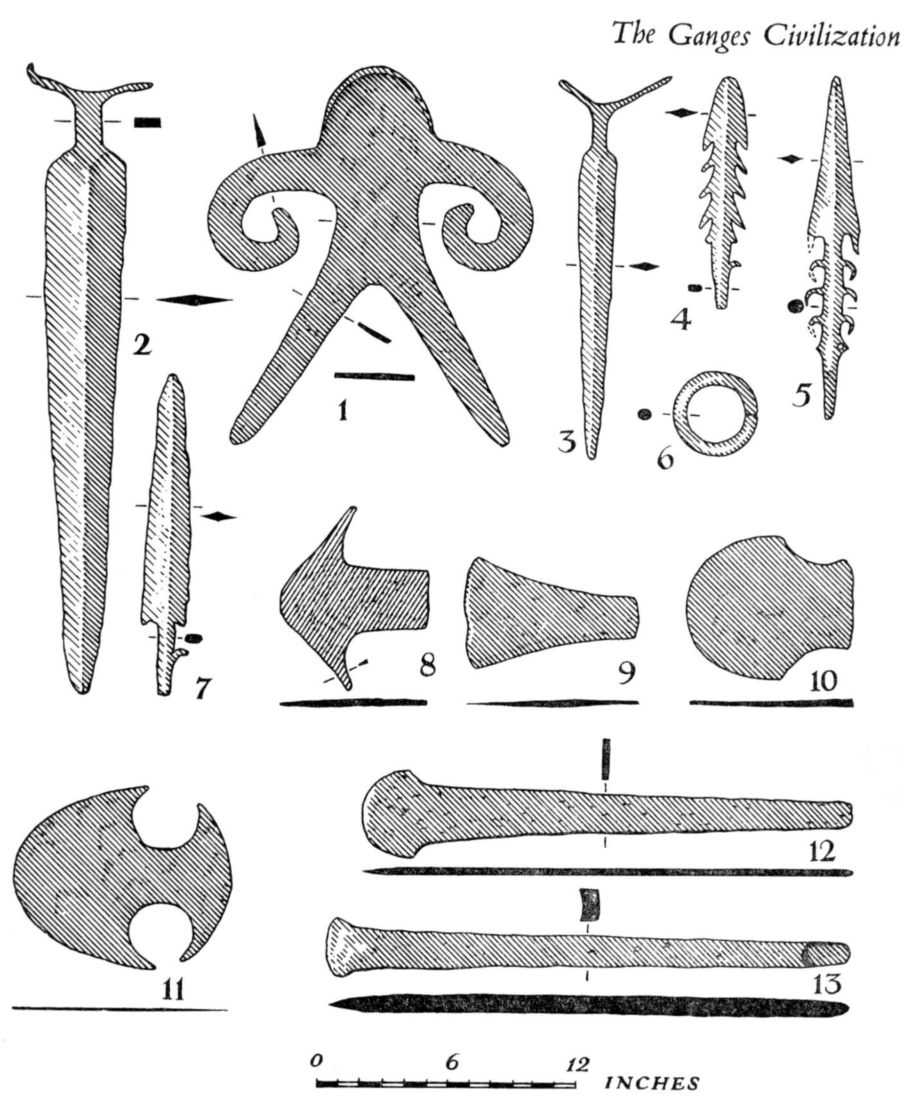

Fig. 26 From 'Gangetic' copper hoards: 1, 'anthropomorph' from Sheorājpur; 2–3, antennae swords from Fategarh; 4–5, harpoons from Sarthaulī and Bisaulī; 6, ring from Pandi; 7, hooked spear from Sarthaulī; 8, axe from Sarthaulī; 9, axe from Gungeriā; 10, axe from Dunriā; 11, double axe from Bhagrā Pīr; 12–13, bar-celts from Gungeriā

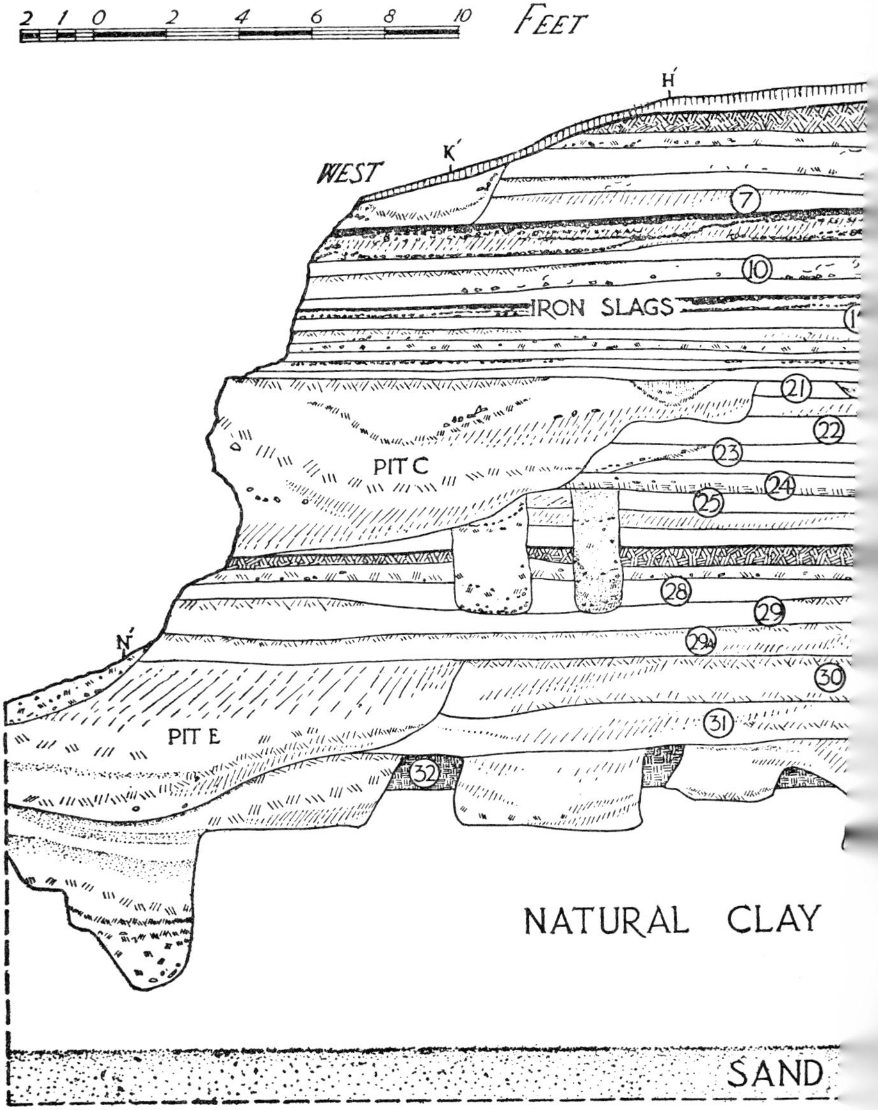

2 1 0 2 4 6 8 10 FEET

H′
WEST
K′
7
10
IRON SLAGS
21
22
23
PIT C
24
25
28
29
29A
N′
30
31
PIT E
32
NATURAL CLAY
SAND

Fig. 27 Section through mound at Hastināpura

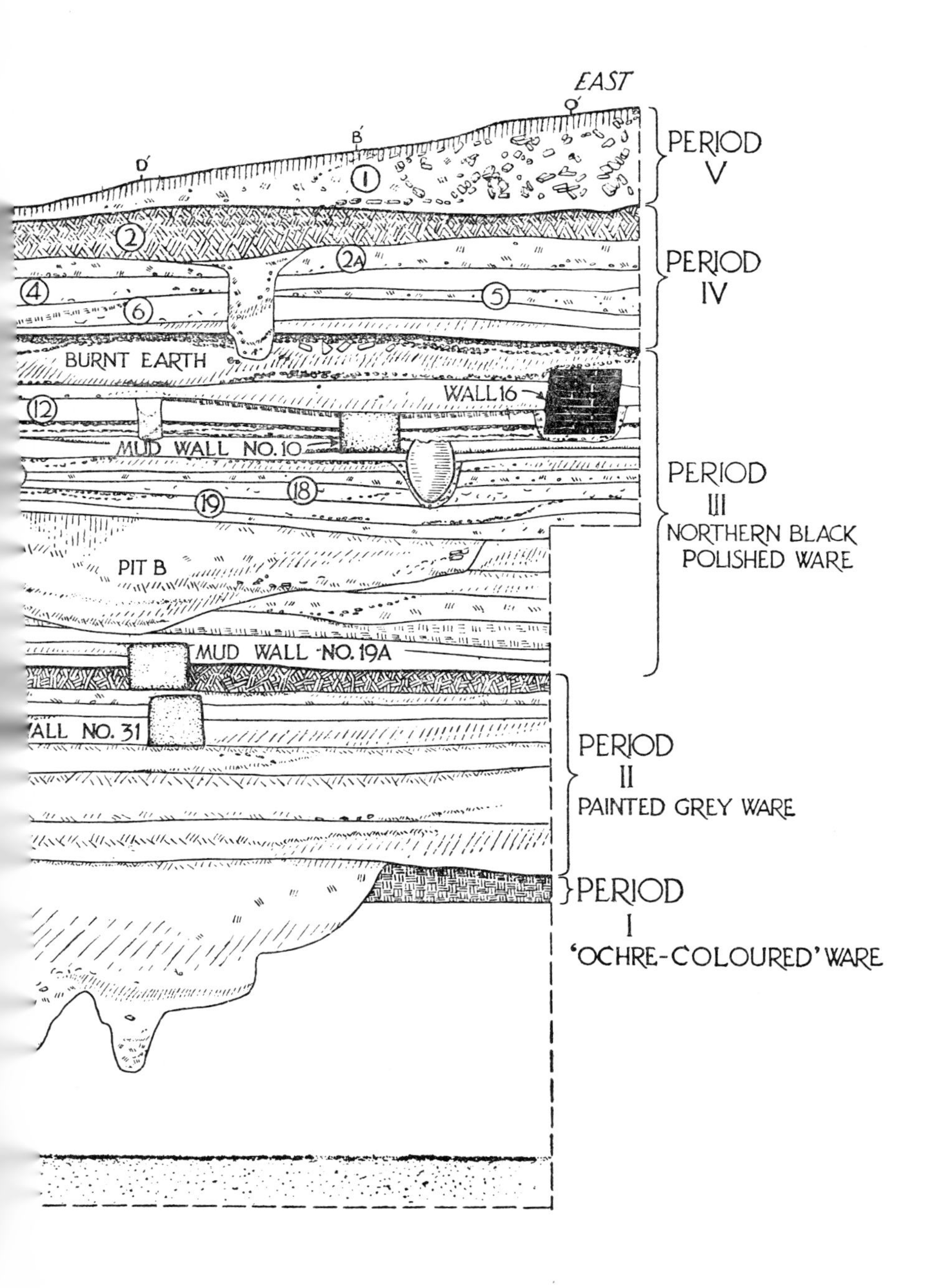

EAST
O'
B'
D'
PERIOD V
PERIOD IV
PERIOD III NORTHERN BLACK POLISHED WARE
PERIOD II PAINTED GREY WARE
PERIOD I 'OCHRE-COLOURED' WARE
BURNT EARTH
WALL 16
MUD WALL NO. 10
PIT B
MUD WALL NO. 19A
WALL NO. 31
1
2
2A
4
5
6
12
18
19

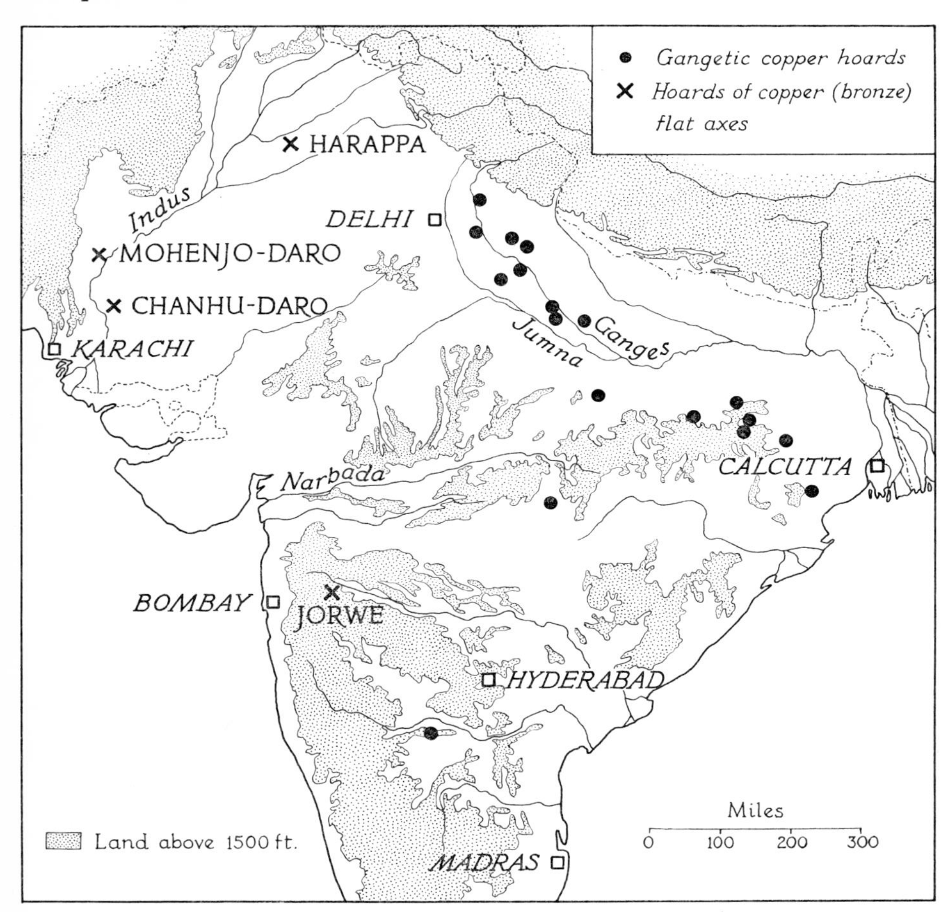

Fig. 28 Distribution of Gangetic copper hoards and hoards of copper flat axes

dark and pathless forest', the *mahāvana*, in which Rāma and the Pāṇḍavas had their being. In this close and tangled country the intruding Aryans at the end of the 2nd millennium B.C. may have found little previous occupation of a settled kind; such at least is the implication of the few sites which have hitherto been probed to the subsoil. The invaders themselves, it may be suspected, here quickly dropped their dominantly pastoral economy in favour of one based on agriculture in fertile riverside clearings. Here the territorial magnate began at no great interval to supersede the traditional tribal chieftain and to build the nations and kingdoms of the Indian epics, of which this is the homeland. Here, in the Middle Country or *Madhyadesha*, developed the 'Inner' category of Indo-Aryan speech, as distinct from the 'Outer' category in the Punjab, Bengal and Assam. Here emerged the essential India, with its imperial dynasties and its great religious teachers. At present, all this achievement is strangely lacking in palpable roots.

Most detached of the available evidence is the famous series of copper hoards which have been found on upwards of thirty-four sites between the upper Ganges and Orissa.[63] Something like six hundred objects is involved, comprising eight main types: (i) flat axes, usually of stocky sub-rectangular form with splayed edge; (ii) shouldered axes with a clear kink or set-back at the points where the curved edge meets the stem of the implement; (iii) 'bar-celts' or chisels, up to two feet long, consisting of a nearly parallel-sided bar and an expanded chisel-edge in one of the lateral planes, not central as in the axes; (iv) rings made by bending a rod of circular section until the ends meet; (v) harpoon-heads strangely like the Magdalenian or Azilian horn harpoons of the West, with bilateral barbs and a loop or projection for the attachment of a cord; (vi) spearheads (sometimes called swords) with strong mid-rib and often with a projection from the tang for the attachment of a cord; (vii) swords, usually with the hilt, of one piece with the blade, bifurcated like antennae; and (viii) strange anthropomorphic objects, up to eighteen inches long, which might be taken to represent a human form with straddled legs and incurved arms. Their purpose and whether indeed their anthropomorphism is intentional are alike unknown.

Figs. 26 and 28

Analysis shows the presence of copper and a small amount of nickel and arsenic, in proportions consistent with an Indian origin for the ore. A few of the implements are of bronze; one of the antennae-swords from Kallūr, in Raichūr district in the Deccan, contains 9·5 per cent of tin,* i.e. is of an alloy suited by strength, elasticity and toughness for its martial purpose. The nearest ancient copper-workings to the Ganges basin are in Rājasthān and in Singhbūm, southern Bihar; of these alternatives the latter, in view of the distribution of the hoards, is the likely source.

In no instance has a hoard or distinctive hoard-type been found in a stratified deposit, and even the precise find-spot of most of the hoards is forgotten. At Rājpur Parsu, in the Bijnor district beside the upper Ganges, a hoard came from the periphery of a mound 'which is 5–7 feet high and covers an area of nearly 4 square furlongs'. Another hoard, from Bisauli in the Badaun district a little farther south, was ploughed up in a field that is 'almost flat without any signs of a mound'. At both these sites Mr. B. B. Lal dug exploratory trenches; at neither did he find further implements, but both sites yielded scraps of ill-fired thick ochre-washed ware, mixed at Bisauli with sherds of well-fired red-slipped ware with black designs. All the Bisauli pottery was near the surface—as indeed the hoard had been—but the groups of sherds were distinguished by the freshness of the red ware and the worn aspect of the ochre ware. Yet another hoard-site, at Bahādarabād eight miles west of Hardwār on the upper Ganges, has also produced ochre sherds. A comparable ochre fabric has been found by Mr. A. Ghosh farther west, in the Dṛishadvatī valley of Bikaner, and has there been called, a little ambitiously perhaps, the 'Sothi Culture', from a place near the sub-divisional town of Nohar. More significantly, it characterized the lowest (earliest) occupation of the Ganges site at Hastināpura, to which we shall come

* Analysis made in 1945 by the Archaeological Chemist in India.

in a moment. Little is at present known of this Ochre Ware; even the shapes of the pots have not been determined; and its association with the copper hoards is not proved. But a considerably more advanced exploration of the succeeding Painted Grey Ware levels in the Ganges-Jumna basin has failed to reveal in them any of the more distinctive hoard-types, and the impression for the moment is that these precede the Grey Ware and the full development of urban life in the region. In a chronology which is at present largely guesswork, I should say that that implies a date for the hoards before the 8th century B.C.; my Indian colleagues might prefer a somewhat earlier terminus.

What do the hoards themselves tell us? The flat axes with more or less expanded blades are the only possible link with the Indus Civilization, and the type is too generalized and widespread to support the view that the hoards represent 'the colonization of the Ganges basin by refugees and displaced persons from the Punjab and the Indus valley during the time of the break-up of the Harappā empire and the coming of raiders from the west'. The only important parallelism between the copper hoards and the Indus bronzes is the absence from both of the hafting-socket, which had been familiar in Mesopotamia and farther north since the 4th millennium. But the really distinctive elements of the hoards—the barbed harpoons, the spearheads with basal projection, the 'bar-celts', the so-called anthropomorphs, the shouldered axes—are not Indus types; and *per contra* the distinctively Indus blade with curved end is absent from the copper hoards. Analogies to the swords with antennae have been recognized in the Koban culture of the Caucasus and may be significant,[64] but intermediate links are at present missing. In all the circumstances, the alternative theory that the hoards may be 'in fact traces of the Indo-Aryan migration' is equally difficult to sustain. Indeed, archaeologically our Ganges evidence is not ready for equation with any major historical event or speculation of the kind, and the Aryans in particular should, I suggest, be given a holiday for the time-being. It is best to admit that no proto-Aryan material culture has yet been identified in India.

Nevertheless, these hoards are not completely dumb. The axes, up to a foot in length and five or six pounds in weight, are excellent woodmen's tools. The barbed harpoons, based perhaps on bone or horn prototypes, proclaim extensive food-gathering in the fishful rivers near which they are found. That they were also used for hunting animals as formidable as the rhinoceros is shown, as B. B. Lal reminds us,[63] by cave-paintings of unknown date in the Mirzapur district of the Ganges valley, south-west of Banaras. The unbarbed spear-heads anticipate in general fashion the iron spears which the peaceful peasantry sometimes carry in these regions at the present day. Only the swords which occur on four of the sites imply a more military element, symbolical perhaps of rank rather than recurrent peril. The general inference is that the hoards represent semi-nomadic food-gathering communities, capable of clearing patches of jungle and perhaps (though this we do not know) of some sort of garden-agriculture, but living mainly by hunting and fishing. The likelihood fits well into far more modern pictures of tribal India.

It has been inferred that the deposition of the hoards 'itself suggests a time of insecurity and economic instability, and and may mean that the refugees from the Indus Civilization were not left undisturbed for long, as the Aryan invasions gathered momentum and pressed on, beyond the old frontiers of the Harappā kingdom and down into the Ganges valley'. This is to force the evidence beyond its warrant. The copper implements are shown, by their frequently specialized character and skilful casting and hammering, and by their distribution over 800 miles of jungle landscape, to have been the work of substantially whole-time experts who were probably also (as in other parts of the world) itinerant. The perils of one kind and another which must have beset them in their vagrancy and led to the occasional loss of their stock-in-trade were not necessarily more formidable than those which man and beast would normally impose upon the wandering craftsman and tradesman in the rough circumstances of the age. Once more it is unnecessary or premature to conjure up cosmic causes such as Aryan invasion to explain these sporadic casualties.

As the evidence goes, then, we are confronted by a striking and individual development of metal-craftsmanship in the Ganges basin and the Orissa hills somewhere about 1000 B.C. amongst folk who were primarily hunters and probably lived in temporary villages in jungle-clearings. (Incidentally, none of the ochre sherds referred to above as possibly contemporary with the hoards has been found in association with built foundations.) Insufficiently large and wealthy to maintain specialists individually, these communities shared, it seems, in a nomadic craftsmanship for which there are many parallels. The sources from which this craftsmanship drew its initial inspiration are not clearly defined; it may be supposed that its ideas germinated in the metal traditions of the north-west (the Indus region and beyond), though it would not be surprising to discover trans-Himālayan sources in the north and north-east. This uncertainty, whilst emphasizing our present ignorance, also points the likelihood that much of the kind and quality of the hoards was due to the inventive skill of the Ganges coppersmiths themselves. Archaeology, in its search for ultimate origins, can readily overlook the possibility that those origins may lie very largely at our feet.

From these *disjecta* we turn to the great urban sites which came into being in the Ganges valley during the 1st millennium B.C. and have sufficiently homogeneous elements to justify the name of the 'Ganges Civilization'. Culturally, their common denominator is the presence successively of Painted Grey and Northern Black Polished Wares, described above (p. 26). Some of these sites, even in the dusty and ruinous condition in which we find them today, are truly stupendous. Overlooking the junction of the Ganges and the Jumna opposite Allahābād is the immense mound of Jhusi, its riven sides oozing with sherds, including the famous Northern Black Polished or N.B.P. Ware of the middle and second half of that millennium. The mound has not yet been explored, but both its key-position and its size indicate its importance. And there are many others, ranging from the little fortified town of Bhīṭā, eighteen miles south of Allahābād, to the mighty Kaushāmbī beside the Jumna, thirty-two miles to the west, or to metropolitan Mathurā (Muttra) itself, by the same kingly river. Bhīṭā is merely 400 yards square, though its mounds stand boldly above the plain. It may have been the Vichhī or Vichīgrāma mentioned on certain sealings found on the site, but the scrappy excavations carried out there half a century ago were incompetent even for their age, and only the occurrence of N.B.P. Ware hints at the antiquity of the place. Kaushāmbī, on the other hand, has a circuit of some four miles and is one of the great sites of India. Before and after the time of the Buddha (*c.* 500 B.C.) it was the capital of the Vatsa Kingdom of the Purāṇas, and here stood one of Ashoka's edict-pillars (p. 174), now in Allahābād Fort. Slight excavations were carried out on the site in 1937–8, and since 1948 its systematic exploration has been undertaken for Allahābād University by Mr. G. R. Sharma. The results have not yet been published, save for interim notes.[65]

Plates 26, 28

The ramparts, over 30 feet high and armed at regular intervals by bastions, were built of mud revetted externally with a battered facing of baked bricks which, as excavated, presents an imposing frontage. They were built before the introduction of N.B.P. Ware, but overlapped the arrival of this fabric, and a central date in the 6th century B.C. provisionally meets the evidence. The facing of baked brick closely recalls that of the Harappā citadel (p. 97), but whether across the many inter-vening centuries a significant structural tradition had been preserved is more than doubtful; the idea of a sloping brick revetment is scarcely so highly specialized that independent invention is excluded. After the original construction of the Kaushāmbī walls, rectangular towers of baked brick were imposed upon the bastions, and the defences were re-newed more than once. Within them, courtyard houses of the later centuries B.C. and possibly later still have been uncovered, together with the site of a large enclosed Buddhist monastery which has been identified with the Ghositārāma described by the Chinese traveller Hiuen Tsang, who came this way in the 7th century A.D. The monastery marked the site where the Buddha preached, and the excavator ascribes the first construc-tion of the main stūpa or relic-shrine to the century of the Buddha's death. The general wealth of the city, in the midst of its fertile landscape and beside its great river-highway, is sufficiently indicated by the vast quantity of material, including many hundreds of terracotta figurines, which has been found here by the present excavators and by less orthodox predecessors.

But of published work on the ancient sites of the *doāb*, the most significant is that carried out in 1950–2 by Mr. B. B. Lal at Hastināpura near an old course of the upper Ganges.[66] The excavation was designed mainly to reveal the culture-sequence, and was so far successful; the character and function of the buildings sampled at the successive levels remain to be in-vestigated, as they should be, by wider digging. Five main phases of occupation were recognized. The earliest, Period I, was represented by a thin layer, never more than $1\frac{1}{2}$ feet thick and often less, with no structures but with a few much-worn fragments of the Ochre Ware. Neither the shapes nor indeed the technique of the pottery could be ascertained. No implements

Fig. 27

were found, but the possible association of this ware with the copper hoards has been discussed above.

There was no overlap with Period II, which contained the Painted Grey Ware described on p. 26, together with remains of mud or mud-brick walls, but with no clear evidence of the use of baked bricks. Copper was found in the form of an arrowhead, a nail-parer, an antimony rod and a few fragments; there were no stone implements and no iron objects, though in the uppermost levels lumps of iron ore were encountered. Two glass bangles from these strata seem to be the earliest yet recorded from India. The humped bull was represented both by terracotta figurines and by actual bones, which occurred in large numbers with those of buffalo, horse, sheep and pig. Whilst these represent considerable domestic herds and flocks, the bones of deer indicate that hunting supplemented farming; but more notable was the discovery of charred grains of rice which, with other rice recently recovered from Chalcolithic Nārḍā Tolī (p. 142), carry back rice-cultivation in the sub-continent many centuries behind the earliest date previously recorded (the 3rd century B.C.). Altogether, the remains of this period, dated roughly to 800–500 B.C., show a developed township with an economy based on mixed farming, and with adequately constructed houses of which at present little is known.

The occupational strata of Period II had reached a height of 6–7 feet when a flood swept across the site and, for a time occupation ceased. When habitation was renewed (Period III) the Painted Grey Ware had given place to the Northern Black Polished Ware, ascribed above (p. 30) to the 5th–2nd century B.C., and baked bricks were now used alongside mud and mud-brick. Again, no details of house-plans were revealed in the trial-trenches, but baked-brick drains were encountered, and 'soak-wells' or 'soak-pits' of superimposed jars with perforated bases or of superimposed terracotta rings about 2 feet

Plate 27

in diameter now begin to appear. Soak-pits and ring-wells of these types are characteristic of Indian towns from the latter half of the 1st millennium B.C. onwards.

In Period III iron was regularly used for the first time: barbed and socketed arrowheads, chisels and sickles of this metal are recorded, although copper was retained for antimony rods, nail-parers and a variety of other purposes. Terracotta figurines of animals, especially the elephant, are better modelled than in the preceding period. Money now comes into use in the shape of punch-marked rectangular pieces of silver with symbols which include the 'crescent-on-hill' and the 'sun'; with them were a number of cast copper coins, both rectangular and round, bearing similar symbols. The indication is that of increasing and increasingly systematized trade.

Within the limited area trenched, there was in Period III an accumulation of 5–9 feet, with evidence of 3–6 sub-phases; and it seemed that the Period had ended in fire. That the event occurred in or very little before the 2nd century B.C. is suggested by the facts that the N.B.P. Ware now ceased and that 5 coins of the rulers of Mathurā, attributed to that century, were found in the lower (earlier) strata of the succeeding Period IV. Both that Period, which is carried by coinage through a number of sub-phases into the 3rd century A.D., and a medieval occupation (11th–15th century), which followed after a long gap, lie outside our present scope.

A not dissimilar sequence is indicated by the more imposing site of the ancient city of Ahichchhatrā, near Ramnagar in the Bareilly district of U.P. and close to a tributary of the Ganges.[67] The city was the capital of the kingdom of North Pāñchāla which, in the *Mahābhārata*, was wrested from the king of Pāñchāla by the Kurus. It retained something of its metropolitan status until about A.D. 1100, when it was replaced by the modern Badaun. Today the deserted city looms majestically over the plain, with towering ramparts 3½ miles in circuit, the tall fragment of a medieval temple within them. Inconclusive excavation in 1940–4 showed two successive earthen ramparts below a stout wall of baked brick, and P.G. Ware is said to have been found below, as well as in, the earlier rampart. If so, the rampart should not be later than 500 B.C. and may be somewhat earlier. The excavators recognized nine main strata in the total life-span of the town, and observed that each stratum had its own individual plan, with differing building-alignments. As at Hastināpura, coins (square and round) came into use during the N.B.P. Ware period.

Between them, the two sites of Hastināpura and Ahichchhatrā, imperfect though our knowledge be of both, proclaim the emergence of a comfortable and organized city-life in the Jumna-Ganges basin sometime in the first half of the 1st millennium B.C. To this period belongs the earliest settled occupation known to us in the Delhi region; at the Purāṇā Qila (Indrapat), which may fairly be described as the first Delhi, and Tilpat thirteen miles to the south. In 1955 a list of thirty-four Painted Grey Ware sites was published,[68] and the number is constantly increasing. Nothing that we know contradicts the impression that this Ganges Civilization was as widespread as it was prosperous. We may recognize in it the general urban background of the *Mahābhārata* without too much labouring of detail: a picture of wealthy and jealous dynasties and polities, based upon a limitless and fertile soil and serviceable river-communications. About the middle of the millennium, a knowledge of iron-working spread through the region, doubtless introduced from Persia where iron-smelting had been familiar for five or six centuries. Its arrival meant no overwhelming revolution in the mode of life of the cities of the Indian plains. Some of their pots and pans underwent a technical change about this time; more important, the introduction of coinage, also from Persia, betrays a quickening of the commercial sense. But, once established, the

Ganges Civilization endured through the centuries with a changelessness which the modern age has not altogether shaken. Ahichchhatrā may be dead, but Banaras swarms busily and immutably upon a buried past of similar antiquity.

Of two other great cities of the Ganges basin—Rājgīr and Pāṭaliputra—something must be said in a later context (p. 173).

CHAPTER VII

Early Civilization in Central India

FROM THE GANGES BASIN it would be logical to move eastwards into Bengal or, turning the eastern corner of the central hills, veer southward into Orissa, where the coastal flats are an extension of the great northern plains. In Orissa two imposing sites have in fact been carefully sampled, but their urban origins are unlikely to go back beyond 300 B.C. At Shishupālgarh, near Bhubaneshwar, a part of a somewhat earlier settlement was powerfully fortified, apparently in the 3rd century B.C., with a clay rampart thirty feet high laid out on a remarkably symmetrical square plan.[69] The sides of the enclosure were three-quarters of a mile long, and in each of them, apart from posterns, were two magnificent projecting gateways, built of squared laterite blocks and equipped with flanking staircases. The unusual excellence of the masonry and the extreme regularity of the planning indicate administrative authority of a high order, and it might not be unduly rash to ascribe the fortress or fortress-town, as an imperial instrument of pacification, to the emperor Ashoka after his famous victory over the Kaliṅgas of these parts about 264 B.C. Historically at least, the defences are most unlikely to have been constructed during the following half-century.

Plates 29, 30

Fig. 29

Seemingly about the same time at Jaugaḍā, district Ganjām, beside the Rishikulyā river in southern Orissa, a developed Iron Age culture and an earthen rampart twenty-five feet high were imposed upon a site previously occupied by villagers who had used stone axes of oblong section and, apparently, Black-and-red Ware (p. 161).[70] Here the association of the new work with Ashoka is perhaps encouraged by the presence of his fourteen rock-edicts in the immediate vicinity.

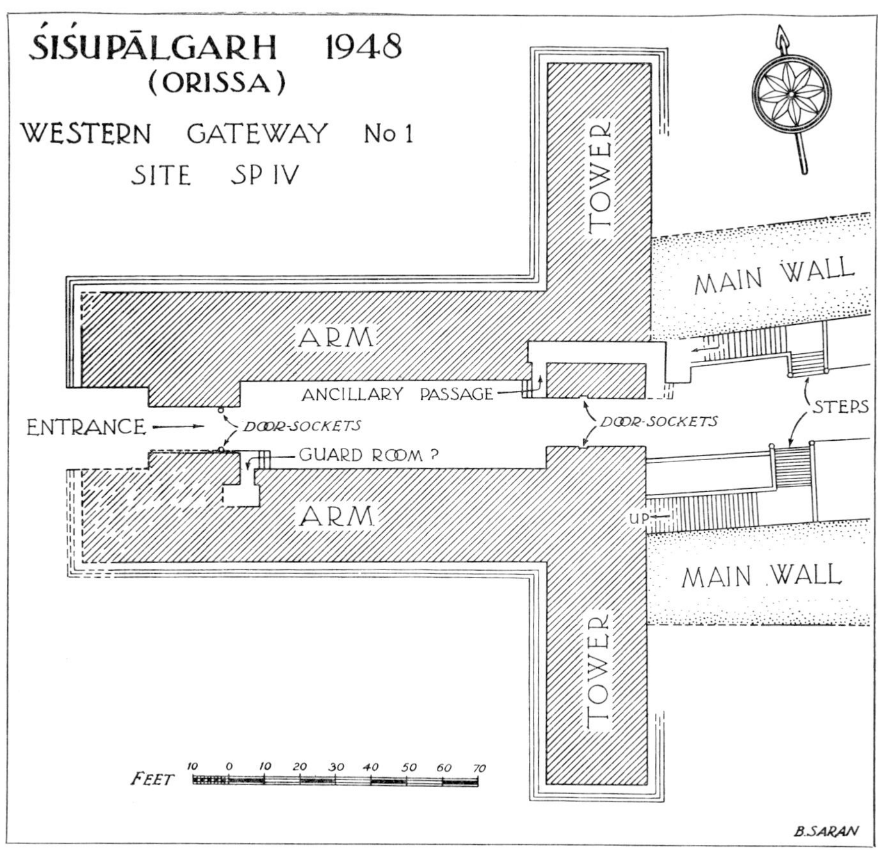

Fig. 29 (Cf. pl. 29)

In Bengal, too, on both sides of the present national frontier, intermittent excavation carried out on obviously important sites, notably Maināmatī near Comilla,[71] Mahāsthān in the Bogra district,[72] and Tamluk (Ptolemy's Tamalites) at the head of the Hooghly estuary,[73] has begun to present a similar picture. At Tamluk trial-excavations have revealed a scanty assortment of 'neolithic celts and an ill-fired pottery' at the lowest level (compare Jaugaḍā, above), followed by a Gangetic culture (with cast copper coins) ascribed to the 3rd–2nd centuries B.C., and succeeded in turn by a deposit containing much Rouletted Ware of the 1st century A.D. Whether these occupations were continuous is not stated, but it would appear that here, as on the other sites mentioned, substantive settlement began in or about the 3rd century B.C., that is, in the Mauryan period. Incidentally, Mahāsthān has produced an interesting inscription on a limestone slab, recording the earliest known Bengal famine and the measures taken by the local authority to meet it by the issue of paddy from reserve stocks, which were to be replenished when opportunity offered. Both alphabet and language resemble those of Ashoka's pillar-edicts of about 250 B.C. (p. 174). Future exploration may show that civilization came late to the dense monsoon-ridden jungles of eastern India, and that these, like the Assam and Orissa hills down to modern times, had previously been the camping-ground of small disarticulate societies in an essentially Neolithic condition.

Plate 52

But south of the great plains, in a belt of central India which includes the Narbadā and the upper Godāvarī and extends roughly from Ujjain in the north to the borders of Mysore in the south, a number of town-sites have been dug into in recent years, and a consistent cultural sequence is beginning to appear. Of the full meaning of this sequence little can be said until vertical probing has been followed in its proper sequence by large-scale lateral clearance. For the time being we have to content ourselves with a mosaic of fragmentary indications.

Nevertheless, the mosaic does already seem to make something of a pattern, and the pattern is this. There is in central India, at any rate outside Gujarāt, no recognizably urban phase which can be equated with that of the Painted Grey Ware of the plains, i.e. prior to 500 B.C. Future exploration may modify this view; but at present it would appear that along the great central rivers organized civic life began with the introduction of iron shortly after the middle of the 1st millennium B.C., following a phase of Chalcolithic village life in which copper was itself comparatively rare and costly—in other words, trade was rudimentary and the social horizon essentially a local one. If this provisional conclusion is supported, the spread of civilization in India assumes a logical shape: beginning with the fertilization of Middle Eastern ideas along the north-west coast and up the Indus valley about the middle of the 3rd millennium; then spreading southwards, on the one hand, as far as the Narbatā estuary, and overflowing from the upper Punjab on the other hand through the Pānīpat-Delhi corridor into the great plains of the Ganges-Jumna *doāb* in the first quarter of the 1st millennium B.C.; and later, between the 5th and 3rd centuries B.C., percolating eastwards to the Ganges estuary and southwards amongst the Chalcolithic communities of central India. Farther south again, in peninsular India, it is likely enough that city-life was somewhat later still in its inception.

Between the north and the centre, the main connecting link prior to the Iron Age appears to have lain in Gujarāt. Other lines of access doubtless contributed, and after the middle of the 1st millennium more central routes, such as that from the Jumna valley up the Chambal river and past Ujjain[74] took the lead. But as knowledge stands, it is in Gujarāt, and particularly in the Kāthiāwāḍ peninsula, that a measure of continuity can be traced between the earlier civilization of the north-west and the central Indian complex. In this context the key site for the moment is Rangpur, near the head of the Gulf of Cambay. Archaeologically, Rangpur has had a chequered history. It was hailed in 1934 as the most southerly site of the Indus Civilization; in 1947 further exploration was thought to disprove its Indus association, but six years later renewed excavation replaced it on the Indus map.[75] Still insufficient investigation suggests that the earliest occupation was marked by crude microliths of jasper and agate, without pottery. This was succeeded by a settlement protected by a mud-brick wall over six feet thick and marked by a culture which may be described as a provincial variant of that of the Indus Civilization. It included triangular terracotta 'cakes', faïence and steatite beads, a chert blade, and pottery with a peacock pattern, all allied to Indus types. Its thick red pottery, on the other hand, painted in black or chocolate with loops, dots, criss-cross, and horizontal and oblique lines, is less distinctively Harappān. It is to be expected that dilution or partial survival of this sort should occur near the periphery of the Civilization.

This sub-Indus culture merged into a succeeding phase characterized by a lustrous red ceramic painted in black with stylized antelopes and less ambitious designs, and this was followed in turn by Black-and-red Ware of a kind which will be discussed later in connection with the South Indian megaliths (p. 161). Crude microliths still appear, but sherds of Northern Black Polished Ware indicate a date after 500 B.C. Substantially from the sub-Indus phase (latter half of 2nd millennium?) to the N.B.P. period, the occupation of the site seems to have been continuous.

For the rest, the Chalcolithic of central India—a phase to which the term 'civilization' cannot at present be applied although villages were already merging into towns—lacks any clear initial link with the Indus, unless the occasional animal-patterns on pottery and certain types of flake implements are an echo from the Indus borderland. Instead, within a generally coherent scheme, it shows a wide diversity of detail, based upon local tradition and initiative. The most northerly site of the series is at Nāgdā, on the east bank of the Chambal north-west of Ujjain, where the uppermost third of a partially natural mound ninety feet high represents three cultural periods.[76] The earliest, twenty-two feet thick, includes massive mud and mud-brick structures of which one may possibly have been the bastion of a rampart. Alongside a few scraps of copper are many microliths, mostly parallel-sided blades with one side occasionally retouched and the other (the working side) often serrated. A few blades show a crested ridge. The pottery, mainly red but sometimes cream-coloured, is painted in black or chocolate with concentric circles, wavy lines, hatched lozenges, 'sun-symbols', spotted deer, and peacocks. The date is roughly the earlier half of the 1st millennium B.C.; for the phase is succeeded without appreciable break by an iron-using culture with 'megalithic' Black-and-red Ware. This is followed by the limited introduction of baked bricks and by N.B.P. Ware, with more iron. A potsherd and a terracotta ball from the upper levels bear inscriptions of about the 2nd century B.C.

Here we have, then, earlier phases marked by a microlithic industry and in part by a ceramic which is essentially local though perhaps, in its animal-decoration, influenced at long range by the cultures of the Baluchistan frontier; and a later, iron-using phase in which, as the N.B.P. pottery indicates, elements that certainly included a new trend towards urbanization found their way southwards from the developing civic centres of the Jumna-Ganges *doāb*. The absence of Painted Grey Ware and the presence of iron closely followed by N.B.P. pottery shows that this penetration from the northern plains occurred not appreciably earlier than the 5th century B.C.

A similar process is indicated by a dozen other sites which have been trenched in the great central region. Here examples must suffice. A site of great promise is that of Maheshwar, probably the Māhishmatī of the *Mahābhārata*, on the northern bank of the middle Narbadā, with the confronting site of Nāvḍā Ṭolī on the south side.[77] As the opposed sites suggest, Maheshwar was an established crossing which carried the highroad from Ujjain and the Ganges basin into the Deccan. Its mounds rise to a height of 100 feet and have produced four main cultures. Like many other central Indian settlements, this was founded on the fertile Black Cotton soil which no doubt yielded a tolerably easy livelihood to an undeveloped community equipped with microliths but lacking both metal and pottery and not yet, therefore, commercially-minded. The microliths are not of an elaborate kind; they include small to medium-sized scrapers of chert and jasper, made mostly on flakes with faceted platform, and irregular and sometimes fluted cores. After a break, of uncertain implication, a more advanced microlithic industry, with backed and crested blades, lunates and points and associated with copper flat-axes, chisels and hooks, introduces the now-familiar central Indian chalcolithic. Querns and slingstones appear, and an abundant pottery, some ochre-washed but predominantly red and often painted with parallel lines, hatched triangles, circles and foliage, occasionally with antelopes and dancing human figures. This deposit is from five to eight feet thick, and may be ascribed to the second quarter of the 1st millennium B.C. It is followed by a deposit no less than twenty feet thick containing a number of occupation-layers marked by large baked or mud bricks, soakpits lined with bricks or pottery-rings, iron implements (sickle, hoe, nails, arrowheads, spearheads), punch-marked coins, N.B.P. Ware and 'megalithic' Black-and-red Ware, a little of which had seemingly appeared also in the preceding deposit. Here once more we have the familiar complex of the second half of the 1st millennium B.C.: a mixture of dominant 'Ganges' elements with certain others of a more southerly kind. Above this deep deposit occurred a finely burnished red ware with 'sprinklers' of a type found at Chandravalli (Mysore) and in western India at Kolhapur, Baroda and elsewhere in layers dating from the early centuries A.D. From this crowning deposit, the 'megalithic' Black-and-red Ware was absent.

Cf. Plate 52

Cf. Plate 31

Nāvḍā Ṭolī, the suburban site across the river, is a group of four mounds about 350 by 200 yards in extent and ten feet high,

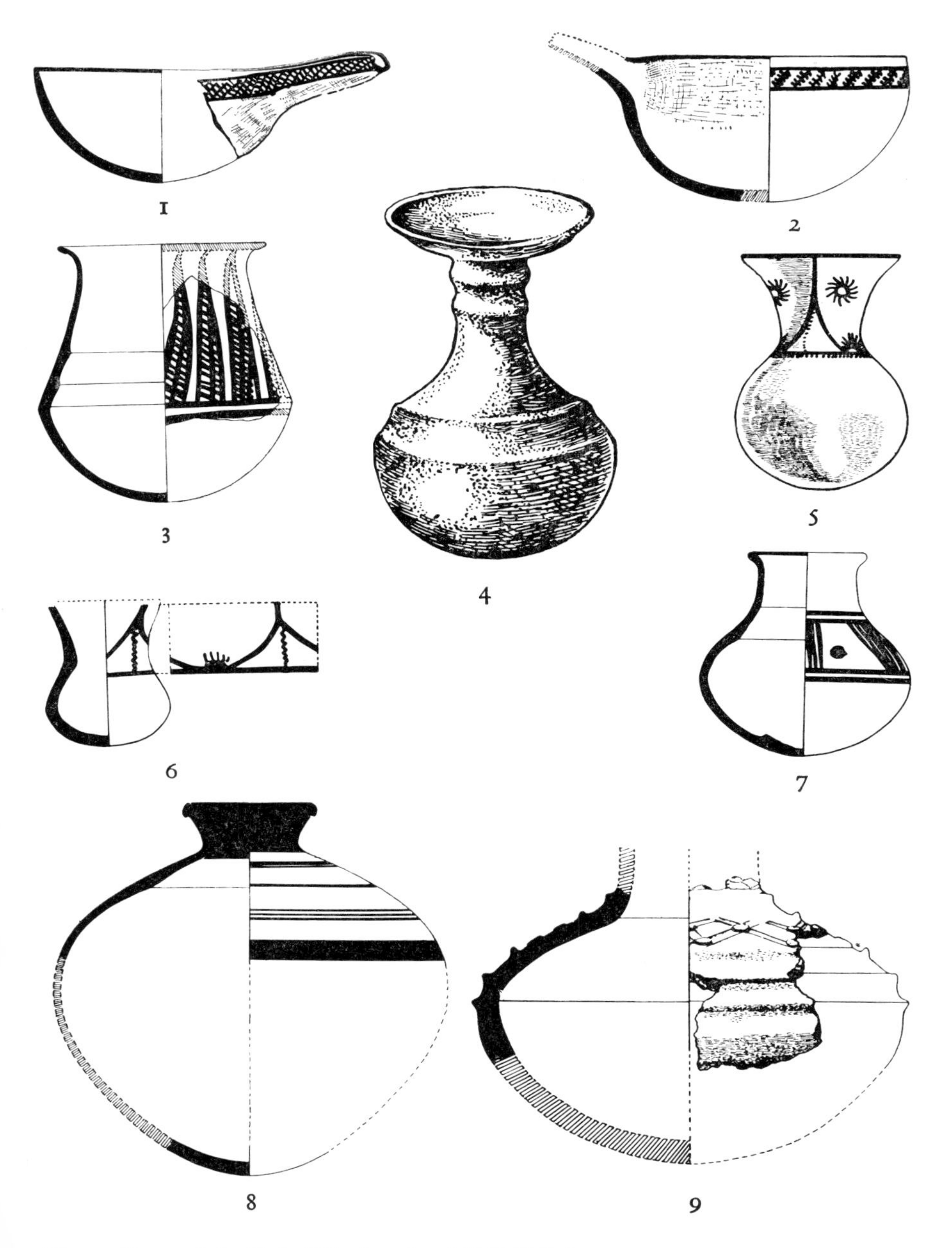

Fig. 30 Pottery of the Chalcolithic phase from Nāvḍā Ṭolī. $\frac{1}{4}$

Figs. 30 31 containing huts indifferently rectangular or round on plan and built of wattle and daub with plastered walls and floors. The suggestion of the excavators that it was essentially a boatmen's village (as indeed the name implies) is probably near enough to the truth. Nevertheless, the Chalcolithic levels immediately below a crowning Iron Age stratum with N.B.P. Ware of the 5th century B.C. or later produced distinctive pottery of a type not yet recognized elsewhere in India; notably, pedestalled goblets and channel-spouted 'tea-pots' which Dr. Sankalia has compared with the spouted pots of Hissar III, or of 'Cemetery B' at Sialk in central Iran. 'Cemetery B' was dated by Ghirshman to *c.* 1000–800 B.C.,[78] and a recent C14 dating from an equivalent deposit at Hasanlu in Azerbaijan gives the confirming date of 812 BC ± 130 years.[79] How significant the suggested resemblance with the (much simpler) Nāvḍā Ṭolī pots may be remains to be seen, particularly if a recent C14 dating for a late Nāvḍā Ṭolī deposit (1336 B.C. ± 125, see p. 83) is confirmed. Intermediate examples between Persia and Nāvḍā Ṭolī are at present lacking. A wide range of foodgrains included rice.

Plate 31

Fig. 30

Seventy miles north of Maheshwar, beside the Sipra river, stands the classic site of Ujjain, one of the seven sacred cities of India, rival even to Banaras in Hindu esteem.[80] In the semihistory of the period, Ujjain was the capital of the kingdom of Avanti, known later as Mālwā, but the excavations in progress at the time of writing under the skilled direction of Mr. N. R. Banerjee have not yet clearly identified any corresponding 7th-century occupation. At present it would appear that, as a developed city, Ujjain began substantially with the impact of an iron-using culture of Gangetic type about 500 B.C., when an area a mile long and three-quarters of a mile wide was enclosed by a great clay rampart with a basal width of 200 feet and a surviving height of forty-two feet. The rampart was reinforced against the flow of the river by transverse barriers of

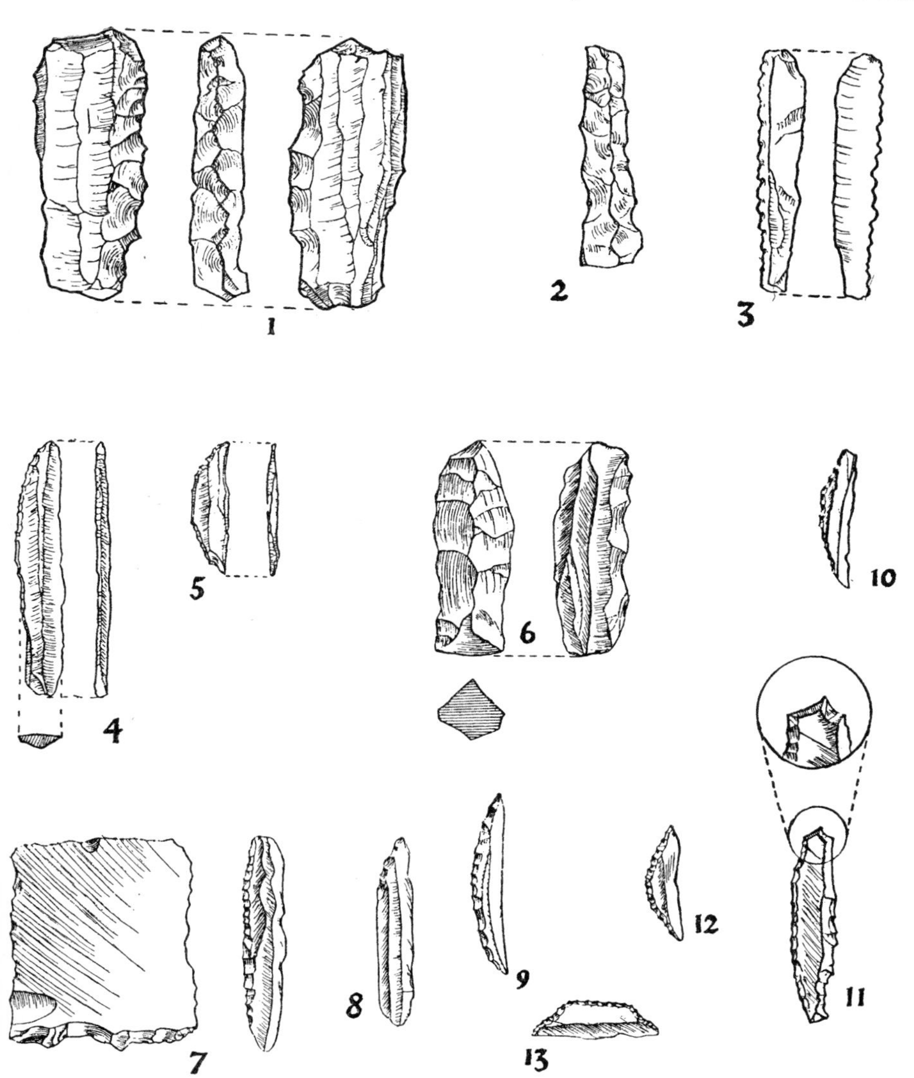

Fig. 31 Chalcedony microliths of the Chalcolithic phase: 1–5, from Nāvḍā Ṭolī; 6–9, from Jorwe; 10–11, from Pravarā Sangam; 12–13, from Nāsik. $\frac{3}{4}$

interlocked timbers vaguely recalling the timber-work of the riverine site of Pāṭaliputra (below, p. 176), and was subsequently revetted in part with baked brick. Outside it, where necessary, was a ditch eighty feet wide and twenty-two feet deep. On the trunk-route from the Ganges to the Arabian Sea, the fortress town of Ujjain was clearly a power to be reckoned with during the last five centuries B.C. In later epochs, changing circumstance and, in particular perhaps, the development of sea-traffic, robbed it of some of its arterial importance, but the ancient site remains a formidable ruin.

In its earliest civic phase, represented by six feet of strata, it included stone and baked-brick structures associated with arrowheads of bone and iron, spearheads and choppers of iron, and evidences of copper-working. Some of the pottery was the Black-and-red Ware already encountered elsewhere; with it were a black-slipped fabric and sherds of unslipped and red-slipped vesiculated ware, some of it made without the wheel. In the body of the rampart two sherds of Painted Grey Ware—the southernmost examples known—are not likely to be much later than 500 B.C.

In the succeeding phase, represented by an accumulation fourteen feet thick, buildings were of baked or unbaked bricks and were roofed with oblong tiles. Streets were made of rubble bound with clay. The soakpits built of pottery-rings or pierced pots, which were to be characteristic of Indian towns for a thousand years, now made their appearance. Oval clay-lined ovens, blackened cooking-pots, grinding-stones and mortars represent kitchen-equipment; iron spearheads and arrowheads, with bone arrowheads which included one 'stained with the blood of a bird', were the principal outfit of the hunter and the soldier. N.B.P. Ware was found in large quantities and in varieties which were partially perhaps local products, some of them diversified with bands of black or saffron paint. The coarse vesiculated ware of the preceding period continued

Indeed Phase II grew naturally out of Phase I under increasing Gangetic influence. Two ivory seals inscribed in an early Brahmi script of the 3rd or 2nd century B.C. marked the upper range of Phase II, but this in turn melted into Phase III, of the Shuṇga period and later, with which we are not here concerned.

Less metropolitan in character than Ujjain were three towns which may be taken as typical of the region south-south-west of Maheshwar: Bahal in the district of East Kandesh beside the Girna, tributary of the Tapti;[81] Nāsik in the district of that name north-east of Bombay; and Jorwe in the district of Ahmadnagar.[82] The last two are in the upper Godāvarī system, a region thickly occupied in the 1st millennium B.C.

Bahal began with what may now be called the 'regulation' microlithic industry of central India: mostly parallel-sided blades of chalcedony, agate or jasper, sometimes serrated, with occasional lunates and trapezes. This microlithic occupation falls into two sub-phases. Phase IA is marked by thick grey hand-made bowls with flared rim, of a kind which occurs also farther south at Brahmagiri in northern Mysore, and a few sherds of thinner grey ware painted on the rim in red ochre. Phase IB produced fine red wheel-turned ware, painted in black with a rich variety of designs—horizontal bands with hatched diamonds, triangles, ladders, concentric circles, criss-cross and wavy lines, foliage, and rarely animals (antelope or horse?). A few sherds of lustrous red-slipped ware are reminiscent of post-Indus Rangpur (p. 138). In the upper levels are spouted vessels of the Nāsik-Jorwe type (below), and sherds of a burnished Black-and-grey Ware with oblique lines painted in white, akin to the 'megalithic' Black-and-red Ware. A shapeless lump of copper justifies the appellation 'Chalcolithic', but it is at least certain that the quantity of metal used in this Phase was negligible. The two sub-phases are thought to have been separated by a break in the occupation, and the ceramic changes are consistent with a shifting population.

At Tekwāḍā, across the river from Bahal, four burials of Phase IB have also produced Black-and-grey Ware of 'megalithic' types.

Again, it is with the arrival of iron in Phase II that the settlement first assumes a purposeful and urban aspect. So far as we know, houses were indeed still of timber, but their equipment now includes legged querns with grains of rice and millet, and the microliths are replaced by abundant tools and weapons of iron—spearheads, arrowheads, knives, sickles. N.B.P. Ware of the Ganges tradition once more marks the source of inspiration. The excavator, M. N. Deshpande, observes that iron here occurs some ten feet below the lowest N.B.P. sherd, recalling a less marked priority for iron also at Nāgdā (p. 138); but on sites relatively so remote from the Ganges *doāb* the utile metal may understandably have penetrated ahead of the less essential ceramic, and the two innovations may be ascribed to the same main source. Burnished 'megalithic' Black-and-red Ware also occurs in the form of rimless bowls and shallow dishes, and there are red globular jars with a gritty core. Massive ear-disks (for wearing in the extended lobes of the ears) of semi-precious stones recall others ascribed to the Mauryan period, roughly the 3rd century B.C., at Rājgīr and Pāṭaliputra.

In Phase III the N.B.P. Ware continues but the Black-and-red drops out. The former may not merely have arrived late on this site, but may have continued somewhat later than usual if its apparent overlap with Sātavāhana coins of the 1st century B.C. is significant.

Both Nāsik on the Godāvarī and Jorwe on the tributary Pravara work to rule in the microlithic phase;[82] indeed, Jorwe never got beyond that phase, though it mitigated its scraps of chert and chalcedony with six flat-axes and a bangle of low-grade bronze which is probably in fact a natural copper alloy. The presence of the copper axes here and at Maheshwar (p. 140) may represent a hang-over from the Indus or sub-Indus culture of the north-west coast; it is less remarkable than is their general absence from these microlithic sites, where their utility in the recurrent process of jungle-clearance must have been cardinal. It is a constant question how these communities, with their miserable microliths, coped with the luxuriant vegetation which certainly surrounded them, although their preference for sandy and relatively open spots such as Langhnāj is a partial explanation. In other parts of the world, microlithic communities have similarly sought a negative milieu.

Nāsik is a mound about 800 by 400 feet with a height of 100 feet of which only the uppermost twenty feet are man-made. Its Phase I produced lunates, trapezes and two-edged blades, and it was observed that 60 per cent of the microliths were 'usable'; in other words, no factory site was included and, to that extent, the limited exploration suggests a measure of specialization or professionalization. With the microliths was ochre-washed and orange-coloured pottery, both wheel-made and handmade and occasionally painted with red or black bands. A distinctive type is that of a spouted vessel, sometimes painted after baking. This type, already noted at Bahal (p.145), is found also at Jorwe and at Nevāsā north-east of Ahmadnagar, and is probably related to a spouted vessel from the levels marked by stone axes and microliths at Brahmagiri in northern Mysore. A similar affinity may be recognized in the large round-bottomed vessels with high rims found at all three sites.

The microlithic phase at Nāsik ended characteristically with the introduction of iron, though an intervening 'weathered horizon', of uncertain implication, is recorded. The Iron Age occupation was marked by iron spearheads, arrowheads, knives, choppers and caltrops, by four-legged saddle querns and pottery-ringed soakpits, and by N.B.P. and Black-and-red Wares. Traces of mud-walled houses were identified, but their plans are unknown. Above this phase come Russet-coated ('Āndhra') wares and 'sprinklers' of red polished pottery, all characteristic of the 1st century A.D.

It is unnecessary here to follow further the exploratory trenching which, over a wide area, has begun to make sense of the cultural sequence of central India without, as yet, throwing much light upon its social significance. That will follow, be it emphasized, when determined lateral excavation over a long period succeeds these easy and quickly rewarding forays.

Meanwhile, with the possible exception of Ujjain, which may be found to have an earlier nucleus but owes its formidable urban character to advancing Gangetic interests about 500 B.C., the sites mentioned above, with others of their kind, have their origins in a widespread and often rudimentary microlithic culture—if the term culture can be so narrowed. Sometimes, as at Rangpur and Maheshwar, this primary culture or industry is thought to have been devoid at first of associated pottery; but at more than one site two to four successive phases of microlithic occupation have been marked by differing pottery-groups and have suggested a certain mobility in locally variant communities at a uniform economic and technological stage of development. In so far as generalization is feasible, we may say that there was in central India, in the earlier half of the 1st millennium B.C., a considerable village-population which used microliths, a little copper or low-grade bronze, and rather coarse painted pottery, often but not always wheel-turned, with a certain community of types that included large round-bottomed bowls with flaring rims and spouted, carinated 'tea-pots'. This population extended from the Vindhya Range 600 miles southwards into northern Mysore.

Towards the south of that area, the microlithic culture lasted perhaps until the 3rd century B.C. Towards the north, but occasionally as far south as Amarāvatī on the Kistna river, it was replaced in the 5th or 4th century B.C. by a vigorous iron-using culture which seems, in the main, to have come from the Jumna-Ganges *doāb*. With the arrival of iron, the microliths went suddenly and almost completely out of use. (Rangpur may provide an exception, but much further work is needed at this site.) Shortly afterwards that typical Ganges product, the steel-like N.B.P. Ware, came in, preceded or accompanied here and there by the more local 'megalithic' Black-and-red Ware of which more will be said in the next chapter. These features, supplemented by native industries, mark the real beginning of civic life in central India. Houses were sometimes still of timber, but mud, mud-brick and baked brick now appear, and pottery-lined soakpits represent a new measure of urban sanitation. Fortifications are not normal, or at any rate have not been widely recognized. It would appear that an undisputed *Lebensraum* was still available for most of the overflow from the northern plains and for the newly-enlarged and elaborated communities of the Deccan.

In summary terms, the contrast between the first urbanization of the northern (Gangetic) plains and that of the Deccan is this. In the north, urbanization began in the developed Bronze Age, during the earlier half of the 1st millennium B.C.; and when, about 500 B.C., iron and the parallel innovations of coinage and a new ceramic technique appeared upon the northern scene, they were absorbed into the existing social system without any drastic change of personality. In the Deccan, on the other hand, the Iron Age descended from the north as a sudden imposition upon a Chalcolithic (largely microlithic) local tradition of altogether lower grade. There, the Iron Age began in the full sense as a revolution.

To the situation in peninsular India, and primarily to its Megalithic Problem, we must now turn.

CHAPTER VIII

South Indian Megaliths

BY WAY OF PREFACE to this chapter, it may be recalled that the term 'megalith' is derived from the Greek words *megas*=large and *lithos*=stone. It is applied primarily to structures of a rudimentary character built wholly or partly of large rough stones, but includes comparable structures of a more sophisticated kind in which the stones may be crudely or even, as at Stonehenge, elaborately dressed. A secondary condition is that the monument fulfilled a funerary or commemorative or religious function.

The megaliths of India are extensive and peculiar. They are in fact the jungle of a problem, and a little preliminary clearing may be helpful, though the procedure is not without risk. In the present context it would appear to be justifiable to set aside at once the megaliths of that region of north-eastern India, extending from Assam to Bastar on the northern flank of the lower Godāvarī, where megalithic 'cultures' (if so they may be called) are a more or less living tradition of the aborigines. To exclude these living or moribund cultures, which have been extensively studied,[83] may seem a wilful rejection of potentially useful comparative evidence; but they do in fact differ in general type and concept from most of the south Indian material, and Christoph von Fürer-Haimendorf's observation that they belong essentially to south-eastern Asia—Indonesia, Oceania, the Philippines, Formosa—matches the evidence, whatever be the truth of his plausible guess that they were introduced into north-eastern India by Austroasiatic immigrants (see also p. 89). The Bastar Gonds and the Khāsis and Nāgas of Assam alike erect single standing stones (menhirs) or alignments of stones in honour of the dead, who are thereby encouraged to help their living kinsmen. In Assam, as well as in Indonesia and Oceania, a forked wooden post of Y-shape is an alternative to the menhir, and both posts and menhirs are associated with ox-sacrifice. An identical custom occurs in Bastar; and the Koyas and Raj Gonds of Hyderabad erect small forked posts carrying the tails of sacrificial cows on graves or the site of memorial feasts. In all these regions it is the widespread belief that the soul or 'virtue' of the dead man is attached to the stone or post and benefits his survivors and the village-crops. Alternatively, the Bondos and Gadabas of Orissa erect a dolmen (table-like cist above ground), often of small size, as the seat of the dead; and this seat may be associated with a stone circle. Generally, the setting-up of menhirs, dolmens and stone-circles links the Orissa tribes both with the Khāsis and Nāgas of Assam and with the Gonds of Bastar. The Khāsis indeed (though not the Nāgas) approach more nearly to the dominant megalithic custom of peninsular India in that they collect periodically the bones of clan-members and deposit them in 'a free-standing cist, as big as a small house, built of enormous single slabs'.[84] So too do the Mundas of Choṭā Nāgpur who, in addition to setting up memorial-stones of north-eastern type, bury excarnated bones of members of a family in dolmen-like graves consisting of a cover-slab supported by smaller stones. Here it may not be irrelevant that the Munda languages have been regarded as a mixture of elements from continental India on the one hand and further India on the other. Chotā Nāgpur is geographically well situated for such an interchange: it remains to discover any equivalent cultural overlap which might explain the Khāsi cists.

The problem, then, of interrelationship (or its absence) between megalithic areas and customs is not an easy one. On the whole, however, in spite of occasional and partial analogies, the differences between the megaliths of the tribal areas and the ancient tombs of the Deccan and peninsular India are far more impressive than their resemblances. As von Fürer-Haimendorf

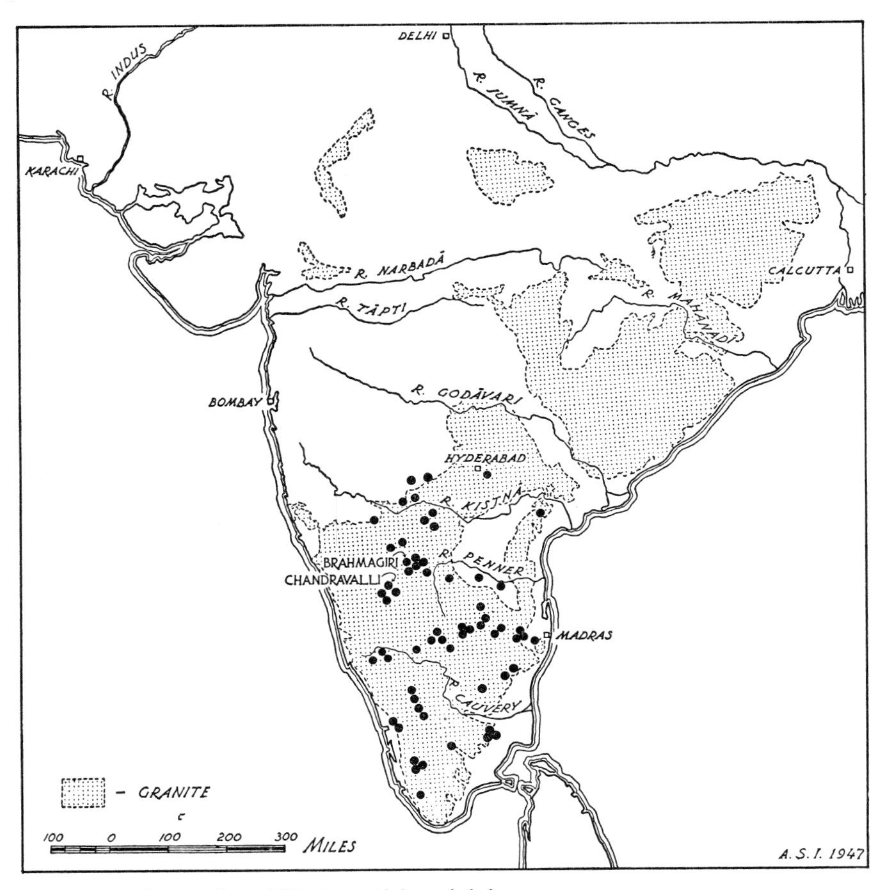

Fig. 32 Distribution of megalithic cists with 'port-holes'

observes, 'I have seen the monuments of the Nāgas and Khāsis, of Gadabas, Bondos and Gonds, and I have seen many of the prehistoric dolmens and cromlechs of Hyderabad, but was never struck by any close resemblance. This alone would, of course, not prove the absence of a genetic connection. More important are the differences in function and meaning of the monuments. The megaliths of the tribal folks of today are, with comparatively few exceptions, memorials unconnected with graves or burning-grounds. Those of prehistoric times are in the majority graves or closely associated with graves.'[84] He adds that the distinctive 'port-hole' opening which will be found to characterize many of the megalithic cists of southern India 'does not occur among any of the tribes of middle India who bury their dead in megalithic graves, such as the Mundas and Hos'. The time-factor is another consideration to which much further attention is needed. The south Indian megaliths seem to have come to an end in the 1st century A.D.; those of middle India and the north-east represent a living tradition of entirely unknown antiquity. If we add to these various diversities and difficulties the almost complete geographical exclusiveness of the two great groups, their essential separateness is at present a fair premise.

The main bulk of the south Indian megaliths lies to the south of latitude 18, which runs a little north of Hyderabad (Deccan); in other words, it begins south of the Godāvarī system, and is characteristic of peninsular India. Much of that region is marked by outcrops of granite or gneiss, of which a large proportion of the megaliths are constructed; fires lit upon the surface of the rock buckle it along lines of cleavage, and iron wedges do the rest—a practice in vogue today as in ancient times. Along the fringes of the granite are derivative deposits of laterite (p. 47), which cuts like cheese when fresh but hardens on exposure. It is in the nature of things that the granite monuments are rough-hewn, if hewn at all, and that the laterite monuments are relatively trim and shapely.

Fig. 32

In 1944 a systematic survey of the south Indian megaliths was begun under the leadership of V. D. Krishnaswami and, although not yet complete, has, with subsequent excavation, produced a reasonably comprehensive catalogue of types.[85] They are as follows.

1. *Dolmenoid cists*, a phrase here limited to cists built of rough granite blocks, now above ground, within a circle of similar blocks which enclose an area from 20 to 140 feet in diameter. The uprights, four or more in number, are (or were) crowned by a massive single or double capstone, which may be either covered by a low cairn, or flush with a low cairn, or emergent from the traces of a denuded cairn. The eastern upright is occasionally pierced with a 'port-hole', and the eastern end may be approached by a short blocked passage. In the Chingleput (Madras) region, where these cists are best known, they are liable to include one or more terracotta legged sarcophagi (sometimes as many as five) with pots and iron objects. A sarcophagus 2½ feet long in the Madras Museum from Sankavaram in Cuddapah district schematically resembles a ram; it contained an iron spearhead, the fragment of an iron knife, and huddled fragments of human bones, and was surrounded by pots of characteristic 'megalith' type. Another sarcophagus, from Pallavaram in Chingleput district, resembles an elephant; but such theriomorphs are exceptional.

Plates 32, 34
Plate 35
Plate 36
Plate 37

It may here be observed that two of the rock-cut caves in Kerala (see below) produced small legged sarcophagi, each about two feet long; and that round-ended cylindrical sarcophagi, without megaliths, have been found at Maski in Raichūr district, Hyderabad. But they are by no means a universal feature of the south Indian megaliths and do not occur, for instance, in the Pudokkoṭṭai cists or at Brahmagiri.

It may be added that in the gneissic uplands of the Kerala region, south-western India, a single stone circle may enclose more than one dolmen; in one instance, as many as nineteen.[86]

2. *Slabbed cists* of granite or laterite, also within a stone circle, are oblong and about six feet in length and height. The eastern upright is normally pierced with a 'port-hole' which may be either circular with a diameter of four to twenty inches, or trapezoidal, or semicircular and cut into the upper edge of the

Plates 34, 38

slab immediately below the capstone; the hole was evidently designed for the insertion of bones and offerings. Excavated examples at Brahmagiri, northern Mysore, showed that there the cists were sunk to half their height below the surface and were surrounded at the old ground-level by dry-stone walling. Their port-holes were closed by an additional external slab and were approached from the outside by a lined passage which had been blocked when the tomb was sealed. In the cists were pots and iron objects with the fragmentary skeletons of a number of individuals. Comparable cists at Suttukeni, near Pondicherry, had a simpler surround and minute, non-functional port-holes; typologically they may be thought to be later than the Brahmagiri series. In Pudukkoṭṭai, south of Madras, laterite cists with port-holes are approached through a slabbed ante-chamber as large as the main cist, and are sometimes called 'transepted cists'. Generally, it may be affirmed that a cist was finally covered up to or even above the capstone by a barrow or cairn, circular on plan and generally outlined by stone blocks or slabs. According to local custom or the nature of the subsoil, the cist may be built on the natural surface, or partially or completely sunk below the natural surface. Thus in the Hyderabad region they are often deeply buried; the Brahmagiri cists were half-buried; whilst in a large megalith cemetery in the jungle near Savandurg, twenty-two miles west-south-west of Bangalore, there are free-standing port-holed 'dolmens' intermingled with identical port-holed cists at all stages of submersion below the natural surface down to capstone level.

3. *Shallow-pit burials*, without a cist, are sometimes found within stone circles, which may then be less than twelve feet in diameter. The pit may contain one or more pots or a terracotta legged sarcophagus. A variant type, best illustrated by an excavated example at Porkalam in Cochin,[87] may be restricted to the very individual megalithic complex below the ghats of

Kerala in south-west India. Here the pit, in the centre of a sixteen-foot circle of roughly dressed laterite blocks, was itself covered by a granite slab. The pit was 4½ feet deep and contained a large urn enclosing many smaller ones, three iron objects, and a few crushed bones. At Kunnattur, in the Chingleput district, a similarly sealed pit within a circle contained a terracotta sarcophagus, Black-and-red pottery, two iron bracelets, and scraps of bone.[88]

4. *Deep-pit burials*, within a stone circle but without a cist, and as much as eight feet in depth, were found at Brahmagiri, where there may have been something like a dozen of them amongst three hundred megalithic cists. On the floor of each of the pits, amongst many pots with iron implements and a few human bones, were four flat slabs, placed as though to support a table or bier. I have suggested that these deep pit-circles may have been macerating pits where the dead were laid out for the process of excarnation which certainly preceded burial in the neighbouring cists; but I do not press the hypothesis. Comparable pit-circles, but without the four floor-slabs, have been found at Maski in the Deccan.[89]

Plate 39

5. *Umbrella-stones* or *hat-stones* (*topi-kal* or *kudai-kal*) are alternative names given to a type of monument which is peculiar to Kerala and in particular to Cochin. It consists of a circular laterite capstone in the form of a low and solid dome resting on four inwardly leaning and tapering stones about four feet high, standing so that their base-lines constitute a square with a diagonal approaching the diameter of the capstone. These monuments have not been explored methodically but are known to cover pit-burials. Their similarity to umbrellas, which are both honorific and, in the monsoon-ridden climate of the Kerala coastland, particularly utile, may not be accidental.

Plate 40

6. *Hood-stones* are dome-shaped laterite blocks, similar to the cap of the umbrella-stones but resting on the surface of the

Plate 41

ground. They too belong to Cochin and may be supposed to cover pit-burials like that under the untrimmed granite slab described under 3 above.

7. *Multiple hood-stones*, also in Cochin, are intermediate between 5 and 6 in that they consist of from five to twelve inwardly-leaning uprights of dressed laterite, some three feet in height. Whether a capstone in fact completed the monument is not known. The structure presumably enclosed a burial-pit.

8. *Menhirs* or standing-stones occur in the Deccan and Kerala but are otherwise not common in south India. At Anapāra, near Trichur in Cochin, a granite monolith twelve feet high is thought locally to mark a battlefield, and another at Kuttūr is dreaded by the local people as the haunt of ghosts; but the name *naḍu-kal* given to menhirs in the Tamil Shaṇgam literature (poetic anthologies) of the early centuries A.D. indicates a commemorative function, which in a general sense recalls that of some of the standing-stones of north-eastern India (p. 150). At Maski, in the Raichur district of the Deccan 'a number of roughly aligned menhirs' occur in close vicinity to burial-circles,[90] but excavation showed no burials actually beside them. On the other hand, at Devikulam in Travancore a burial-urn containing four pots and an iron axe was found beneath a menhir, and similar discoveries are affirmed elsewhere in that region. A single alignment of menhirs ranging up to 12¾ feet high at Komalaparathela in Kerala is the only monument of the kind known to me south of the Hyderabad area; but in that area, particularly in the districts of Raichūr, Gulbarga and Mahbūbnagar, apart from the possible example at Maski, is a large number of serried groups of granite or, rarely, sandstone menhirs from three to twenty-five feet in height and arranged either in parallel lines or as a quincunx.[91] The over-all orientation is roughly to the cardinal points. More than half of these alignments adjoin burial-circles, as at Maski,

Plate 42

and the indications are that they and the circles are contemporary; but their function is unknown and guesswork scarcely profitable. They are not similar in lay-out to the alignments of north-eastern India, and are not obviously derived from there.

Plate 44

To these categories, of which 1 and 2 are the most widespread, should be added an extensive series of *burial-caves*[92] which have been cut into the laterite of Kerala, since their contents, so far as known, are similar to those of the megaliths. The laterite lies on the foot-hills between the alluvial coast and the granite ghats. The caves have been made first by scooping out a square stepped pit in the rock, approached by rock-cut steps; then by cutting one or more doorways in one or more sides of the pit, each doorway about 1½ feet high and just large enough to admit the workman; and finally by opening up beyond the doorways a dome-shaped (rarely flat-roofed) cave or caves, normally circular but sometimes rectangular on plan and sometimes with a central rock-cut pillar of rectangular section rising to the roof. Often there are rock-cut benches along the sides, and occasionally there is a central opening in the dome of the cave.

Much nonsense has been written about these caves, but the suggestion that, as tombs, they may represent the huts, or even the umbrellas, of the living is not necessarily extravagant. What their relationship may be to the cists with circular or rectangular port-hole is less certain. It has more than once been postulated in Europe that megalithic tombs are in some measure simulated caves; and the question may be asked whether the Kerala caves with their small but obviously functional entrances are parental to the port-holed cists of south India. After all, cave-cutting was a widespread Indian accomplishment, whether amongst the Buddhists, the Jainas, or the Hindus. Nevertheless, it would seem more likely that the reverse relationship was the case. The Buddhists, Jainas and

Hindus imitated free-standing structures in cutting their cave-temples and monasteries, and it would appear more likely than not that the Kērala caves, with their limited distribution, followed a parallel course, and were in fact quarried adaptations of the free-standing cists in the viable laterite of the Kerala lowlands.

So much for the structural types of megalithic or allied monuments in south India. A passing mention may here be made of the few megaliths recorded, more or less inadequately, from the north and north-west.

In the neighbourhood of Karāchi more than one observer a century or so ago recorded the existence of large stone cists similar to those of south India save for the absence of the port-hole.[93] In particular, they were noted on the hills near Waghodur, twenty miles east of Karāchi, and on the road to Shāh Billāwal in Baluchistan. Following these hints, I have indeed found the remains of a rough sandstone cist 5½ feet long, with the major axes east-south-east, in the sand 3½ miles north-east of the village of Murad Memon, about twenty miles east-north-east of Karāchi; it is said to have been demolished since 1950. The name 'Kaffir's grave' applied to it by the villagers safely indicates a pre-medieval antiquity. Other 'Kaffir's graves' of smaller size, 3–3½ feet in length, can also be seen in the sand about half a mile north-west of the nineteenth milestone on the Karāchi-Kotri highroad. One of them appears to be surrounded by a stone circle twenty-seven feet in diameter.[94] By virtue of their position on the map, these cists would repay investigation.

The apparent (though not proved) absence of the distinctive port-hole from the Karāchi series seems to extend to the few other cists which have been recorded, though not recently seen, in the north. These include cists, with cairns and stone circles, noted long ago 'in the hilly districts of Delhi, Mirzapur, and Orissa'; and another 'six feet square and about four feet in height' at Deosa, a village thirty-two miles east of Jaipur in Rājasthān; and yet others eighteen miles south-east of Almora in U.P., and in the remoter depths of the Himālayan massif in the Leh valley of Ladakh, near the western border of Tibet. The fact remains, however, that, whatever future research may reveal in the north, it cannot upset the huge preponderance of megalithic cists in the south, particularly of the significant port-holed type.

Two other megalithic monuments in the north may be noted: an irregular group of standing-stones in the vicinity of Srinagar, Kashmir,[95] and a circle of standing-stones about ten feet high near the village of Asota, seventeen miles east-north-east of Mardan in the former North-west Frontier Province.[96]

We return to south India. There it has been shown that megaliths, particularly port-holed cists, are widespread, but that other types are locally present and there are clear local variations. For example, in northern Mysore the cists are carefully walled and have sizeable and functional port-holes, whereas in the Pondicherry region they are roughly enclosed and their port-holes are small and presumably vestigial.[97] Along the ghats and the isolated coastal strip of Kerala there are, as we have seen, several individual types, though their contents seem to indicate approximate contemporaneity both with one another and with the south Indian megaliths generally. And not only that; the megalithic problem cannot be considered as a whole without some reference to the non-megalithic urn-burials or urn-fields which have been recorded chiefly from the eastern plains south of the Kistna river; notable sites being Ādichchanallūr in the Tirunelveli (Tinnevelly) district of the extreme south, the environs of Pondicherry, the Madras region,[98] Amaravatī near the mouth of the Krishna, and Maski in Raichūr district on the Deccan plateau. In all this heterogeneous assemblage of funerary customs there are significant common factors which must now be defined. They are three in number.

First, where adequately recorded, the burials are those of bones collected after excarnation or flesh-removal elsewhere. I know of no clear instance of the burial of an articulated skeleton in an Indian megalith or urn-field.[99] Furthermore, although the bones of several individuals (up to six or more, as represented by skulls) might be included, they were normally bundled together as a single parcel; very rarely is there a suggestion that the same tomb may have been used more than once.

Secondly, the tools and weapons normally included in all these categories of burial are of iron, ranging from axes, knives, bill-hooks, hoes, wedges and horses' bits to all-metal spears more than six feet in length. Bronze is used for bangles, rings and other non-utile objects, and also for bowls; gold beads occur occasionally; but a liberal and developed iron industry is the outstanding feature.

Plate 43

Thirdly, there is the pottery. The distinctive ware of the megaliths, and only less so of the urn-fields, is the Black-and-red to which passing references have already been made. This is typically the product of inverted firing, so that the top and inside of the pot, in direct contact with the fire, turn black whilst the lower part (upper in the firing) is a terracotta red or, rarely, as at Bahal and Tekwāḍā (p. 145), grey. Sometimes the whole pot is black. The ware is slipped and polished, usually fairly thin, and is wheel-turned. It is said in some instances to have been salt-glazed, with a resultant shining and crackled surface. Resemblance of the blackened pots or sherds to the Northern Black Polished Ware is only superficial; the 'megalithic' ware has been fired at a lower temperature and altogether lacks the metallic hardness and lustre of the N.B.P. fabric. Shapes are for the most part simple and utilitarian: bowls and dishes, globular vessels, and occasionally tall lids. Most of the vessels are round-bottomed, and cylindrical or

Plate 46

concave-sided pot-stands are not uncommon. A jar with three or four feet is characteristic of certain areas, notably northern Mysore and Kerala. Decoration, when present, is rudimentary and consists of horizontal grooves, incised herring-bone or leaf impressions, or, rarely and usually early, simple painted linear patterns, usually in white; but graffiti, scratched after firing and of unknown meaning, are common. Within a general similarity of type and fabric, local preferences or phases are discernible.

Before these various factors are further considered, something must be said of the date of the megalithic series. This can now be stated in general terms, but within them no detailed chronology is yet available. The lower limit at least is fairly clear. At Brahmagiri, where a town-site alongside the megaliths was explored with this problem in view, it was found that the megalithic culture overlapped a different and more elaborate successor which was dated by the occurrence of Rouletted Ware (p. 31) to the 1st century A.D. This evidence was confirmed forty-five miles away at Chandravalli where the successor-culture was marked, not only by Rouletted Ware, but also by imported silver coins of the Roman Principate, dating from the first three or four decades of the 1st century A.D. Again, 300 miles to the south-east, at Arikameḍu near Pondicherry, a brick-built commercial town which yielded imported Arretine and other wares of the first half of the 1st century A.D. succeeded, apparently without a time-gap, a village characterized by the 'megalithic' Black-and-red Ware.[100] As long ago as 1817 a Roman silver coin of Augustus (23 B.C.–A.D. 14) is recorded to have been found in a megalithic cist in the Coimbatore district; it may of course have been intrusive. A port-holed cist at Tiruvilvamala in Cochin contained russet-coated pottery with white or yellow curvilinear patterns, allied to a similar ware with rectilinear patterns dated to the 1st century A.D. at Brahmagiri and Chandravalli.[101] The evidence as a whole, though not abundant, is consistent, and some of it is well-documented. The megalithic complex ended in the first half of the 1st century A.D.

The earlier time-bracket is less firmly defined. On the town-site at Brahmagiri the 'megalithic' strata were three to four feet in vertical depth. What this accumulation represents in time is very conjectural, but two to three centuries might not appear unreasonable. I have in fact suggested 200 B.C. as a schematic date for the beginning of the 'megalithic' occupation there. The guess may err on the short side, but a date not earlier than the 3rd century B.C. would be consistent with the recorded finding of a bronze coin of Eran, ascribed to the 3rd or 2nd century B.C., in a port-holed cist at Sulur, again in the Coimbatore district.

In review, there is at present no evidence for ascribing any south Indian megalith to a date earlier than the 3rd century B.C., and the 3rd century B.C.–1st century A.D. is here accepted as a provisional time-bracket.

It may be added that only at Brahmagiri, at Sanganakallu (p. 85), at Kunnattur in Chingleput,[88] and at Maski has a 'megalithic' settlement been excavated, and very few such settlements have been identified. Only at Brahmagiri was the evidence definitive in a chronological sense. The town lay along the lower slopes of the hill in the vicinity of a tank, and the cists, of which there must have been many hundreds (about 300 survive) are spread about the adjacent plain, amidst what are, and doubtless were, the fields of the inhabitants. In the Madras (Chingleput) region, the relative position of the living and the dead is apparently reversed; there, the megaliths are commonly on the slopes of the hills or amidst rocky outcrops, with the implication that the living dwelt amongst their fields on the adjacent plain. Here, too, ancient tanks are found in the neighbourhood, and it is a fair assumption that the megalith-builders practised tank-irrigation.

It remains to ask, Where did they or their culture come from? Their iron-industry at least is no insoluble problem. Its impressive quantity and quality owe much to the accident of preservation in protective tombs. The scrappy remains of iron-work from the 'megalithic' levels of the Brahmagiri town would never, unsupported, have suggested the extent of the industry. *Per contra*, had megalithic tombs been built beside the Gangetic cities of the Iron Age, there can be no doubt that their display would have been correspondingly striking. There is in fact no more difficulty in deriving the early ironwork of south India in the 4th and 3rd centuries B.C. from Gangetic sources in the 5th and 4th centuries—and ultimately from Persian sources at the end of the 6th century (p. 24)—than in deriving the ironwork and N.B.P. Ware of the towns of the upper Deccan from the same northern region. The distinctive ceramic fashion of the *doāb*, as is not unnatural, was gradually left behind in the Deccan, but the use of the splendid and abundant new metal quickly penetrated southwards into the Peninsula. At the risk of complicating the matter with a gratuitous historical intrusion, I here add the suggestion that the southward extension of the Mauryan Empire into the Peninsula at the beginning of the 3rd century B.C., probably in the time of Ashoka's father, Bindusāra,[102] provides an apposite context. The sharp and sudden difference at Brahmagiri between the magnificently equipped megalith-builders and their relatively primitive stone-using predecessors is exactly consonant with a tremendous historical event of the kind.[103] On this view, the three copies of Ashoka's Minor Rock-edict at Brahmagiri were appropriately addressed to the southernmost colonists of his father's empire, and not, as I had previously conjectured, to their bucolic precursors.

Plates 39, 43

All this may be claimed to make good sense, but what of the 'megalithic' Black-and-red Ware? How does that fit into the picture? Not too badly. In recent years the Black-and-red

Ware has been creeping steadily northwards on the map, and there is more than a suspicion that some of the northerly examples are also amongst the earliest; in other words, that the pottery, like the iron, may have been derived by the south from the north. Indeed a few scraps of the Black-and-red have occurred with Indus or sub-Indus valley wares at Lothal and elsewhere in Kāthiāwāḍ.[104] The peripheral Indus site of Lothal may well be late in its series but must be placed somewhere in the 2nd millennium B.C. Are its Black-and-red sherds truly significant in this context? The basic technique of Black-and-red Ware is widespread in space and time: for example, it occurs in ancient Egypt and modern Africa. Is the Black-and-red pottery of India necessarily a unitary problem? The door must be kept open to doubt; the more so since at Rangpur, only a short distance from Lothal, more substantial vestiges of Black-and-red Ware were separated from the sub-Indus culture of the site by a distinctive intervening phase (p. 138). But evidence of continuity in the Black-and-red wares of India is in fact accumulating within the general limits of the 1st millennium B.C., and the problem should solve itself beyond doubt in the near future.

The most northerly occurrences of the fabric are in the fertile south-eastern parts of Rājasthān, on the eastern flank of the Arāvalli Range. There, in the districts of Udaipur, Chitorgarh and Mandasor, bowls with everted rims, black internally and largely red externally, and occasionally painted with simple rectilinear or circular patterns in white, are found sometimes with and sometimes without microliths, rarely with a scrap of copper. At Āhāṛ, close to Udaipur railway-station, an ancient site of some recorded importance showed over thirty feet of occupational deposit in which two main cultures, separated by a break, have been recognized. The later is of the historical period, but the earlier, nearly twenty feet thick, showed three sub-phases, all characterized by Black-and-red sherds. From the lowest sub-phase the ware is described as rather coarse, and polished only on the exterior; in the middle sub-phase the fabric is finer and the pots are polished both inside and outside; in the final sub-phase, decay has set in and new wares begin to dominate the field. In the upper levels of this culture were pottery-ringed soakpits of the kind which began to characterize the cities of northern and central India in the latter half of the 1st millennium B.C. Only two microliths were noted.[105]

The initial date of this Rājasthān series is undetermined, and the pottery bears only a generic resemblance to that of the megaliths. It continues, however, towards the south-east, to the Mālwā Plateau and the Narbadā valley, where both its date and its affinity with the megalithic ware become less dubious. At Nāgdā on the Chambal, north-west of Ujjain, the Black-and-red belongs to the Iron Age and is presumably therefore after 500 B.C. At Ujjain itself the evidence is similar; the Black-and-red Ware is associated with iron but precedes the arrival of N.B.P. Ware which, on this tolerably remote site, may have arrived relatively late. At Maheshwar on the Narbadā, the Black-and-red Ware is found mainly with N.B.P. Ware, but a little appears in the preceding Chalcolithic culture (p. 140). Farther south, at Bahal the sequence is identical; the first sherds of Black-and-red are in the top of the Chalcolithic, and the ware continues alongside N.B.P. pottery and iron. At Nāsik on the upper Godāvarī on the other hand, the Black-and-red is uncompromisingly equated with the N.B.P. Ware.

The trend of the evidence is clear: in the Rājasthān-Mālwā region and along the great central rivers, Black-and-red pottery is liable to occur about or just before the middle of the 1st millennium B.C., and may anticipate the arrival of iron and N.B.P. Ware. The probability of an earlier date in Kāthiāwāḍ depends upon a further examination of Lothal or some equivalent late-Harappān site. The ware does not occur in the Jumna-Ganges *doāb*; it would appear rather to be at home between the

Arāvalli and the Vindhya Ranges and to have survived there and farther south as a folk-craft after the foreign and technically better N.B.P. Ware had arrived upon the scene. With local modifications in form, decoration and skill, it subsequently penetrated southwards with an improving technique, and was ultimately perfected by the megalith-builders and urn-field-users of peninsular India. The time-table, as at present known, fits this suggested diffusion of the Black-and-red Ware as it fits that of the 'megalithic' iron-industry. The two cultural streams, one from the northern plains, the other from the Mālwā Plateau, unite in the Deccan.

To sum up so far; it is here postulated that about 300 B.C. certain cultural elements, with iron as their major component, were infiltrating southwards into a variety of Chalcolithic communities, when their progress was suddenly stimulated and given a new political coherence by the southerly extension of the Mauryan empire from its homeland in the northern plains. Between the invading complex and the crude Chalcolithic cultures upon which it impinged there was no organic transition, save where the advancing iron outpaced its own N.B.P. Ware and absorbed the makers of the Black-and-red Ware farther south. For the most part, the invader passed over the invaded like the tide over the sand. It was a case of cultural conquest, nothing less.

If this historical reading of the archaeological evidence be provisionally accepted—and it fits the factors of time and space as they are known at present—there remains one unexplained factor, and that a formidable one. Whence came the urge and the art of building the megalithic structures themselves? To that question there is no present answer. The general, indeed the specific, resemblance between the south Indian port-holed cists and others in the Caucasus, Transcaucasia, the Jordan valley, North Africa, the Spanish Peninsula, France, Central Germany, and the British Isles has long been recognized.

Most of these analogues are over a thousand years earlier than the Indian series, but the structural likeness is often astonishingly close. Is there a causative link through all this diffuse geography? Or did the south Indians evolve their tombs from their own inner consciousness, without foreign aid? Certainly some of the Kerala types are unique and therefore local. But in regard to the cists we do not know. One thing, at least is certain: in the 3rd century B.C. there was no monsoon-borne sea-traffic, no short cut, direct to peninsular India; that was a discovery of the 1st century B.C.[106] Any link with the West must have been closely coastwise or overland, and has presumably left intermediate traces. If the little-known cists of the Karāchi region turn out, on excavation, to be of the series, a solution is perhaps on the way. That, however, remains to be seen.

It would, of course, produce a tidy geographical solution of the problem if we could with any confidence derive the southern megaliths, or at any rate the idea embodied in them, from the megaliths of Orissa, Chotā Nāgpur and north-eastern India. With C. von Fürer-Haimendorf, however, I see no ready help in that direction.[84] In spite of rare and incomplete resemblances, I prefer to return to the initial premise of this chapter and to accept the differences manifest in the north-eastern series as too numerous and extensive to justify affiliation. The structural problem—and that alone—of the south Indian megalith culture seems to me at the present time insoluble save by extravagant guesswork.

In this outline of the megalithic problem I have said nothing about its linguistic aspects. I am not a linguist, nor, in any case, is the evidence adequate to support anything more than speculation. Von Fürer-Haimendorf has boldly recognized the megalith-builders as primary speakers of Dravidian languages;[107] and it is certain that, within measurable range of the earliest Dravidian records, there is no rival and commensurate cultural phenomenon. It may indeed be averred categorically that the megalith-builders were also Dravidian speakers. But this affirmation does not carry us far in a search for the 'origins' of the Dravidian tongue, unless in one respect. The map of the Dravidian languages, with their north-western outlier (Brahui), bears an alluring likeness to that of the megalithic cists with their little-known but sufficiently definite north-western groups. Did both in fact come in from the north-west? There is at present no new answer to this question.

CHAPTER IX

Ashoka

THIS BOOK IS NOT A HISTORY, but in its last chapter the impersonal *disjecta* of prehistory may fittingly be assembled for a moment in the likeness of a man. Ashoka came to the throne about 268 B.C. and died about 232. Spiritually and materially his reign marks the first coherent expression of the Indian mind, and, for centuries after the political fabric of his empire had crumbled, his work was implicit in the thought and art of the subcontinent. It is not dead today.

It is just possible that Ashoka had Seleukid blood in his veins; at least his reputed vice-royalty of Taxila in the Punjab during the reign of his father would have introduced him to the living memory of Alexander the Great, and, as king, he himself tells us of his proselytizing relations with the Western powers. But, though on one notable occasion he used Greek and Aramaic as his vehicle, it is as an Indian that he speaks to us through the graven rocks and pillars that bore his message to his people, from Afghanistan and the North-west Frontier to Mysore: his message of Moderation and Gentleness and Tolerance and Piety; his exhortation to forgo silliness and superstition and to regard the sacredness of life. And then, 'Let small and great exert themselves', he proclaims sharply from the granite slopes of that Brahmagiri which, with its ancient town-site and its megaliths, has recurred more than once in this survey. The alternation of a meekness which sometimes partakes of sentimentality with a recurrent and redeeming toughness is a dual character that has reappeared down to modern times amongst the greater Indian leaders.

Here we are not concerned with the details, true or suppositious, of Ashoka's life and administration. The writings of Vincent Smith and F. W. Thomas are accessible[108] and, in spite of needed modifications and additions,[109] wear well with time. It will suffice to recall that Ashoka's grandfather, Chandragupta, who in 326 B.C. had met Alexander the Great in the Punjab, usurped the throne of Magadha beside the Ganges in Bihār within the next two or three years, and so established the Maurya dynasty at the head of the most powerful and wealthy kingdom in northern India. About the same time he attacked and destroyed the garrisons left by Alexander in the Indus basin; and the attempt by Seleukos, one of the four heirs to Alexander's empire, to recover the lost ground in the latter years of the century ended in victory for Chandragupta and a patched-up peace. The peace-terms may possibly have included a marriage between the victor and a daughter of Seleukos.

The Mauryan kingdom, from its Gangetic homeland, now reached out to the Hindu Kush in the west and to Bengal in the east. Its southerly limit at the death of Chandragupta in 398 B.C. is less certain; but his successor Bindusāra, surnamed Amitraghāta or 'slayer of enemies', extended it into the Peninsula, and when Ashoka came to the throne the southern end of his empire lay across northern Mysore. Nor was this vast amalgam a merely nominal holding. It was integrated by a highly organized civil service, and the king himself was tireless in its supervision, touring the land and, in his own words, 'beholding the country and the people'. In archaeological thinking, the scene was set for a wide pervasion of dominant cultural ideas and standards over an almost infinite diversity of local traditions.

And that, as I see it, is what we find. I have already suggested (p. 24) the likelihood that at the end of the 6th century B.C., when Achaemenid Persia acquired its Indian province, Persia supplied India, not merely with administrators, but also with new materials and ideas: above all, with the use of iron, which now appears in India for the first time, and the idea of a currency, which was minted at Taxila in native guise but on

Persian standards, and emerged in the Ganges basin in or shortly after the 5th century B.C. Persia moreover lent India the Aramaic alphabet which, with Aramaic speech, had been the official medium of communication throughout the Achaemenid empire. In India this script was modified to suit the local Prākṛit language and, as Kharoshṭhī, was used by Ashoka for his inscriptions in the north-west. Even as far south as Brahmagiri, the Ashokan scribe has added a word in this alien Kharoshṭhī, though elsewhere in metropolitan India the Brāhmī script was unchallenged.

But the Persian contribution to India did not end with iron and currency and Kharoshṭhī. These were the symbols of that new security which advancing imperial rule imposed along the highways, and of a new burgeoning of inter-regional trade. Local capitals which were also caravan-cities sprang up beside the main routes: probably Begram north of Kabul; certainly, as recent work has shown, Chārsada (Pushkalāvati or 'Lotus City') on the Peshāwar plain; and far-famed Taxila in the Punjab. These derelict and dusty sites are memorials to the *pax Persica* of the latter half of the 6th century B.C. And two centuries later, when Alexander the Great brought his travel-stained troops to the Indus, he came as the successor to the Great King of Persia, whose empire he had grasped. He came to claim the Achaemenid province of India; albeit that his curiosity ever marched ahead of him, and his horizon was a mirage. But in the long view what mattered to India was less the arrival of Alexander than the destruction of the Persian power. Under the Achaemenid emperors, the arts and crafts—particularly but not only those of architecture—had achieved resplendent distinction. With the burning of Persepolis in 330 B.C., two centuries of royal patronage came to an abrupt end. The accumulated artistry of Persia was out of work.

Plates, 54, 55

The successor-empire, to which Alexander and his heir Seleukos pointed the way, was that of Chandragupta and his

Mauryas. Here was the greatest empire that India had ever produced, greater even than that of the Indus valley two thousand years previously. Here was the patronage of a dynasty with, as yet, no confirmed artistic tradition of its own in any way comparable with its wealth and its ambition. Here was a new home for the accomplished artists and craftsmen of Persia. And hither they came.

It is not an exaggeration to say that this Indo-Persian phase marks the beginning of masonry architecture in India. There had of course been stone and brick buildings far back in the 3rd millennium, but little to which, so far as we know, the proud term 'architecture' can fairly be applied. Subsequently to the 3rd millennium, the earliest stone structures in India to which an approximate date can be attached are the remnants of the great defences of Old Rājgir in Bihār. These defences, twenty-five miles in length, enclose the site of the city which was associated in the 6th century B.C. with the Buddha and Mahāvīra during the first formative period of the Buddhist and Jaina faiths.* The work consists of a massive wall, dry-built of large unshapen stones, with square bastions at frequent intervals. These rugged structures, too, can scarcely claim the name of architecture. Nor can those of the early Taxila in the Punjab, visited though it was by Alexander in 326 B.C. There, on what is now the Bhīr Mound, the local king received his Greek visitor and showed him the sights. They were humble enough; the excavator of Taxila, Sir John Marshall, himself admits that at this time the town had 'no architecture worthy of the name'.[110] With rare exceptions, its buildings were a rambling conglomeration of ill-aligned and ill-built walls of

Plate 47

Plate 50

* Limited excavation within this huge site has shown, at one point, N.B.P. Ware at the lowest level, and at another point a preceding layer containing 'a medium to coarse red ware mixed with a few fine black sherds'. There is at present no indication of any very long occupation prior to 500 B.C. See *I.A.* 1953–54, 9, and 1954–55, 16.

plastered rubble, resembling rather the slum of a poverty-stricken suburb than the central lay-out of a capital city. Almost the only architectural 'feature', if such it may be called, is the occasional use of untidy stone pedestals designed to carry wooden roof-posts. The general culture of the city was of the same inferior order: only at the end of the 4th century, at or shortly after the arrival of Alexander, do considerable hoards of sophisticated jewellery, including three superb gems of Achaemenian workmanship,[111] enliven the monotony of the scene. It is likely enough that these hoards were either Persian loot brought to Taxila by Alexander's following, or were otherwise a sequel to the devastation of the Persian empire and the dispersal of Achaemenian craftsmanship.

Plate 51

Indeed, in 'Aryan' India the term 'architecture' can first be applied unreservedly to the famous sandstone columns, once more than thirty in number, which Ashoka set up as memorials after his conversion to Buddhism, and on some of which he subsequently carved his pious injunctions to his subjects. It has long been recognized that these columns, without precedent in Indian architectural forms, represent *in partibus* the craftsmanship of Persia. Actually, the name 'Persepolitan' which is commonly given to them by writers on Indian architecture is not altogether happy, since the innumerable columns of Persepolis are invariably fluted, whereas those of Ashoka are unfluted,[112] as indeed was the normal Persian custom. But if for 'Persepolitan' we substitute 'Persian' or, better still, 'Achaemenid', there can be no dispute. The Chunār sandstone from which Ashoka's columns are wrought is superbly carved and is finished with a lustrous polish of a kind which in India is characteristic of no other age. This is a Persian accomplishment; the masonry of the palaces of Darius and Xerxes 'goes to the extreme of highly polished stones, looking, when well preserved, like mirrors of black marble'.[113] Equally Persian are the famous lions which crowned the Ashokan column at

Sārnāth, near Banaras, and have been assumed as the Republican badge of India. The setting-up of memorial or religious pillars (of wood) was indeed an Indian, not a Persian, habit,[114] but the Ashokan form and craftsmanship are a completely alien rendering of this tradition. And, once established in India by the great Buddhist emperor, the Achaemenid column, with its bell-shaped lotus capital and with or without its animal impost, entered into the fabric of Indian architecture and was reproduced, in modified forms, by architects or rock-carvers, Buddhist and other, for several centuries after Ashoka.

Plate 56

The mention of rock-carvers recalls another debt of Ashoka's to Persian prototypes. From the 7th century B.C., if not earlier, tombs in the likeness of pillared halls had been cut into the cliffs of Media and Persia. In India, the first of a long and distinguished series of rock-cut 'structures' were carved in the time of Ashoka out of the hard gneiss of the Barābar hills, nineteen miles north of Gayā in southern Bihār.[115] It is significant that they reproduce wooden buildings: a round hut with a thatched roof, an oblong hall or shrine with a vaulted 'wooden' roof, a monumental doorway imitating bamboo and timber. In other words, the more grandiose Persian idea is adapted to the Indian idiom. At the same time the Persian tradition of polished stonework is faithfully and laboriously followed; the hard granite surface of the interiors of these humble cells has been burnished until it resembles glass or metal. And incidentally the Barābar caves were dedicated by Ashoka to the use of the Ājīvika ascetics, who were rivals to Buddhists and Jainas alike, though with a bias to the latter. The dedication is a tribute to the reality of the tolerance which the Buddhist emperor preached.

Plate 57

Lastly, there can be no doubt that, in carving his precepts upon rocks, Ashoka was once more adapting a Persian precedent. The Bisutūn or Behistūn rock-inscription of Darius I dates from *c.* 518 B.C.; there is in India no precursor to the rock-edicts cut at the bidding of Ashoka in and after 257 B.C. True that, save for an occasional formula, nothing could be more unlike the commemorative and administrative records of the proud Persian despots than the gentle exhortations of the Buddhist emperor. But yet again, as so often, we are confronted with the transmutation of a manifestly inherited idea.

In one way and another, then, the Mauryan was heir to the Great King. There is, however, an archaeological time-gap in the process of transmission. Persepolis was burned in 330 B.C., and the earliest relevant works of Ashoka shortly antedate the middle of the 3rd century. What in the interim had happened to the homeless Persian craftsmen? I am inclined to think that Megasthenes and Pāṭaliputra, between them, come to the rescue.

Megasthenes was sent by Seleukos as ambassador to the court of Chandragupta at Pāṭaliputra, adjoining Patna on the Ganges, about 302 B.C. He compiled a valuable account of the Mauryan court and administration, and extracts from it are preserved by later classical writers. The Indian towns, he says, 'which are down beside the rivers or the sea are made of wood; for towns built of brick would never hold out' against rain and flood. 'But the towns which are built on elevated places out of reach, these are made of brick and clay.' Pāṭaliputra he describes as situated at the junction of the Son and Ganges, and as being more than 9 miles long and 1¾ miles wide; in other words, it was stretched out along the bank of the Ganges in a fashion similar to that of the modern Patna. The city was surrounded by a wooden palisade with loopholes for archers, and outside the palisade was a wide and deep ditch, which served both as a defence and as a drain. Along the palisade were 570 towers and 64 gates. In the royal palace, as we are told by Aelian, following Megasthenes, there was much that was 'calculated to excite admiration, and with which neither Susa, with all its costly splendour, nor Ecbatana, with all its magnificence, can vie. In the parks tame peacocks are kept, and pheasants which have been domesticated; and cultivated plants . . . and shady groves and pastures planted with trees, and tree-branches which the art of the woodman has deftly interwoven. . . . There are also tanks of great beauty in which they keep fish of enormous size but quite tame.' The whole description is significantly reminiscent of a Persian paradise.

Of the splendour that was Pāṭaliputra little is known today in material form, but that little is precisely what we have been led to expect.[116] As long ago as 1896 a summary excavation brought to light a column-capital of a familiar Achaemenid pattern. It has the stepped impost, side-volutes and central palmettes of its Persian prototypes, and its design if not its execution is attributable to an early phase of the transplanted Achaemenid craftsmanship. Two stone legs of a throne of Persian type were also found. Subsequently, in 1912, a more ambitious but still very incomplete excavation seems to have uncovered some part of a large pillared hall, represented by an unframed cluster of some eighty monolithic columns showing the Persian polish. In front of them is a row of massive timber rafts, presumably designed to carry a platform or monumental staircase over the unstable subsoil. Inadequate though the evidence be, it is tolerably clear that we have here a Persian *diwan* or *apadana* or audience-hall, and that we are confronted once more with a deliberate 'Persianization' that bespeaks the presence of imported ideas and imported master-masons.

Plate 49

The general credibility of Megasthenes is supported by a further discovery: that of a part of the wooden fortification which he describes. In 1926–7 digging disclosed a double line of upright timbers, 15 feet high, $14\frac{1}{2}$ feet between the parallel lines, and bonded together by a 'floor' and a 'roof' of cross-timbers. The strange structure was interrupted by a transverse timber drain, but appeared to the excavator to 'extend almost

Plate 48

indefinitely'. Whether it was a passage within an earthen rampart or whether, as is more likely, it was filled with earth and formed its core or revetment, was not ascertained but could be determined, no doubt, by trained observation. Unless the timber breakwaters of Ujjain be included (above, p. 144), this type of fortification is at present without analogy in India, though it fits in happily with the remarks of Megasthenes about the use of timber on riverine sites.

The excavation of these various constructions was clumsy and produced no associated evidence as to date. A little recent digging[117] on this difficult and often water-logged site has recognized five periods, ranging from that of the N.B.P. Ware (*c.* 5th century B.C. or later) to the Islamic 17th century. The earliest stratum lay on the natural surface and, with the N.B.P. sherds, yielded 'a good number' of polished sandstone pieces, including one large slab showing the typical Mauryan or Persian polish and bearing a palmette and bead-and-reel pattern of appropriate type. Somewhere under the vast site lies doubtless an earlier nucleus, if we may believe that the foundation of Pāṭaliputra as a Magadha border-fortress occurred in the time of the Buddha, about 494 B.C.[118] No site in India would better repay sustained and large-scale excavation.

As is wholly natural, therefore, it is at the Mauryan capital, Pāṭaliputra, that we may expect to discover the two missing generations of Achaemenid craftsmen. By the time of Ashoka their transference from the dead Persian empire to the living and expanding Indian empire had become something more than an accident of history. The displaced masters had already begun to train Indian pupils in their Achaemenid skills, and a certain non-Persian element in some of the Ashokan carvings—a trend towards softness and reduced precision, as in the bull from Ashoka's column at Rāmpūrwā in Bihār, and even in the lively animals round the pedestal of that most Persian

Plate 56

creation of Ashoka's bestiary, the lions of Sārnāth—anticipates the Indianization which was to become more apparent in the succeeding Shuṅga period. Indeed, the whole episode of which this forms a part, taking place as it did on the historic stage, is an instructive finale to Indian prehistory. We are present at the passage of ideas, forms and techniques from one great region of Asia to another, from one religious and ethical and physical environment to another, not as blue-prints but as intelligent stimuli. Stated otherwise, the process is not altogether unlike that of biological evolution: history suddenly presented India with a whole complex of notions and variations from which she selected those best adapted for survival and development in her particular intellectual climate. The Mauryan empire of India was the sequel to the Achaemenid empire of Persia, not its reflection.

And in greater or lesser degree this is the recurrent implication of Indian prehistory. It may be that the industries of the Old Stone Age of the subcontinent should be approached on these lines, with Africa directly or indirectly as a major though not exclusive source. More certainly, the derivation of the Indus Civilization from Mesopotamia may be understood in this fashion; and the Gangetic Bronze or Copper Age, in which the individuality of the northern plains first asserted itself, demonstrates the extent to which borrowed ideas and materials could be transmuted by the genius of a borrower supported by a prolific environment and drawn by imaginative ambition. So too in the succeeding Iron Age we observe this recipient India of the plains adopting the new metal with an avidity that amounted, nevertheless, to a technical rather than a social revolution; and then spreading it southwards to the more isolated and archaic populations of the central plateau, and southwards again—if I am right, as a parcel of Mauryan encroachment—into the Peninsula. And behind this interplay of material and geographical opportunity lies the Mind of India which, for all the recklessness inherent in so immense a generalization, may be said to show a surprising uniformity of response amidst an infinite diversity of background. For on the one hand Indian prehistory—it is not my function to extend this assertion into history—displays, like the Indian landscape, wide expanses of uniformity: a monotonous and interminable Palaeolithic, a diffuse Microlithic, centuries of Indus Civilization, centuries of Ganges Civilization, leagues of Megaliths. But on the other hand, again like the Indian landscape, this monotony is broken by sudden changes and heights; ever and anon India leaps from its sleep and grasps new ideas, new opportunity, with quick and prehensile intelligence. Let me say again that a prehistorian is writing.

Notes

CHAPTER I

[1] See T. H. Holditch, *The Gates of India* (London, 1910); Aurel Stein, 'The Indo-Iranian Borderlands', Huxley Memorial Lecture, 1934, *Journ. of the Roy. Anthropological Inst. of Gt. Britain and Ireland*, LXIV (1934); and generally, J. F. Richards, 'Geographic Factors in Indian Archaeology', *Indian Antiquary*, LXII (1933), 235–243—the best sketch of the historical geography of India yet published. Also, O. H. K. Spate, *India and Pakistan: a General Regional Geography* (London, 1954).

[2] Wheeler, 'Roman Contact with India, Pakistan and Afghanistan', in *Aspects of Archaeology, Essays presented to O. G. S. Crawford*, ed. by W. F. Grimes (London, 1951).

CHAPTER II

[3] For these and some other geochronological methods see F. E. Zeuner, *Dating the Past* (4th ed., London, 1958), and L. S. Palmer, *Man's Journey through Time* (London, 1957).

[4] See pp. 106, 142, and Walter A. Fairservis, *Excavations in the Quetta Valley, West Pakistan* (American Mus. of Nat. Hist., 1956), p. 356. Recently the University of Pennsylvania has been very co-operative in this matter, and C14 dates are slowly accumulating.

[5] W. F. Libby, *Radiocarbon Dating* (Univ. of Chicago, 1952), and a large literature.

[6] *A.I.* no. 1 (1946), 58–9; nos. 10–11 (1955), 32–3, and 138–41.

[7] *A.I.* no. 1 (1946), 55–8; nos. 10–11 (1955), 50–2, and 143–6. N.B.P. ware has been mistaken for Greek black gloss, but, as Miss M. Bimson of the British Museum laboratory points out, there are several differences. Thus, a razor blade will run smoothly across the Greek black, whereas it will cut into the Indian black. If very small fragments are held near a magnet, Greek black is attracted to the magnet, whereas Indian black is relatively non-magnetic. Greek black, when refired, is consistently stable at temperatures of *c.* 1000° C., whereas Indian black shows considerable variation in its resistance to such temperatures.

[8] *A.I.* no. 2 (1946), 45–9; no. 4 (1948), 308–10; and Wheeler, *Rome Beyond the Imperial Frontiers* (London, 1954), pp. 149–51.

[9] *I.A.* 1954–55, 19–20.

[10] Unpublished: in the National Museum, Karachi.

CHAPTER III

[11] For general surveys, see V. D. Krishnaswami, 'Stone Age India', *A.I.* no. 3 (1947), 11 ff.; and 'Progress in Prehistory', *Ib.*, no. 9 (1953), 53 ff.

[12] H. de Terra and T. T. Paterson, *Studies on the Ice Age in India and Associated Human Cultures* (Carnegie Inst. of Washington, 1939); Jacquetta Hawkes, Christopher Hawkes and H. de Terra, 'Yale North India Expedition: Palaeolithic Human Industries in the Northwest Punjab and Kashmir and their Geological Significance', *Memoirs of the Connecticut Academy of Arts and Sciences* (New Haven, 1934). See also F. E. Zeuner in *Dating the Past* (4th ed., London, 1958), pp. 274–7.

[13] B. B. Lal, 'Palaeoliths from the Beas and Banganga Valleys, Panjab', *A.I.* no. 12 (1956), 58 ff.

[14] *I.A.* 1956–7, 1 f.

[15] F. E. Zeuner, *Stone Age and Pleistocene Chronology in Gujarat* (Deccan College Monograph Series 6, Poona, 1950); B. Subbarao, 'Archaeological Explorations in the Mahi Valley', *Journ. of the M. S. University of Baroda*, I (1952), 33–72; H. D. Sankalia, *The Godavari Palaeolithic Industry* (Deccan College Monograph Series 10, Poona, 1952).

[16] F. E. Zeuner, 'Das Problem der Pluvialzeiten', *Geologische Rundschau*, Bd. 41 (Stuttgart, 1953), 242 ff.

[17] De Terra and Paterson as cited, n. 12.

[18] H. D. Sankalia, *Investigations into the Prehistoric Archaeology of Gujarat* (Baroda, 1946).

[19] V. D. Krishnaswami and K. V. Soundara Rajan, 'The Lithic Tool-industries of the Singrauli Basin, District Mirzapur', *A.I.* no. 7 (1951), 40–59.

[20] N. K. Bose and D. Sen, *Excavations in Mayurbhanj* (Calcutta, 1948).

[21] H. D. Sankalia, 'Animal-fossils and Palaeolithic Industries from the Pravara Basin at Nevasa, District Ahmadnagar', *A.I.* no. 12 (1956), 35–52. (On p. 36, Nevasa is erroneously placed in 'District Ahmadabad'.)

[22] L. A. Cammiade and M. C. Burkitt, 'Fresh Light on the Stone Ages in Southeast India', *Antiquity*, IV (1930), 327 ff. Also, F. J. Richards, L. A. Cammiade and M. C. Burkitt, 'Climatic Changes in South-east India during

Early Palaeolithic Times', *Geological Mag.* LXIX, no. V (1932); and M. Seshadri, *The Stone-using Cultures of Prehistoric and Protohistoric Mysore* (Univ. of Mysore, 1956).

[23] For Africa, see L. S. B. Leakey, *Stone Age Africa* (Oxford, 1936); Sonia Cole, *The Prehistory of East Africa* (Pelican Books, 1954); and H. Alimen, *Préhistoire de l'Afrique* (Paris, 1955), translated as *The Prehistory of Africa* (London, 1957).

[24] K. V. Soundara Rajan, 'Stone Age Industries near Giddalur, District Kurnool', *A.I.* no. 8 (1952), 64–92.

[25] So V. D. Krishnaswami, *A.I.* no. 9 (1953), 62.

[26] H. L. Movius, *Early Man and Pleistocene Stratigraphy in Southern and Eastern Asia* (Papers of the Peabody Museum, Harvard Univ., XIX, no. 3, 1944), and 'Palaeolithic Archaeology in Southern and Eastern Asia, exclusive of India', *UNESCO Journ. of World History* II, nos. 2 and 3 (Paris, 1955).

[27] *Indian Geolog. Survey Rec.* XIII, pt. 3 (1881), p. 122; hence de Terra and Paterson, *Studies on the Ice Age in India . . .* (Washington, 1939), p. 313.

[28] Cited by G. H. R. von Koenigswald, *Meeting Prehistoric Man* (London, 1956), p. 173.

CHAPTER IV

[29] De Terra and Paterson as cited, n. 12.

[30] H. D. Sankalia, 'Animal-fossils and Palaeolithic Industries from the Pravara Basin at Nevasa', *A.I.* no. 12 (1956), 35 ff.

[31] *Proc. Prehist. Soc. of E. Anglia* VII (1932), 39–40. See also K. R. U. Todd, 'The Microlithic Industries of Bombay, *A.I.* no. 6 (1950), pp. 4–16; and, more generally, D. H. Gordon, 'The Stone Industries of the Holocene in India and Pakistan', *A.I.* no. 6 (1950), 64–90.

[32] H. Alimen, *Préhistoire de l'Afrique* (Paris, 1955), p. 81.

[33] B. Subbarao, *The Personality of India* (Baroda, 1956), p. 32.

[34] F. E. Zeuner, 'The Microlithic Industry of Langhnaj, Gujarat', *Man* 1952, 182; H. D. Sankalia and I. Karve, 'Early Primitive Microlithic Culture and People of Gujarat', *American Anthropologist* LI (1949), 28–34.

[35] F. E. Zeuner and Bridget Allchin, 'The Microlithic Sites of Tinnevelly District, Madras State', *A.I.* no. 12 (1956), 4 ff.

[36] R. E. M. Wheeler, 'Brahmagiri and Chandravalli, 1947', *A.I.* no. 4 (1948), 222 ff.

[37] De Terra and Paterson, as cited, n. 12.

[38] *A.I.* no. 13 (1957), 89 ff.

[39] *A.I.* as n. 25; B. Subbarao, *Stone Age Cultures of Bellary* (Poona, 1948), pp. 31 ff.; F. R. Allchin, 'The Neolithic Stone Industry of the North Karnataka Region', *Bulletin of the Sch. of Orient. and African Studies* XIX/2 (1957), 321 ff.; E. C. Worman, 'The "Neolithic" Problem in the Prehistory of India', *Journ. of the Washington Acad. of Sciences*, 39 (1949), 181–201. The last paper is partially out of date but includes a good bibliography.

[40] *I.A.* 1956–57, 19.

[41] *I.A.* 1955–56, 8.

[42] Particularly in the Somrong Sen culture and in Tongking. See P. Lévy, *Recherches préhistoriques dans la région de Mlu Prei* (Hanoï, 1943); V. Goloubew, 'L'âge du bronze au Tonkin et dans la Nord-Annam', *Bulletin de l'École française d'Extrême Orient*, XXIX.

[43] D. J. Finn, *Archaeological Finds on Lamma Island near Hong Kong* (Ricci Publications, University of Hong Kong, 1958), p. 44. Finn's dating, based on Menghin, is wild. Uncritical, too, is his acceptance of Heine-Geldern's very speculative equation of supposed 'waves' of cultural migration with the spread of language-groups. See R. Heine-Geldern in *Anthropos* XXVII, 543 ff. For Szechwan, see Cheng Te-K'un, *Archaeological Studies in Szechwan* (Cambridge, 1957), pp. 54, etc.

[44] B. Karlgren, 'Some Weapons and Tools of the Yin Dynasty', *Bulletin of the Museum of Far Eastern Antiquities, Stockholm* (Stockholm, 1945), 103 ff.

[45] This suggestion has been developed by Dr. A. H. Dani, whose Ph.D. thesis on the 'Prehistory and Protohistory of Eastern India' (University of London Library) is a scholarly study of the whole subject.

[46] The map seems to me to be decisively against the opposite view that the Indian axes were 'derived ultimately from the neolithic stoneworking techniques of the Middle East and Iran'. F. R. Allchin as cited in no. 39, p. 325. Of course China *may* have got its axe-types from western Asia by some trans-continental route like the later Silk Route. But there is at present no connecting evidence.

[47] *Man* 1948, 99.

CHAPTER V

[48] E.g. V. Gordon Childe, *New Light on the Most Ancient East* (London, 1952); Stuart Piggott, *Prehistoric India* (Pelican Books, 1950); Wheeler, *The Indus Civilization* (Cambridge, 1953); D. H. Gordon, 'The pottery-industries of the Indo-Iranian Border', *A.I.* nos. 10 and 11 (1954–55), 157–91.

[49] Wheeler as cited in n. 48.

[50] *I.A.* 1956–57, p. 1. For the Kāthiāwāḍ or Saurashtra sites, see *I.A.* 1953–54, 7; 1954–55, 1, 11–12; 1955–56, 6–8; 1956–57, 15–16; 1957–58, 12–13; and S. R. Rao, 'The Excavations at Lothal', in *Lalit Kalā*, nos. 3–4 (1956–57). Incidentally, Lothal seems to have possessed a considerable granary, with underlying air-ducts, built of mud-bricks on a platform 15 ft. high. The structure is strangely identified as a 'kiln' by its excavator. See Rao as cited.

[51] *I.A.* 1955–56, 6.

[52] *A.I.* no. 4 (1948), 91.

[53] *Illustrated London News*, 24 May, 1958.

[54] S. L. Hora, 'Angling in Ancient India', *A.I.* nos. 11–10 (1954–55), 152–6.

[55] For an important discussion of these records, see A. L. Oppenheim, 'The Seafaring Merchants of Ur', *Journ. of the American Oriental Soc.*, 74 (1954), 6–17.

[56] See *Kuml*: *Årbog for Jysk Arkaeologisk Selskab* (*Århus*), from 1954, for interim reports. Also *Ill. Lond. News*, 4 and 11 Jan. 1958, and *Antiquity*, XXXII, Dec. 1958, pp. 243–6.

[57] C. J. Gadd, 'Seals of Ancient Indian Style found at Ur', *Proc. Brit. Academy* XVIII (1932): and Wheeler, *The Indus Civilization* (Cambridge, 1953), p. 85.

[58] J. Marshall, *Mohenjo-daro and the Indus Civilization* (London, 1931), I, 110 ff.

[59] D. H. Gordon in *A.I.* nos. 10 and 11 (1954–55), 174.

[60] *Man* LVI (1956), 151.

CHAPTER VI

[61] Babur *v.* Ibrahim Lodi, 1526; Akbar *v.* Himer, 'Ādil Shāh Sūr's general, 1556; Afghans *v.* Marathas, 1761.

[62] *A.I.* nos. 10 and 11 (1954–55), 141.

[63] B. B. Lal, 'Further Copper Hoards from the Gangetic Basin and a Review of the Problem', *A.I.* no. 7 (1951), 20 ff., with bibliography.

[64] R. Heine-Geldern, 'The coming of the Aryans and the End of the Harappa Civilization', *Man* LVI (1956), 151.

[65] Interim notes in *I.A* 1953–54, 9; 1954–55, 16; 1955–56, 20; 1956–57, 28. Also information kindly provided by Shri G. R. Sharma.

[66] *A.I.* nos. 10–11 (1955), 5–151.

[67] A. Ghosh and K. C. Panigrahi, 'Pottery of Ahichchhatrā (U.P)', *A.I.* no. 1 (1946), 37–59; V. S. Agrawala, 'The Terracottas of Ahichchhatrā',

A.I. no. 4 (1948), 104–79; M. G. Dikshit, 'Beads from Ahichchhatrā, U.P.', *A.I.* no. 8 (1952), 33–63.

[68] *A.I.* nos. 10–11 (1955), 138–41; *I.A.* 1954–55, 13.

CHAPTER VII

[69] B. B. Lal in *A.I.* no. 5 (1949), 62–105.

[70] *I.A.* 1956–57, 30–1.

[71] Wheeler, *Five Thousand Years of Pakistan* (London, 1950), pp. 101–2. Since 1950 the Pakistan Depart. of Archaeology has carried out further work on the site.

[72] *Ib.*, 102–3 and 142.

[73] *I.A.* 1954–55, 19–20.

[74] An important introductory study of Indian trade-routes has been prepared by Dr. Moti Chand but is at present available only in Hindi: *Sārthavāha* ('Caravan Leader') (Bihār Rāshtra Bhāshā Parishad, Patna, 1957).

[75] *I.A.* 1953–54 7; 1954–55, 11–12.

[76] *I.A.* 1955–56, 11.

[77] H. D. Sankalia, B. Subbarao, and S. B. Deo, 'The Archaeological Sequence of Central India', *Southwestern Journal of Anthropology*, vol. 9, no. 4 (University of New Mexico Press, Albuquerque, 1953); H. D. Sankalia, 'Excavations at Maheshwar and Nevasa and their Possible Bearing on the Puranic History', from the Sardhashatabdi Commemoration Volume (As. Soc. of Bombay, 1955); B. Subbarao, 'Chalcolithic Blade Industry of Maheshwar', *Bull. of the Deccan Coll. Research Inst.* XVII (1955–56); H. D. Sankalia (on Nāvḍā Ṭolī) in *Ill. Lond. News*, Sept. 20, 1958; and especially H. D. Sankalia, B. Subbarao and S. B. Deo, *The Excavations at Maheshwar and Navdatoli 1952–53* (Deccan Research College and M.S. Univ. Publication no. 1, Poona and Baroda, 1958).

[78] R. Ghirshman, *Fouilles de Sialk* II (Paris, 1939), p. 94.

[79] Reported in *Archaeology*, vol. 11, no. 2 (New York, 1958), p. 128.

[80] *I.A.* 1955–56, 19; 1956–57, 20–8; M. B. Gardes in the *Annual Administration Report of the Arch. Dept., Gwalior State*, 1938–39; hence B. C. Law, *Ujjayini in Ancient India* (Gwalior, 1944). Also information kindly provided by Shri N. R. Banarjee.

[81] *I.A.* 1956–57, 17–19.

[82] H. D. Sankalia and S. B. Deo, *Report on the Excavations at Nasik and Jorwe 1950–51* (Poona, 1955).

[83] E.g. W. V. Grigson, *The Maria Gonds of Bastar* (London, 1938); J. H. Hutton, 'The Meaning and Method of the Erection of Monoliths by the Naga Tribes', *Journ. Roy. Anthrop. Inst.* LII (1922), and 'The Use of Stone in the Naga Hills', *ib.*, LVI (1926); C. von Fürer-Haimendorf, *The Naked Nagas* (London, 1939); R. von Heine-Geldern, 'Die Megalithen Südostasiens und ihre Bedeutung', *Anthropos* XXIII (1928); V. D. Krishnaswami, 'Megalithic Types of South India', *A.I.* no. 5 (1949), 41–3.

[84] C. von Fürer-Haimendorf, 'The Problem of Megalithic Cultures in Middle India', *Man in India* XXV (1945), 73–86.

[85] V. D. Krishnaswami, 'Megalithic Types of South India', *A.I.* no. 5 (1949), pp. 35–45; K. R. Srinivasan and N. R. Banerjee, 'Survey of South Indian Megaliths', *A.I.* no. 9 (1953), pp. 103–115; N. R. Banerjee, 'The Megalithic Problem of Chingleput in the Light of Recent Exploration', *A.I.* no. 12 (1956), 21–34.

[86] *A.I.* no. 5, 38.

[87] B. K. Thapar, 'Porkalam 1948', *A.I.* no. 8 (1952), 3–16.

[88] *I.A.* 1955–56, 23.

[89] B. K. Thapar, 'Maski 1954', *A.I.* no. 13 (1957), 33.

[90] *Ib.*, 35.

[91] F. R. Allchin, 'The Stone Alignments of Southern Hyderabad', *Man* LVI (1956), 150.

[92] Y. D. Sharma, 'Rock-cut Caves of Cochin', *A.I.* no. 12 (1956), 93–115.

[93] References in *A.I.* no. 4 (1948), 301–3.

[94] Wheeler, *Five Thousand Years of Pakistan* (London, 1950), pp. 34–6.

[95] De Terra and Paterson, as n. 12, 233–4 and pl. XXIV; de Terra, 'Excavations at Burjhama', *Miscellanea of the Amer. Phil. Soc.*, 1936.

[96] D. H. Gordon in *Journ. Ind. Anthrop. Inst.*, new series, I, 18 (Calcutta, 1945).

[97] J. M. and G. Casal, *Site urbain et Sites funéraires des Environs de Pondichéry* (Paris, 1956), pp. 30 ff.

[98] *A.I.* no. 5 (1949), 37; *I.A.* 1954–55, 20–2.

[99] Meadows Taylor, in his account of pit-circles at Jiwārji in the Gulbarga district of Hyderabad, illustrates skeletons in articulation, but his description makes it clear that they were in fact disarticulated fragments. See his *Megalithic Tombs and other Ancient Remains in the Deccan*, papers collected and republished by the Archaeological Department of Hyderabad State, 1941. At Maski, complete burials of approximately the same period occur, but without any megalithic structural feature.

[100] J. M. Casal, *Fouilles de Virampātnam—Arikamedu* (Paris, 1949), pp. 20 ff.

[101] For references, see *A.I.* no. 4 (1948), 200 and 300.

[102] Vincent Smith, *The Oxford Hist. of India*, 3rd ed., 1958, p. 99; and N. P. Chakravati, *A.I.* no. 4 (1948), 15 ff.

[103] The view which I state here supersedes that which I put forward in 1947: *A.I.* no. 4 (1948), 201–2. From a different angle it tallies with that of C. von Fürer-Haimendorf. See his Presidential Address to the Anthrop. and Arch. Section of the Ind. Sc. Congress, Poona, 1950.

[104] *I.A.* 1956–57, 15.

[105] *I.A.* 1954–55, 14; cf. 1956–57, 8.

[106] Wheeler, *Rome beyond the Imperial Frontiers* (London, 1954), pp. 126–30.

[107] C. von Fürer-Haimendorf, 'New Aspects of the Dravidian Problem', *Tamil Culture* II, 2 (1953).

CHAPTER IX

[108] Vincent Smith, *Aśoka* (Oxford, 1901); F. W. Thomas in *The Cambridge History of India* I (1922). For a reassessment of Ashoka's dates, see P. H. L. Eggermont, *The Chronology of the Reign of Asoka Moriya* (Leiden, 1956).

[109] E.g. new rock-edicts in the Ṭhāna district (*I.A.* 1955–56, 29), more recently at Gujarrā near Jhānsī, and, above all, the newly discovered denunciation of hunting embodied both in Greek and in Aramaic on a rock at Kandahar: see G. Pugliese Carratelli and G. Levi Della Vida, 'Un Editio Bilingue Greco-Aramaico di Aśoka', *Serie Orientale Roma* XXI (Rome, 1958); and D. Schlumberger, L. Robert, A. Dupont-Sommer, and E. Bannister, 'Una bilingue gréco-araméenne d'Asoka', *Journ. Asiatique*, 1958.

[110] J. Marshall, *Taxila* (Cambridge, 1951), I, 20.

[111] *A.I.* (1946), 33–4. The gems are there described as Ionian Greek, but I prefer to regard them as Achaemenian.

[112] There is no evidence of fluting or faceting in India certainly earlier than the faceted column of Heliodorus at Besnagar in Central India, *c.* 140–130 B.C. or a little later.

[113] E. Herzfeld, *Iran in the Ancient East* (Oxford, 1941), p. 321.

[114] *A.I.* no. 4 (1948), 24.

[115] Percy Brown, *Indian Architecture* (*Buddhist and Hindu*) (Bombay, 1942), p. 12, etc.

[116] References by Wheeler and Piggott in *A.I.* no. 4 (1948), 95–103.

[117] *I.A.* 1955–56, 22–23.

[118] *Camb. Hist. of India* I (1922), p. 184; Vincent Smith, *Oxford Hist. of India*, 3rd ed. (1958), p. 73.

Bibliography

Cambridge History of India I (1922). (Much out of date but still useful.)

STUART PIGGOTT *Prehistoric India*, Pelican Books, 1950

VINCENT A. SMITH *Oxford History of India*, 3rd ed. (1958)

B. SUBBARAO *The Personality of India*, M.S. University of Baroda, 2nd ed. (1958)

D. H. GORDON *The Prehistoric Background of Indian Culture*, Bhulabhai Memorial Institute, Bombay, 1958

A. L. BASHAM *The Wonder that was India*, London, 1954

Ancient India published annually by the Director General of Archaeology in India, New Delhi. (Here abbreviated as *A.I.*)

Indian Archaeology ditto. (Here abbreviated as *I.A.*)

Sources of Illustrations

For many of the plates and text-figures, grateful acknowledgment is due to Shri A. Ghosh, Director General of Archaeology in India, Dr. F. A. Khan, Director of Archaeology in Pakistan, Dr. H. D. Sankalia, and Shri G. R. Sharma.

THE PLATES

2

3

5

6

10
11
12

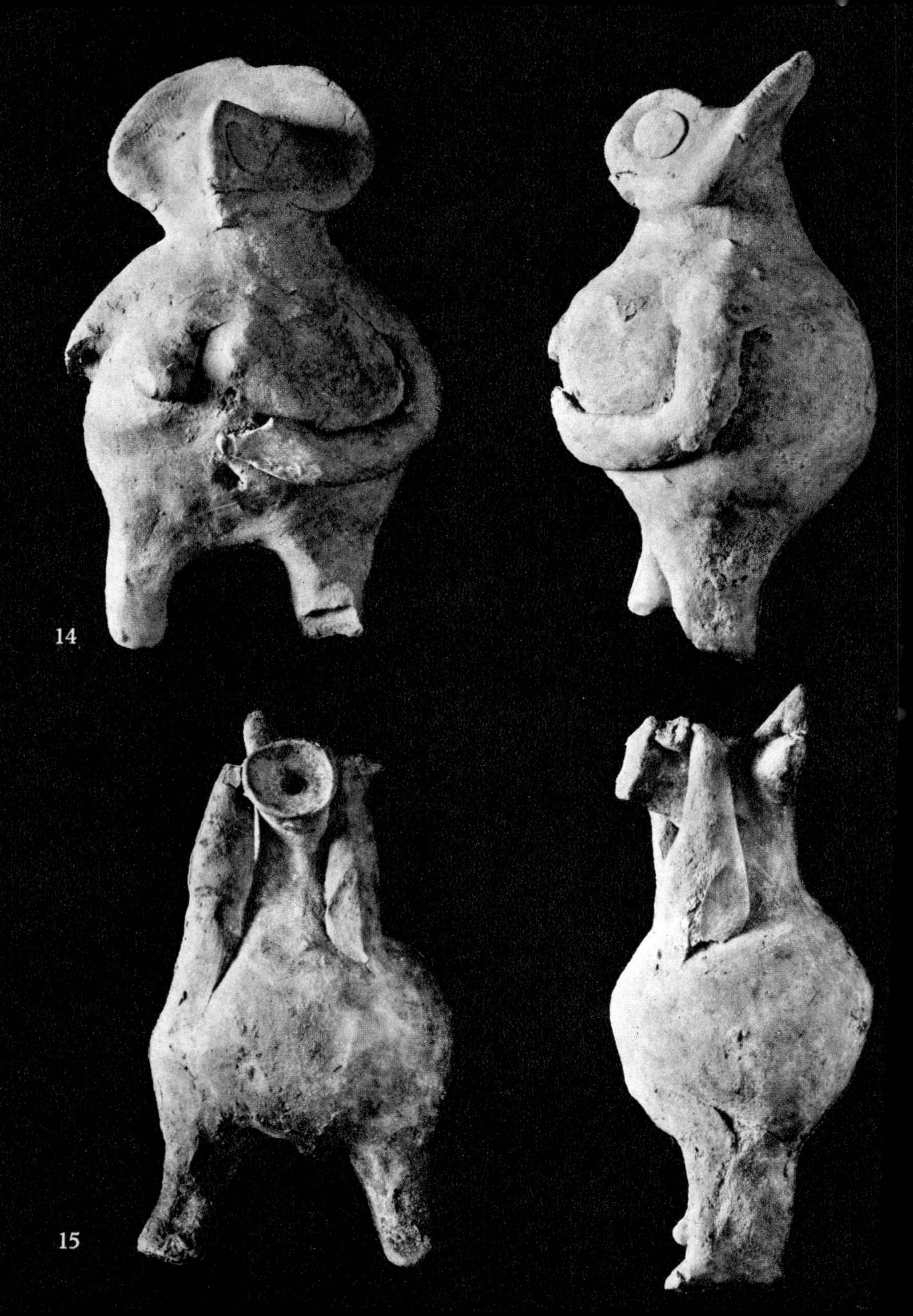
14
15

16

20

22

23

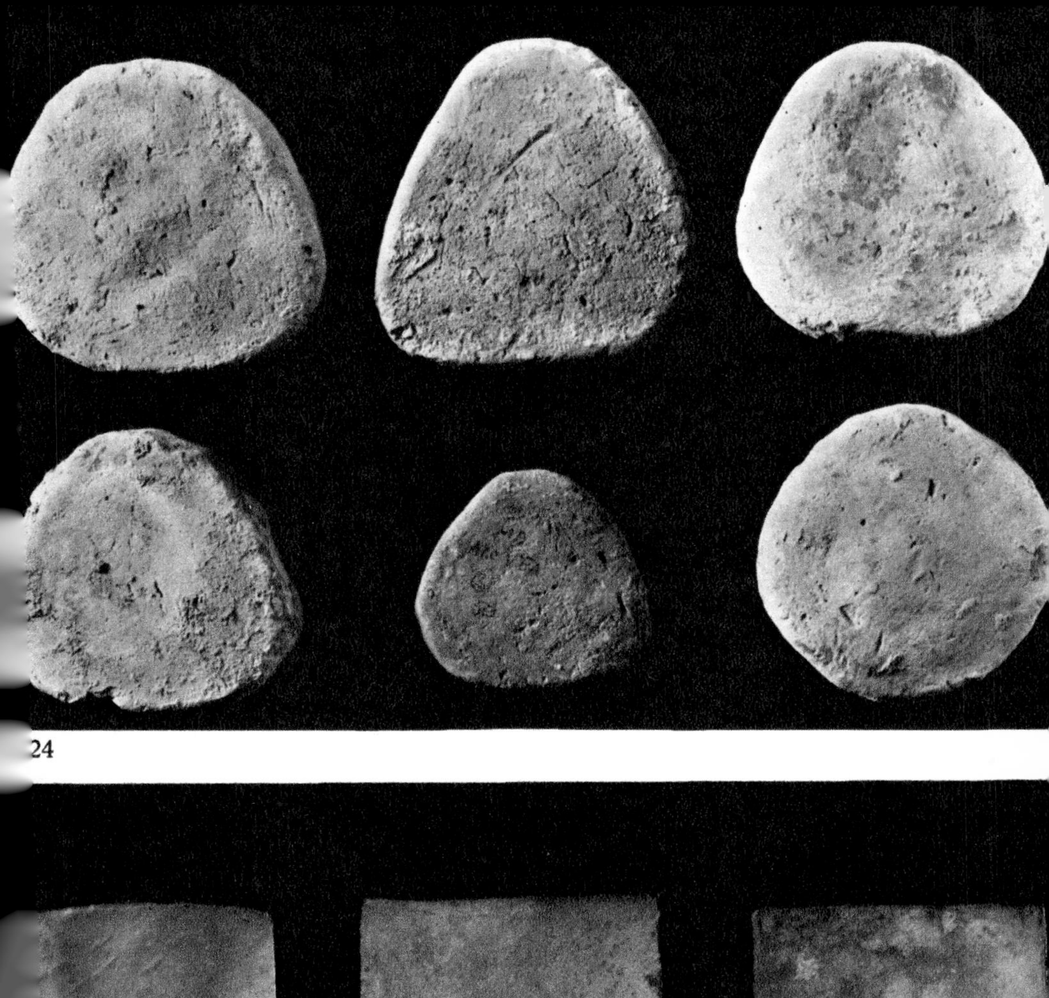

24

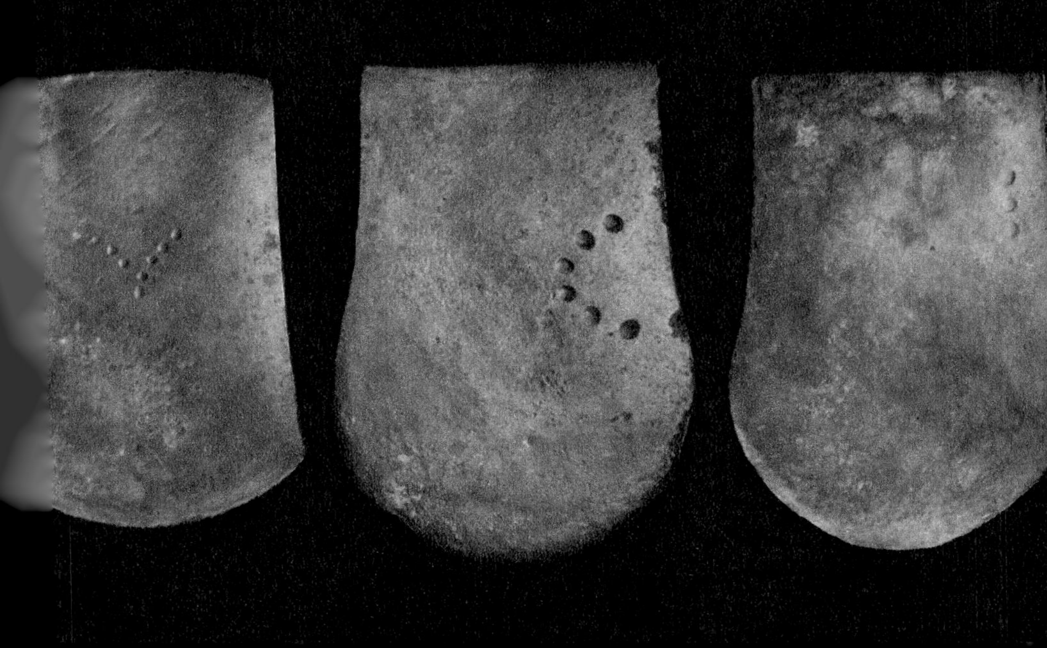

28

29

31

33

34

36

37

39

42

43

45
46

48

49

51

52

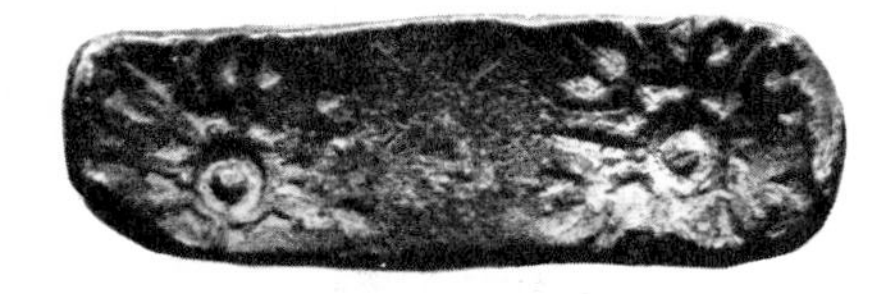

3

55

JB

Notes on the Plates

1 Rouletted ware from Brahmagiri, Chitaldrug district, Mysore, p. 31 ($\frac{1}{2}$).

2 Polished stone axes from Brahmagiri, p. 84 ($\frac{1}{2}$).

3 Shouldered stone hoe from Midnapur, West Bengal, p. 87 ($\frac{1}{1}$).

4 Mohenjo-daro: loading-bay and platform of the Great Granary, excavated 1950, p. 97.

5 Harappā: baked brick revetment (two periods) of the mud-brick defence of the citadel, p. 97.

6 Mohenjo-daro: the tank on the citadel, p. 97.

7 Mohenjo-daro: defensive towers at the south-east corner of the citadel, excavated 1950, pp. 97 and 102.

8 Mohenjo-daro: 'Low Lane', p. 97.

9 Mohenjo-daro: street with drains, p. 97.

10 Mohenjo-daro: bronze statuette of dancing girl ($\frac{1}{1}$).

11 Mohenjo-daro: stone head of 'priest-king' or deity ($\frac{1}{2}$).

12 Mohenjo-daro: stone head ($\frac{1}{2}$).

13 Mohenjo-daro: terracotta figurine with 'pannier' head-dress ($\frac{1}{1}$).

14, 15 Mohenjo-daro: grotesque terracotta figurines ($\frac{1}{1}$).

N

Early India and Pakistan

34 Megalithic cist with 'port-hole', Vengupattu, North Arcot district, p. 154.

35 Terracotta sarcophagus in megalithic cist, Mandurantakam taluk, Chingleput district, p. 154.

36 Terracotta sarcophagus from Sankhavaram, Chingleput district. Now in the Government Museum, Madras, p. 154 (length $2\frac{1}{2}$ ft.).

37 Terracotta sarcophagus at Pallavaram, Chingleput district, p. 154.

38 Megalithic 'port-hole' cist at Brahmagiri, Chitaldrug district, p. 155.

39 Burial-pit with grave-goods and four stones to support bier, Brahmagiri, Chitaldrug district, p. 156.

40 'Umbrella stones' in the Talapalli taluk, Cochin, p. 156.

41 'Hoodstone' over burial, Talapalli taluk, Cochin, p. 156.

42 Stone avenues near Gogi, Gulbarga district, p. 157.

43 Iron hoes or ploughshares found below a megalithic cist at Polechattiche-rugudda, Warangal district, p. 161 ($\frac{2}{5}$).

44 Entrance-chamber to four rock-cut caves at Katakampal, Talapalli taluk, Cochin, p. 158 (scale of ft.).

45 Pottery from a burial-cave at Eyyal, Trichur taluk, Cochin ($\frac{1}{5}$), p. 161 ($\frac{1}{4}$).

46 Black-and-red pottery from Brahmagiri ($\frac{1}{5}$), p. 161 ($\frac{1}{3}$).

47 Old Rājgir, Bihar: dry-built city-wall at the Bānganga defile, *c.* 6th century B.C., p. 173.

48 Pāṭaliputra, Bihar: defensive palisade at Bulandibāgh, *c.* latter part of 4th century B.C., p. 177.

Early India and Pakistan

49 Column-capital in Persian style, from Pạ̄aliputra, *c.* late 4th–early 3rd century B.C. In the Patna Museum, p. 177. (Height 2 ft. $9\frac{1}{2}$ in.).

50 Taxila: air-view of part of the earliest city, on the Bhīr Mound, 5th–2nd century B.C., p. 173.

51 Three Achaemenid gems, with impressions, from Taxila (Bhīr Mound), *c.* 300 B.C. ($\frac{1}{1}$). Found with the bent-bar coins, pl. 53. In the National Museum, New Delhi, p. 174 ($\frac{2}{1}$).

52 Mauryan inscription from Mahāsthān, East Bengal, p. 136 ($\frac{1}{1}$).

53 Silver bent-bar coins from Taxila (Bhīr Mound), *c.* 300 B.C. ($\frac{9}{7}$).

54 Chārsada, North-west Frontier: defensive ditch and post-holes for postern and bridge, part of the early fortifications of the Bālā Hisār or High Fort, *c.* 4th century B.C., excavated 1958, p. 172.

55 Terracotta figurine of goddess, from Chārsada; 3rd–2nd centuries B.C. ($\frac{1}{1}$).

56 The Ashokan lion-capital at Sārnāth, *c.* 245 B.C., p. 174. (Height 7 ft.).

57 Entrance to the Lomas Rishi cave in the Barābar hills near Gaya, Bihar, time of Ashoka, p. 175.

Index